Painting The Shadows

Dedication

This book is dedicated with love to the memory of my mentor and my hero.

Painting The Shadows

The Extraordinary

Life of

Victor Hoo

Mona Yung-Ning Hoo

ELDRIDGE & CO

First published in 1998 by Eldridge & Co
24 Altior Court
Shepherds Hill
London N6 5RJ

Distributed by Gazelle Book Services Limited
Falcon House Queen Square Lancaster
England LA1 1RN

British Library Cataloguing in Publication Data
A catalogue record for this book is available from the British
Library

ISBN 0-9533455-0-5

Typeset by Amolibros, Watchet, Somerset
Publication of this title has been managed by Amolibros
Printed and bound by Professional Book Supplies, Oxford,
England

Contents

List of Illustrations

The Trusteeship Visiting Mission to Cameroon, November 1949

Secretary General of the United Nations, U Thant

Following page 226

Victor with Hammarskjold (center) and Chief of Protocol, Count Jehan de Noüe (right)

Victor, representing the Secretary General at the Security Council, sitting next to Andrei Gromyko (Yacov Malik behind Gromyko)

With Krishna Menon of India and Fernand van Langenhoven of Belgium.

Victor welcoming Pope Paul VI to the United Nations

Victor welcoming Lyndon and Lady Bird Johnson to the United Nations

United Nations Headquarters, New York City (reprinted here with the kind permission of the United Nations)

A rare evening out together, for Victor's sixtieth birthday

Mona with Mrs Patricia Tsien, daughter of Dr V K Wellington Koo, New York, 1995

Acknowledgements

It was in May 1989, seventeen years after my father's death, that I was approached by a United Nations representative of the Beijing Government. Mr Qiu Yingjue was Deputy Director of the Security Council and Political Committees Division at the United Nations. He had never met my father but, he said, the United Nations was still impregnated with Victor Hoo's personality and legacy. This, coming from a staunch Communist regarding a life-long anti-Communist, was remarkable. Mr Qiu impressed on me in an avuncular manner, that someone in the family should write Father's biography; that it was our duty to make his life story available to the masses in China. The climate in China had become liberal. There was a great interest in the lives of successful Chinese people whose careers had taken them abroad.

Father had left a quantity of files covering his working life, including detailed diaries. After his death in 1972, we decided to donate them to the Hoover Institution on War, Revolution and Peace in Stanford, California, for the benefit of future students of history.

With Mr Qiu's counsel in mind, I decided to attempt this task in the belief that Father would have approved. Mr Qiu gave me several useful leads on how to get the book translated and published in China. I was fortunate to obtain financial support from the Pacific Cultural Foundation in Taipei to allow me to travel for my research. I mapped out my travel plans and research programme, but almost at the same time there came news of the Tienanman events. It became obvious that the liberalism and freedom of information would be drastically curtailed. My plans were somewhat spoiled but I decided to start by translating the diaries from the French.

In March 1990 I went to California to delve into the files and diaries deposited at the Hoover Institution. I also visited Ambassador Liu Chieh, Father's old friend and colleague. From him I learned something of the life behind the scenes, both in the Chinese Delegation and at the United Nations. Also on this visit, I spent an afternoon with Alison Stilwell, the daughter of Joseph Stilwell. She had known Chiang Kai Shek and had first-hand appreciation of the situation in China in the forties.

At the end of 1990 I travelled to Taipei to search in the government files. I stayed with my uncle, Raymond Hoo, a former ambassador who was working in the Waichiaopu. Thanks to him I was given access to the government archives and was driven every day in his official limousine, accompanied by my translator, Wu Ya Mei. There I discovered many official reports, in Father's own handwriting, covering the period from the Versailles Treaty to the early thirties. I also found boxes of files covering my grandfather, Hoo Wei Teh's career.

In 1991 I spent my holiday researching the United Nations archives in New York and took the opportunity of interviewing colleagues and friends of my father. One or two refused to be interviewed, others were only prepared to offer platitudes. A handful were able and willing to contribute important facts, in particular, Mrs Patricia Koo Tsien, daughter of Dr V K Wellington Koo, one of Victor's closest friends and collaborators. She had not only known Victor since childhood, but had worked with him from 1947 in the Trusteeship Department of the UN. Her knowledge and candour were most appreciated. The other was K K Tsien, son of Ambassador Tsien Tai, also a family friend who had worked in close proximity to Victor, first in Berne and then at the UN. K K Tsien gave me a unique and frank insight into Victor's working environment, with an unbiased analysis of the international stage setting as Victor would have experienced it. My thanks also go to Lorraine Shea, Bill Sie, Gerry Wen, Charles Chung, Philippe de Seynes, Eileen Pei and Munling Landegger for their contributions.

In 1992 my research took me to the League of Nations archives in Geneva and to a second visit to the Hoover Institution. This time I was able to interview C Y Wu and Professor William Tung, both close colleagues of Victor's at the UN and in Chungking respectively.

I owe a special debt to Phoebe Phillips and my niece Roseanne each of whom in their own way gave me support and encouragement from the beginning and throughout this project.

My greatest thanks and appreciation are due my friend Lynn Bushell who took on the task of weeding out masses of details which, though fascinating to me, threatened to clog up the narrative. As an experienced journalist, she helped me to shape and polish the research material into the finished product.

I would like to thank my consultant, Jane Tatam of Amolibros, for her remarkable competence, her cheerful good nature and her enthusiasm.

Last but not least, I am most grateful to all the members of my family, within which I include Jeremy Eldridge, who contributed reminiscences and anecdotes to achieve a fuller picture of Victor Hoo, the person.

Chronology

Birth:	November 16, 1894 in Washington DC (father was then Secretary of the Chinese Legation)
1899	Went to Russia Kaiser Primary School, graduating 1905 Annan Schule in St Petersburg, graduating 1912, awarded the Kaiser Prize Visits to Japan during this period (father Chinese Minister since 1908)
1912	To Paris École Libre des Sciences Politiques, Section Diplomatique. Graduated and awarded Gold Medal for outstanding academic achievement
1916	Received degree of Licencié en Droit at the Law School of University of Paris
1918	Docteur en Droit. Prix Goullencourt and Prix de Thèse Doctoral Dissertation "Les Bases Conventionnelles des Relations Modernes Entre la Chine et la Russie" Summers in Oxford and Cambridge
1919	Assistant Secretary Chinese Delegation to the Peace Conference in Paris at the conclusion of World War I
1920	Member of Chinese Delegation to the Conference of Associations for the League of Nations, Brussels
1921	Technical Member of the Chinese Delegation to the International Finance Conference for the Suppression of Traffic in Women and Children, Geneva

1921	Technical Adviser of the Chinese Delegation to the League of Nations
1921	Technical Delegate of the Chinese Delegation to the first five Assemblies of the League of Nations and also to many other conferences convened by the League.
1921	Appointed Third Secretary of Chinese Legation in Belgium but did not proceed to his post due to the following appointment
	Appointed Secretary of the Chinese Delegation to the Washington Conference
1922	Appointed Second Secretary Chinese Legation, Berlin
1923	Promoted to First Secretary
1924	Promoted to Chargé d'Affaires in Berlin
1925	Returned from Germany to China to serve in the Tariff Conference at Peking as Assistant Director of the Treaty Dept.
1926	Appointed Sectional Chief in the Treaty Department of the Ministry of Foreign Affairs and Secretary of the Cabinet. Also served as Technical Expert to the Sino-Soviet Conference and Assistant Counsellor of the Ministry of Foreign Affairs, drafting new Sino-Soviet Treaties
1927	Promoted to Assistant Director of the Treaty Department of the Ministry of Foreign Affairs
1928	Appointed Counsellor of the Shanghai City Government and Secretary of the Reorganisation Commission, which position he resigned when he became Secretary of the Ministry of Foreign Affairs of the National Government
1930	Appointed Director of the Department of Asiatic Affairs of the above Ministry

1931	Went to Moscow as Technical Adviser of the Chinese Delegation for the Sino-Soviet negotiations on the Chinese Eastern Railway
1931	Attended the Assembly of the League of Nations as Secretary General of the Chinese Delegation
	Attended all the meetings of the League on the Sino-Japanese conflict
1932	Appointed Director of the Permanent Office of the Chinese Delegation to the League of Nations concurrently with that of Chargé d'Affaires in Switzerland
1932	Attended International Labour Conference as Chief Delegate in Geneva
1932	From May, represented China at the League's Advisory Committee on Opium and Other Dangerous Drugs
1933	Promoted to the rank of Envoy Extraordinary and Minister Plenipotentiary at Berne
	Concurrently, Director of the Permanent Office at Geneva
	Represented his country in various League of Nations' Committees, such as the League's Advisory Committee on Opium and Other Dangerous Drugs, and the Advisory Committee on Social Questions
1942	Returned to China to serve as Vice-Minister of Foreign Affairs to 1945
1944	Attended as Delegate at Bretton Woods and Dumbarton Oaks Conferences
1945	Served as Secretary-General of Chinese Delegation at San Francisco Conference
1945	Served as Technical Expert and Official Interpreter at the Sino-Soviet Conference for the Sino-Soviet Treaty of Alliance in Moscow

1945-46	Substitute Delegate in London to the Executive Committee, Preparatory Commission and General Assembly of the United Nations. Received the rank of
1946	Appointed Assistant Secretary General of the UN in charge of Department of Trusteeship and Information from Non Self Governing Territories
1947	Went to Palestine as the Special Representative of the Secretary General of the UN on the UN Special Committee on Palestine (UNSCOP)
1948	Went in the same capacity to Korea with the UN Temporary Commission on Korean (UNTCOK)
1955	Appointed Under-Secretary for Conference Services
1962	Appointed Commissioner for Technical Co-operation at the United Nations

HONOURS AND DECORATIONS

Blue Cordon of the Precious Jade (China)
Grand Officer of the Brilliant Star (China)
Grand Officer of the Order of the Crown (Iran)
Grand Officer of the Nile (Egypt)
Grand Officer of the White Lion (Czechoslovakia)
Commander of the Order of the Crown (Belgium)
Order of George First (Greece)
Grand Officer of the National Order of the Sun (Peru)
Grand Officer of the Order of the Southern Cross (Brazil)
Commandeur de la Légion d'Honneur (France)

CHAPTER ONE

The Early Years

International Beginnings - Mother's Death - European Education

Victor Chi-Tsai Hoo began life in Washington DC on 18th November 1894, the first of twelve children and the son of Hoo Wei-Teh, Secretary to the Chinese Legation. In consequence of his birthplace, people often wrongly assumed that he was an American citizen. A diplomatic clause, however, meant that, even in the American capital, Victor had been born on Chinese diplomatic soil, thus fulfilling his parents' patriotic expectations.

This was pure accident, as one might well be born in a taxi or on the trans-Siberian. In fact Victor could have grown up to be anything but American. He had no recollection of his life as a small child in the US. Later he took on the cultures of an Oriental, a Slav, a Latin, but never a North American although he eventually grew to feel at home in New York.

Three months before Victor's birth China and Japan had declared war on each other, the outcome of ten years rivalry and intrigue in Korea. It was a catastrophe for China. The European powers and the US tried to mediate but to no avail. The Japanese, superior in both land and sea, scored early victories in several strategic places. The situation looked hopeless.

Though keenly aware of the terrible events unfolding in their homeland, Victor's parents were overwhelmed with joy by the much awaited birth of their first child. Mrs Hoo had had five miscarriages and was convinced that she would never be able to bear a child. During her last pregnancy she could hardly sleep with worry and night after night lay awake praying. Her prayers were answered but, three days after the baby arrived, the Chinese forces suffered a devastating defeat off the Yalu River, at Port Arthur. "We will call the boy Victor," said Hoo Wei-Teh. "He is the symbol of our faith. We have to win over the Japanese."

Less than five months later China was defeated and forced to sign the humiliating Treaty of Shimonoseki. More than ever Victor would symbolise the new hope of one day gaining revenge, although China would have to wait fifty years for this.

The background against which Victor was to play out his role, was colourful by any standards. His father's generation bridged two eras, that of the ancient Manchu Dynasty and, later, the new Republic that replaced it. It was a dangerous time to be alive but Hoo Wei-Teh managed to remain true to both regimes. To the end he continued to serve the last Empress as her faithful Mandarin and, by the time of Victor's birth, had already established himself as a statesman and diplomat of some repute. Being one of the few diplomats then who could speak English and French, Hoo Wei-Teh was ideally suited to the Foreign Diplomatic Service and in the course of his career represented China in countries as diverse as America, Japan, Russia, Peru and France.

He had started life as the child of a peasant family and after the early death of his father, was brought up by his mother and grandfather. It was his good fortune that the latter was able to teach him the classical Chinese that gave Hoo Wei-Teh access to an education. Ambitious and determined to succeed, his diligence at school gained him notice and his dreams finally came true when he was sent to Shanghai to study for the diplomatic service. Hard work was the key to success. It was another lesson Hoo Wei-Teh was to pass on to his son.

Although he was destined to leave the poverty of his origins far behind him, the one aspect of his childhood that never deserted him was his love of the countryside. Victor would always feel most a home in the cosmopolitan atmosphere of great cities but his father's happiest hours were spent in the country house he acquired after the death of his first wife and which he kept until his own death more than a quarter of a century later. Here he would retreat alone, often for days at a time, particularly in his later years.

The house was an old temple with many acres of land and Hoo Wei-Teh was to become a familiar figure on his long walks by the fields. He never forgot his humble beginnings and was as much at ease leaning on a stick and chatting to the local farm workers about agriculture as he was talking to diplomats about affairs of state.

When Victor was two his father was appointed Counsellor (later promoted to Minister) to the Legation in St Petersburg and the family moved to Russia. Victor's earliest recollections of the capital were of an era drawing to a close. The Tsars, Rasputin, Tchaikovsky - all the romance of a dying age - conspired to instil in Victor the nostalgic longings of the Slavic soul. Although his religion was officially "Confucian," he was so moved by the Gregorian chants that he continued to attend Russian services at the Orthodox Church at Easter whenever possible.

It was here too that he was to experience the first of life's tragedies. One cold winter's evening, whilst he was still a toddler, his mother, in keeping with the Chinese custom of politeness, insisted on accompanying an Embassy guest to the front gate, walking through the front garden in her thin Chinese cloth shoes. There was a chill wind blowing and by the time she returned to the house she was shivering. During the night she woke with a fever and over the next few days the symptoms of pneumonia manifested themselves. Despite desperate efforts to save her she had died within the week.

Victor never fully recovered from the wrench of this sudden parting. Throughout his life, he felt excluded from those fortunate enough to have known a real mother. Although later he dug deeply into his memory for recollections of her these were inevitably vague and he was left with an impression, fostered largely by others, of a woman both gentle and devoted, whose joy at his birth had been so tragically short-lived.

Having himself suffered the loss of a parent in infancy, Hoo Wei-Teh was sympathetic to his son's grief but he was a member of the old school and not easily given to demonstrations of affection. Although Victor later described him as approachable and easy-going, Hoo Wei-Teh was an exacting father and as the first and only son of his first wife, it was impressed on Victor from the beginning that the family expected great things of him.

After the death of Victor's mother, Hoo Wei-Teh would normally have married his concubine - who was to bear him six children - as was the custom. This put him in somewhat of a quandary, however. Certain things would be expected of a diplomat's wife that would not necessarily be expected of a concubine - a knowledge of foreign languages for example. Clearly an education was a essential prerequisite and, after much agonising, a Miss Chou was selected to be the second Wife Number One.

Well versed in both Chinese and European literature, Miss Chou came from a upper class family and had a university degree from the US. Not only was she gifted with culture and education she had the additional advantage of wealth. Her parents had undoubtedly expected her to marry a wealthy man and were less than happy with her choice. The fact that she settled for Hoo Wei-Teh suggested that her education had left her progressive enough to appreciate Hoo Wei-Teh's other admirable qualities.

Though never a family man in the conventional sense, in the years that followed Hoo Wei-Teh gave as much attention to his growing family of eight sons and four daughters as his time and inclinations allowed. Outings to Beihai Park with a regiment of youngsters packed into the family car and family dog trailing behind were a favourite treat for the younger children, the last one of whom was born when he was sixty years old.

Because of the gap in age between himself and his younger siblings, and because Victor lived in Europe, when he did have breaks in China he made an effort to get acquainted with them. He would entertain his young brothers with somersaults, pony rides and card tricks. Seeing their amazement as his sleight of hand produced an ace of hearts from his breast pocket or behind his ear, Victor was urged on to feats of ever greater dexterity until one of the children, his eyes riveted on the elusive cards, caught him out and, clapping his hands, shrieked: " I saw, I saw … trick, trick," destroying in an instant Victor's reputation as a wizard. But the laughter echoed.

He had a particular affection for Augustin, who was ten years his junior and, indeed, was largely responsible for the naming of his younger brother. Though not particularly gifted musically, Victor was a perfectionist in all things and his efforts to master *Ach, du liebe Augustin* on the piano had driven the rest of the family to distraction. When the second son of the family was born, it seemed natural to call him Augustin, since by that time the name was embedded in everybody's consciousness.

Apart from the age gap and the respect afforded him as the elder brother, however, there was also a culture gap between Victor and the others. He had been born and educated abroad; they were culturally Chinese. Even the Chinese he spoke was different from theirs. The warmth and intimacy that might have muted his natural reserve was therefore absent and, if anything, increased Victor's sense of isolation. He was not really at ease with children and remained remote from his own in later life.

4

Although she was fond of her stepson and often cited him as an example to her own three sons, Hoo Wei-Teh's second wife proved no replacement for the first in Victor's heart. She had a sharp eye and a sharp tongue and, whilst Victor testified to his respect for her, his feelings fell short of the kind of true filial affection he might have felt for his own mother had she lived. It was not until after his father's death, with its inevitable role reversal, that Victor became her advisor and confidant and their relationship deepened. They conducted a regular correspondence during the thirties whilst Victor was in Geneva in which his stepmother in Peking confided her anxieties over her children and the difficulties of educating them in the face of the Japanese advances into China. In reduced financial circumstances, it was Victor she looked to for help and advice.

From the age of six onwards, in fact, Hoo Wei-Teh's influence over his son was effected largely in his absence. His appointment as Minister in St Petersburg was followed in 1899 by and appointment as Attaché to the Chinese Legation in London. This involved him in frequent trips to Europe and America and taking his father's absence for granted, Victor in his turn would later regard any time spent at home as the exception rather than the norm.

Although Hoo Wei-Teh's career and his second marriage had left him apparently comfortably off, few luxuries percolated down through the family. Hoo Wei-Teh enjoyed the pleasures of social intercourse and banquets almost as much as he enjoyed the quieter pleasures of the countryside but he retained his peasant's frugality and ensured that, even in his absence, household affairs were conducted without any of the vanities common to society.

Whereas most diplomats took their sons with them during tours abroad, Hoo Wei-Teh decided not to interrupt Victor's education and in 1907, when he was appointed Minister to Japan, Victor was placed in St Petersburg with friends of long standing, Prince and Princess Troubetskoy.

For Victor, this change in domestic circumstances, which might have been traumatic for some children, was to afford him a happiness that he had not known since early childhood. Princess Troubetskoy had been seventeen when she married the Prince who was twenty years older. Despite the difference in their ages it was a love match and the couple was very happy. The Princess was related to the Romanoffs and was very refined and well-mannered but a youthful buoyancy and sense of fun broke through the strictures of her class. She was naturally affectionate, showering love on her own two sons and extending it unstintingly to Victor when he was visited upon them.

Victor adored her, although even at this young age he questioned the unswerving allegiance of the Troubetskoys and other Russian aristocrats to the Imperial Family of the Romanoffs. At services in the Russian Church, with its rich litany of chants and incense and golden icons, prayers for the Tsar and his family occupied most of the service. But, if he was sceptical of the focus of their worship, Victor never questioned the trappings of it. The emotionally charged atmosphere of the Orthodox service overwhelmed him and the memory of it remained with him all his life. The fact that the Troubetskoys and most of Victor's school-friends at the elite and aristocratic Annan Schule, which he now attended, were wiped out in the Revolution undoubtedly contributed to his lifelong aversion to Communism.

Apart from his friendships, it was at the Annan Schule that Victor first began to acquire the knowledge of languages that was to prove so valuable to him in later life. The school had originally been German, so German was naturally one of the languages taught there. Although not a military school, the uniforms had a regimental look to them. But if the school itself still clung on to the symbols of the past, the curriculum did not. Victor had the privilege of being educated by some of the finest professors in the land. One of them, a famous poet in his time, was officially charged with teaching classics but his love for modern literature suffused his lessons and Victor, as one of his most impressionable young pupils, was fired by an enthusiasm for literature that endured throughout his life.

As small boys the pupils were called by their Christian names but once they reached the age of thirteen they were addressed by their full names, excluding any titles, to show respect and equality of social class.

There was little need for a strict system of discipline since all the boys came from backgrounds in which courtesy and obedience were taught at home from the cradle. Though neither troublesome nor rebellious, Victor's problem was his desire to converse and be sociable. Silence was not his forte and thus on many occasions he ended up in the corridor outside the classroom, where he was told to stay until he could control his tongue.

The experience was always mortifying and he lived in terror of a reprimand at home although this rarely amounted to more than a stern but affectionate upbraiding from Prince Troubetskoy and the withdrawal of privilege - no play-time after dinner or no skating on a Sunday.

The home of the Troubetskoys was very like that of other Russian aristocrats of the time. Large and always warm in winter, the house was lavishly provided with open fires and the scent of wood smoke percolated through the rooms. In the cold season double windows were put up to keep out the extremes of frost and snow. Between the two layers of glass was coloured cotton, impregnated with a chemical to stop ice from forming.

As in most aristocratic homes, there were more servants than family. Apart from the obligatory governesses, there was also a tutor or répétiteur, usually a young man. In winter, night fell early and when the temperature dropped below minus twenty-five the children stayed at home to be tutored by the répétiteur.

At meal-times, the tutors and governesses sat at table with the rest of the family. The governesses were always foreign and came from good families with a high level of culture and education. In very rich families there would be one for each child. At table the family traditionally spoke only the language of the governess, thus emphasising the respect and affection due to her. It was a tradition Victor carried on later in his own family. Although we all spoke several languages and enjoyed the game of mixing them in front of other people, the governess was never allowed to become the butt of our semantics.

The Troubetskoys' English governess, Miss Gulliver, was from Glasgow and very strict about manners. It was from her that Victor learnt to speak English, so fluently that, when he graduated from the Annan Schule in 1912, he was chosen to deliver the valedictory address in Russian and English.

If Miss Gulliver commanded his respect, however, it was Mademoiselle Lefèvre who commanded his adoration. Half French and half Polish, Mlle Lefèvre had been educated in Russia and was therefore as much a cosmopolitan as Victor himself aspired to be. With her dark eyes and soft voice with its romantic accent, her long flowing skirts and the faint whiff of perfume that lingered in the air after her departure, she was the embodiment of Victor's adolescent longings. Asked why he was so besotted with the new governess, Victor replied dreamily: "Because she's so beautiful." It seems that Victor's weakness for a pretty face developed at an early age.

The German governess, Fraulein Klemperer, who followed Mlle Lefèvre, failed to elicit the same response from Victor, who claimed that she didn't like him and therefore he didn't like her. Where prettiness was not an issue Victor could be inscrutably logical in his feelings.

Prince Troubetskoy had studied in England and punctiliously followed the English custom of dressing for dinner, expecting the entire family to do the same. Despite the seemingly formal atmosphere, however, dinner was a happy, chaotic and often uproarious time, with a babble of voices amongst which Victor's was invariably the most insistent.

Every child, including Victor, had his own room in the house and during vacations the family, with governesses, tutors and servants, decamped to the family Dachas in Finland and the Baltic. Sport was very much encouraged for the boys, particularly horse-riding, and Victor's later decision to purchase his own race horse was the legacy of a love of riding acquired in childhood.

Boxing also interested him and later, in Paris, he continued to look for sparring partners, though most of them turned out to be rough and illiterate and the acquaintance did not extend beyond the ring. One day, when sparring, he accidentally gave one of them a very strong blow to the nose. Immediately, Victor dropped his arms and apologised, whereupon the ruffian gave him an uppercut and put Victor out cold on the canvas.

In spite of the family's wealth, Prince Troubetskoy pursued his career as a high-ranking civil servant, not because of any financial need but simply because it was expected of such people that they would serve their country. In many ways the values acquired by Victor in the Troubetskoy household were those he might otherwise have acquired on his own, the need to serve being one of his primary motivations in later life.

Until they were fifteen, the boys were always accompanied to and from school. The route took them past the Kirov Ballet and, a little further on, the Youssoupov residence - the home of Rasputin's assassin. In winter, there were invariably plates of hot muffins to ward off the cold suffered on the way home and Victor's friendship with the Youssoupovs survived the Revolution and their escape to Paris. Beyond the Youssoupov residence was the fateful Palace of the Romanoffs.

Victor's final years in St Petersburg ran parallel with the dying days of the Manchu Dynasty in China. There, as in Russia, the old order was about to crumble.

The fact that in China full-scale revolution was averted was due largely to the intercession of Hoo Wei-Teh himself. His career so far had been devoted to serving the last Empress. Now it fell to him to tell her that the Dynasty was at an end and that abdication was the only course open if bloodshed was to be averted.

Such courage could easily have cost Hoo Wei-Teh his head. The enormity of the risk involved was demonstrated by the fact that the man whose duty it should have been to present the Empress with the reality of her situation was too frightened to do so. Hoo Wei-Teh had taken on the task in place of the Foreign Minister, Yuan Shih Kai.

Apart from his personal courage, the incident highlighted Hoo Wei-Teh's talents, not so much as an innovator or pioneer but as a conciliator. It was in his power to draw together apparently irreconcilable factions and find common ground between them.

His reward came when, after the difficult birth of the Republic in 1911, he became one the only members of the old regime to be given a prominent place in the new one. In the 1920s, he reached the peak of his career when he served briefly as Prime Minister.

During these years Victor visited his father in Tokyo several times. Tough, ironically still not permitted to walk to school by himself, from the age of fourteen he became used to travelling alone by ship, often during troubled international times and was given a loaded pistol with which to defend himself in case of attack. A picture of him as a boy shows the muzzle of the pistol, pointing upwards from his breast pocket, next to a white handkerchief, his face serious but relaxed.

His experiences had made him self reliant and mature at an early age, qualities that would stand him in good stead in the years that followed.

On completing his secondary education at the Annan Schule, Victor left his school-friends in St Petersburg to join his father in Paris, where the latter was now Minister. He little knew how tragically permanent most of the farewells were to be.

These were the years of the First World War and the Chinese government was in a state of confusion and close to collapse. Hoo Wei-Teh was sincerely in favour of democracy and sent many despatches back to his superiors, trying to convince them of the need to proceed along more modern and democratic lines. Just as he had used his powers of persuasion to avoid a revolution in 1911, he now used them to persuade the Foreign Ministry to join the War on the Allied side. It was largely in consequence of this involvement in 1917 that China was later able to relinquish its position as a backwater nation and take its place in the world as an international power.

9

Victor's university years in Paris furnished the second side of his cultural personality. Whereas his childhood had been steeped in the nostalgic Slav tradition, inculcating him with a love of Russian culture, pre-Revolutionary literature and the haunting cadences of Gregorian chants, Paris gave him an intellectual dimension. His brother Augustin was at the Lycée in Paris. They grew very close and in the years that followed, continued to share everything. Augustin's later decline into an unfortunate marriage, profligacy and debt hurt Victor deeply.

Being already fluent in French as a result of his school years in Russia, Victor adapted easily to the French way of life and thinking. He found great social compatibility with the French, especially with pretty women, whose company he would continue to enjoy well into old age. It was here that Victor set the tone for his future lifestyle, one often more appropriate to a playboy than a diplomat, but with an underlying strength of purpose that kept his life and career, unlike Augustin's, securely on track.

During his university years at the Institut d'Études Politiques and the Faculté de Droit, he spent the summer breaks at Oxford and Cambridge, in order to perfect his English. He found the English way of life very civilised and in Cambridge, particularly, he discovered a kind landlady in a Mrs Highfield, the charm of British culture. A widow whose husband had been killed in the first year of the War, Mrs Highfield's stately Georgian home on Trumpinton Road had been divided into rooms housing young gentlemen from the Colleges. Although Mrs Highfield had been forced by circumstances to offer up her home in this way it was unlikely that she made much profit out of it. The young men were charged very little, they ate a great deal as young men do and the scent of frying bacon was as likely to percolate up the staircase at midnight as at breakfast. This is where Victor acquired a taste for kippers and, whenever in later life he would come to Britain, he always look for a hotel that served good kippers for breakfast.

Fifty years later I drove him to Mrs Highfield's house in Cambridge. It still stood there exactly as it had in his student days. He looked at the house and his eyes filled with nostalgia. We did not get out of the car.

Throughout his life Victor remained a great admirer of the British sense of decency and tolerance, even though the Chinese had suffered unfair treatment and treachery at the hands of British colonialists. He admired British bravery in wartime, both civilian and military and often asserted that their soldiers were the best disciplined of all. Influenced by his father's liberal thinking, he concluded that the British system of government was the model for all democratic systems. He respected the English ability to compromise and adapt to changing needs and above all, he admired the practice of "the gentlemen's agreement" which rarely exists in other countries.

At Oxford and Cambridge, he forged a number of friendships, both English and non-English, that were to endure throughout his life. University friends from the past reappeared at international conferences, sometimes on opposite political sides, though the links between them always remained genial. In Peking in 1930 and later, when he was recalled to war-torn Chungking in the 1940s, Victor was delighted to discover one of these old friends, Berkeley (later Sir Berkeley) Gage installed in what remained of the British Embassy there. The two not only shared an interest in politics but were *bon viveurs* of equal standing. Friendships like these, fostered in youth, did much to ameliorate the privations of the war years. No doubt it was as a result of this close friendship that Berkeley Gage became one of Britain's foremost China experts in the Foreign Service.

Although his sense of fun and capacity for enjoyment were already becoming something of a legend, it was notable that even his enemies were quick to admit that Victor never made the mistake of mixing work and pleasure. As head of his department at the United Nations he would later be renowned for choosing the plainest girls to be his secretaries. Why put temptation in one's way he would say wryly. Likewise, his interest in politics was serious and unprejudiced by personal concerns. His main preoccupation at university was the state of his country and the threat to her from Japan.

Recognising that his son was sincere in his desire to serve his country, Hoo Wei-Teh decided to try and place him in the Foreign Service. In those days it was customary and necessary in China to be recommended personally by someone in a highly placed position. Having received a western education this practice made Victor uncomfortable. However, he accepted that nepotism was practised and his background had instilled in him an obligation of *noblesse oblige*, to help friends and relatives wherever possible. He was in the delicate position during most of his life of receiving requests for jobs, promotions and recommendations, to the extent of being offered bribes and inducements. Torn between his principles and his duties, he tried to make the best of treading a middle course. That meant, usually, doing his duty (helping out) and then regretting it.

During the latter years of the World War I Victor continued to live in Paris where he was devastated by the news of the massacre of the Troubetskoys, the family he had come to regard as his own. At first, in the chaos of the Revolution, only the murder of the Prince and Princess were confirmed. Later he learned that their sons together with most of his schoolmates - the cream of his generation - lost their lives also. He was never to discover the fate of the uncongenial Miss Klemperer, who had been the last governess and stayed on, but his harsh judgement of her as a boy came back to haunt him when he imagined her probable destiny.

In 1918, the last year of the War, he graduated with a Doctorate in Law and Political Science. His thesis had centred on relations between China and Russia, the two countries closest to his heart, and led to the award of the Prix Goullencourt and the Gold Medal for outstanding academic achievement. Hoo Wei-Teh was proud of his son though typically he stopped short of saying so. Victor was similarly reticent. He had grown up believing that his accomplishments were no more than were expected of him. It was only after his death that I found amongst his personal possessions a beautiful gold pendant with his name engraved on it. It had come from the Fabergé workshop in St Petersburg and was the coveted Kaiser Prize awarded him at the Annan Schule in 1913 as the outstanding student of his class. He had never mentioned the prize to us and I only learned of the award from an entry in *Who's Who*.

Having completed his education, Victor was even more eager to start in his chosen career, his sense of politics now sharpened by the horrific events in Russia. At the time Hoo Wei-Teh was Doyen of the Paris diplomatic community and Victor was in the right place at the right time. It was in Paris that the Peace Conference was about to take place.

In the summer of 1918, after the Battle of Verdun, it was felt that the war was finally coming to an end. In October Austria sued for peace. The end came unexpectedly in November. Hoo Wei-Teh was notified that a Supreme Council of Allied and Associated Powers would be set up to consider the terms of peace. He cabled the Government, asking them to appoint a representative to attend the Council, and Dr Wellington Koo was instructed to go to Paris at once.

Victor's opportunity for advancement came when he was appointed Secretary General of the Chinese Delegation to the Peace Conference. Though as yet untried, his western wit and unusual gift for languages soon made him popular, though the people he worked with were still all friends of his father's and he was keenly aware of the need to show himself to be competent. His most obvious shortcoming was an insufficient knowledge of written Chinese, an area woefully neglected during his European education. Since this made it difficult for him to read the documents he vowed to rectify the defect as soon as possible.

In Dr Koo Victor discovered both a mentor and a friend. Koo was only a few years older but was already established as the most brilliant mind to grace the post-war Chinese delegation. Throughout his career it was to Dr Koo that Victor deferred on any issue of which he was uncertain. The two would continue to work closely together, in particular at the League of Nations, until 1946 when Victor left the Foreign Office to work for the United Nations Secretariat. At Victor's funeral Dr Koo gave a moving eulogy to the efforts they had made on China's behalf over the years.

Koo had taken a leading role in resolving some of China's internal problems and was to head the Chinese delegation at all international events from the end of World War I. He spent the final years of his career as Ambassador in Washington and in retirement as one of the Judges at the International Court in The Hague.

As the man responsible, along with Hoo Wei-Teh, for persuading China to enter the War in 1917, Koo was held in great respect by the major Powers. He was a personal friend of the American President Woodrow Wilson, who supported China - albeit with limited success - against the territorial ambitions of Japan. In return Wilson asked for Koo's support in setting up a world organisation to preserve peace. It was the ultimate irony that, having initiated the League of Nations, the American President failed to persuade the Senate to join it.

It was, nonetheless, largely thanks to Wilson that Japan failed in her efforts to exclude China from the Peace Conference in 1918 and although the outcome of the Conference was to prove disappointing, not only for China but for the peace loving community as a whole, at least her presence was established.

Koo's ambition, naturally, was to organise matters to China's best advantage. Of greatest concern was Japan's retention of economic rights in Shantung despite his warning that this would only facilitate the setting up of a Japanese Empire in East Asia. It was not the only fatal mistake on behalf of the negotiating powers.

Demonstrations by Chinese students in Paris and the desperate attempts by Victor and the other delegates to alter the League of Nations Covenant proved futile. General relief at the ending of the war had led to a mistaken belief in the goodwill of all those countries on the winning side.

In his book, *The Economic Consequences of the Peace*, which prophesied the terrible consequences of the errors made at Versailles, J M Keynes had written

'Our power of feeling or caring beyond the immediate question of our own well-being was temporarily eclipsed.'

In his own diary, Victor wrote simply:

After the War people want to forget about atrocities.

————————

As well as his fellow diplomats, Victor foresaw the apocalypse that was likely to result from this attitude, though he sympathised with the euphoria and relief that engendered it. It was an exhilarating time for him too. Few young men could have slotted so effortlessly into their vocation. The launching of his career at the 1919 Peace Conference marked the beginning of a long relationship with Europe.

In 1920 he was appointed a member of the Chinese Delegation to the League Conference in Brussels where he quickly became a favourite of the cocktail circuit. His fluent French, quick wit and liking for socialising also made him a desirable guest amongst local aristocrats. At work he made sure he was appreciated by his superiors for his more sober qualities: his thorough preparation of whatever subject was in hand, his punctuality and his deference.

His enthusiasm and energy were boundless and spilled over irrepressibly into other activities. It would inevitably be Victor who organised sporting competitions, bridge, Ping-Pong tournaments and, of course, visits to night-clubs. He would always be the last one to leave a party and was also developing a reputation as a player of practical jokes which certain friends discovered to their cost.

One evening in Geneva Victor gave a dinner party for fourteen people at one of the best restaurants in town. One of the guests was

Wunsz King, his close friend and colleague. That afternoon he told King that he might be late arriving at the restaurant because of an afternoon meeting, but please would he act as host and start the dinner. This was duly done but as the evening progressed it became apparent that Victor was not coming at all. King, who had the embarrassment of having to pay the bill, did not have enough money on him and this was long before the days of credit cards. Victor enjoyed relating this tale amid gales of guffaws but he had to admit that sometimes *he* would be the victim of his friends' pranks.

———————

In 1921 a posting to Geneva led to another as Technical Advisor of the Chinese Delegation to the League of Nations. This guaranteed him a seat at the League and entry to most of the conferences taking place in Europe.

The dizzying advancements of 1921 were crowned by his appointment as Secretary of the Chinese Delegation to the Washington Conference. Victor was about to return to the place of his birth. Although the Conference promised to be hard work for the Chinese from the beginning, the prospect of seeing Washington was very exciting for him.

By 1921 the fear of Victor and his colleagues and of many far-sighted diplomats regarding the inadequacies of the Peace Treaty were proving well-founded. Japan, who had been with the Allies in World War I, was now, as a result of her claims at the Peace Conference, in a position to dominate the East by control of the sea. She dominated all maritime access to China and Siberia, she controlled access to Manchuria from Korea, and from Shantung she could dominate Peking. With her rail rights in Shantung, she could cut off North China from the centre and maintain effective control of central China from Fukien Province on the coast. China had few friends willing to step in and halt this advance. As Japan's ally England was unwilling to oppose her. Russia had already been defeated by Japan in the war of 1904-05 and had little influence while American interest in the Far East was limited to its commercial market.

The Conference did not therefore bode well for China and although he had relished the opportunity of returning to his birth place, Victor found the American way of life very foreign to him. Politically, however, he continued to believe that the American government was China's only hope; but on this occasion any optimism soon proved unfounded.

Officially the Conference had been called to maintain the status quo in the Pacific. In essence it guaranteed Japan against possible US-GB joint attack. There was no attempt to limit land armament. Thus Japan was free to construct submarines and aircraft suitable for use against the continent, a development that was to have far-reaching and terrible consequences.

Once more Victor was conscious that his country seemed to have no voice, or that its voice remained largely unheard. It suited most western powers, who enjoyed special privileges in most large cities in China, to keep her in a semi-colonial state. It was a frustrating realisation for the enthusiastic and idealistic young diplomat, although his own career was continuing to move at a rapid pace.

In 1922 he was moved to Berlin as Second Secretary to the Chinese Legation there. On arrival, true to character, he immediately got down to perfecting the language, the basis of which he had acquired at the Annan Schule and with Fraulein Klemperer. An awareness that being able to speak the language fluently was an advantage when getting onto terms with the ladies no doubt proved an incentive. Having, as usual, taken the local society by storm, he found himself with plenty of opportunity to practice his German.

Less than a year after his arrival he was promoted again, initially to First Secretary and then to Chargé d'Affaires. It seemed to Victor as if the world were his oyster. Conscious, perhaps, that with each move he was getting closer to the heart of international events, he began to keep a diary.

One of his most powerful memories of this period, which he recorded, was of interceding in a political demonstration by Chinese students outside the Embassy. Victor believed in free speech and was watching imperturbably from the Embassy windows when he realised the protest was threatening to turn ugly. Scuffles had broken out and the police were moving in to arrest the leaders. Anxious not to give strength to the protesters by rising to the bait and aware of the harsh penalties meted out to troublemakers, Victor went down into the street and interceded. Persuaded that the students were guilty of an excess of youthful exuberance rather than anything more sinister, the authorities backed off reluctantly.

Amongst the students, was a face that Victor was destined to come across again in later life, that of Chou En Lai!

His halcyon days in Berlin ended all too prematurely in 1925 when he received an abrupt letter from his father recalling him immediately to Peking. As one of the most socially desirable bachelors on the diplomatic scene, Victor had never been short of attractive young lady friends. There were very few eligible Chinese women in Berlin and his western upbringing had, in any case, left him feeling more at ease with Europeans than with his own people. He had decided to have a good time before settling down, but events overtook him when he fell deeply in love with the daughter of a German aristocrat. For some time the two of them agonised over what to do. Aware that his family would not approve, Victor nonetheless felt bound to write to his father and ask his permission to marry the girl.

For Hoo Wei-Teh the matter was not open to negotiation and Victor, even at the age of thirty-one, was too steeped in tradition to rebel openly. He was relieved of his post and returned to Peking where his father was now Foreign Minister. There he was given a job in the Ministry of Foreign Affairs and served as technical expert to the Sino-Soviet Conference.

It was a bitter blow. Life, which had seemed to be opening up for him on so many levels, had suddenly closed in again. His existence in Peking was a good deal more restricted than in Berlin. Once again Victor was living at home with his father and stepmother and, although on the surface his relations with his stepmother remained warm, it was made clear to him that he must toe the line and behave in the accepted, filial manner.

Any disappointment he felt was kept below the surface. Although it was to be several years before "Lilli" was replaced in his affections, it was not in Victor's nature to spend his time languishing.

On his return home he paid the customary calls to his numerous older relatives and was told in unambiguous terms by all of them that at thirty-one it was time he found a suitable Chinese wife.

With the aim of bringing this about he was invited to a round of parties where mothers were encouraged to bring along daughters seeking a husband. Victor was not too happy with the arranged marriage system, being of a romantic disposition in the western mode and still in thrall of his former love. He showed willing, however, and feigned an interest in the planned introductions, feeling that he need not commit himself.

Naturally all the young ladies presented to him were of suitable family background but after a year a string of parties had failed to produce the desired result. His relations were baffled. Perhaps Victor was simply not in the mood to get married or else he was looking for the perfect girl who did not exist. Amongst others, there had been Miss Chang whose father was the First Secretary under Hoo Wei-Teh in Paris, but she was not attractive enough. Then there was Miss Liao whose father was a high-ranking diplomat and friend of the family, but Victor felt no chemistry between them.

Occasionally Victor had to make trips to Shanghai for his job. He had several relatives and friends there, including his father's young brother's wife, whom he called Sen Niang. The couple had been childless and, as was the custom, had adopted Victor's brother Augustin, Number Two Son in the family. Sen Niang was a very sociable woman who played mahjong in many Shanghai homes and who enjoyed a good gossip.

One fateful night in Shanghai Victor took his aunt Sen Niang to a fashionable restaurant. There he fell prey to destiny, being suddenly confronted by a young lady whose beauty made him stop in his tracks. It was love at first sight.

The girl was Marguerite Chen, second daughter of Shanghai's Foreign Commissioner. She spoke English and French fluently and was popular with many of the bachelors in the foreign service. That evening she had been invited to a party at the restaurant, given by a young New Zealand diplomat who was hopelessly in love with her. Marguerite's brother-in-law, James, had brought her and was coming back to escort her home. Sen Niang knew Miss Chen whose mother was a mahjong friend.

Although Victor was not tall or handsome, as some of her other suitors had been, Marguerite was secretly flattered by his attentions, admiring the agility of his mind and his ability to entertain her with jokes and anecdotes. She had met many up and coming young men, but none as dazzling as this.

Normally Victor would be talking politics with the men. That night he could not be torn away. They talked through the evening, oblivious of the rest of the company, to the extent that Marguerite suffered some teasing from the other women present.

The very next morning Victor went to talk to Mrs Chen whose first thought was that no man over thirty could still be a bachelor. She suspected him of having a wife abroad and was determined that her daughter would never be anything but Number One Wife.

Sen Niang gave her word to Mrs Chen that Victor was single and he in turn gave his word that he would never take concubines. In China at that time it was customary for the bride to live with her mother-in-law, but this bride was a modern woman - having been educated in the western schools of Shanghai. She was determined not to follow the custom and her condition for marrying was that she and Victor would have a separate house in Peking. This flouting of conventions was unprecedented in good Chinese society and for many years Marguerite's request was considered a scandal in Shanghai and even beyond.

Once these basic terms were agreed privately, the marriage negotiations - including the appointment of the indispensable match-maker - went very rapidly. Marguerite's parents were already concerned that, at twenty-four, their daughter was already on the shelf and if she did not marry at this late stage she might never find a suitable husband. They knew and approved of Victor's background; they were impressed by his experience abroad and believed in his potential success. Marguerite was not completely convinced. She was very protected and spoiled at home, and had never been required to exercise any form of responsibility. Still, she did not rejoice in being branded an old maid and she was very flattered at Victor's obvious display of devotion. This man was completely her slave.

Victor had to return to work in Peking but the wedding plans went ahead. Mme Wei Tao-Ming, a college mate of Victor's in Paris, and China's first woman lawyer, was a friend of both families and offered to be the official match-maker. Many years later she would still joke about that outdated custom and would laughingly demand special respect to be accorded to her.

The wedding took place on 1st June 1927, only three months after their first meeting. It was the occasion of the year, a modern wedding similar to that of Chiang Kai-Shek and Soong Meiling the previous year. The bride wore a knee-length white wedding dress, flapper-style, with a head-dress which covered the forehead, and yards of trailing veil. It was as if the couple and their wedding had been designed specifically for the front page of a fashion magazine.

The only thing which marred the occasion for Victor was his father's absence from the wedding. He was financially dependent on his wife in whose house he lived. She evidently felt the trip to Shanghai would be too costly. Augustin was his best man, the only member of the Hoo family to attend besides Sen Niang. Such was Victor's disappointment that his father had not attended that he cried. That was the only time Marguerite ever saw him cry and she blamed Victor's stepmother for what she felt was a cruel act. Marguerite also felt deeply that because the wedding was conducted in the full glare of Shanghai society, it was a personal and intentional discourtesy to her.

After a honeymoon in Hankow, chosen for its romantic setting, Victor was thrown back into his work in Peking. The couple settled in a part of the house belonging to Victor's stepmother. As promised, Marguerite was not required to share the same house with the older generation and a separate courtyard was built for them.

Until 1937 the family remained quite affluent. The house, which had belonged to Victor's stepmother even before the death of her father, was large and comfortable with beautiful gardens, a small pool, central heating and a car and telephone. There were two manservants, two amahs, a cook, a gardener, a chauffeur and an old gatekeeper.

Despite the many charms of the place, however, Victor and his new bride did not remain there long. In the year of his marriage he was promoted again, this time to Assistant Director of the Treaty Department. The following year he was appointed Counsellor of the Shanghai City Government and Secretary in the Foreign Affairs Department of the National Government.

Peking in those days was an enchanting city, especially for the foreign diplomats who enjoyed the best of both worlds. Victor was happy to rediscover some of the contacts he had made as a student in Paris and Cambridge, including the ubiquitous Berkeley Gage who shared his taste for horse riding as well as pretty women, and was destined to continue cropping up at various points in Victor's life.

During the six years that he remained in China, Victor's main problem, paradoxically, was in getting used to the Chinese psychology. He felt he was flexible enough to adapt both to eastern and western traditions but, like many foreign diplomats, he found Chinese officialdom very frustrating. Whilst he was popular, even amongst those who disagreed with him, some of his colleagues were suspicious of his western ways, especially those who had not had a western education.

Although politically there was a determined attempt towards a democratic government at this time and the equipment for it was in place - President, Premier, Parliament, Cabinet - what was lacking was a deep-rooted tradition of representative government. Victor sensed in his heart that he would always feel more at home in the West. However, in his characteristically single-minded manner, he set out to perfecting his written Chinese which always created problems for him when reading documents. He also took a leaf out of his father's book by practising calligraphy with all its attending ceremonials. He carried on practising this form of literary art and as a little girl I would be allowed to make the ink by rubbing the ink stick onto a piece of wet ornamental slate. This I was allowed to do only if I could keep from talking, for it had to be done in unqualified silence.

It was not long before Marguerite discovered she was pregnant but in the third month she miscarried. She really longed to be back in her parents' home where, furthermore, her aunt was a midwife. When she eventually became pregnant again she announced that she would prefer to return to her family in Shanghai for most of the pregnancy and for the birth. She felt the need to be in her home environment where she was indulged and pampered. This would remain one of the most important conditions of her life.

Both Peter and I were, therefore, born in Shanghai, in the maternal grandparents' home where Mother was surrounded by all that was secure and familiar. Here she had always had all she wanted.

Marguerite's health was never strong and she was very weak after Peter's birth. When she broke the news to Victor that she did not feel able to cope with a large family he agreed, on condition that he could have a daughter. When the second child was a girl, Marguerite was too relieved for words. "Now, I have done my duty," she thought.

Peter was a name chosen by Mother who enjoyed reading books in English and thought it to be a noble English name. "Mona" was selected in consequence of a Danish friend of Father's, who was married to the English Lord Beauchamps. I met Mona Beauchamps for the first time as a married woman living in London and she often included me in her ladies' lunches. Everyone wore hats on these occasions, something I was not prepared for and I once overheard Mona "excusing" me by suggesting that "…she looks Chinese, but she is from a good family."

My maternal grandparents' house in Shanghai was a big, rambling, three-storey house in the French Concession. The interior was disorganised and untidy and had an appearance of being extremely lived-in. Just as in St Petersburg there were more servants than family and they formed part of the family. As in all respectable families, too, there was a tailor who catered for all our sewing and clothing needs and a woman from Tientsin whose sole duty was to look after Grandmother's hair-do, an elaborate chignon with jade ornaments woven in.

Grandfather Chen had been Mayor of Shanghai and Foreign Commissioner. As such he had many decorations from foreign powers for he was the intermediary to their comforts, supplying sewage systems, roads, electricity and gas. In spite of his high public office, at home Grandfather had no say whatsoever. Grandmother was the undisputed boss and was feared and obeyed without question. Her days were spent playing mahjong and finding suitable marriage partners for the younger generation. It was perhaps fortunate that she had no sons, for in the Chinese custom her daughters-in-law would have been under her draconian jurisdiction.

In 1930 Victor had been appointed Director of the Foreign Ministry's Department of Asiatic Affairs. In April 1931 he and Marguerite went to Moscow for the Sino-Soviet Conference. The capital, where they remained for several months, was cold and desolate. It was the first time Victor had returned to Russia since he left St Petersburg in 1912 and he was shocked to see how the buoyant spirit of the people had been broken since the Revolution. Retracing his steps in St Petersburg from the Troubetskoy residence, where he had spent so many happy hours as a child, past the long abandoned home of the Youssoupovs' and the grim magnificence of the Romanoff Palace, Victor experienced a pang of unutterable sadness. The Revolution which had promised so much seemed to have given so little to the people. Passing them in the streets, Victor noted in his diary how furtively they walked, how devoid of joy and hope their faces were. Being by nature optimistic and forward-looking, he would never again try to recapture the past in this way.

The one positive aspect of their stay in Russia was the evidence Marguerite presented of her linguistic abilities. Within a few weeks she was able to communicate in simple Russian just by hearing others speak. Victor was impressed - he seemed to have found the ideal diplomat's wife. But Marguerite did not enjoy her time in Russia or the long hours waiting for Victor's return to the hotel when she did not dare to step out on her own. She resolved that in future she would not accompany her husband on short missions.

Married life had not proved to be a happy state for Marguerite. The honeymoon had proved to be a disaster in that she found the physical side of marriage not only distasteful but positively revolting. As an ardent suitor, Victor had been rather engaging, but now she found it impossible to keep up with him intellectually, socially or physically. She also felt that Victor was disappointed in her as a person and his energies soon found their way to seeking other pastures. Like all wives, Marguerite was highly sensitive to public humiliation but if she suspected her husband of infidelities, she was secretly relieved that she was spared from his physical advances.

Whatever course their marriage later took, it was therefore Marguerite who initially decreed that Victor should occupy the political arena alone, without the support that, as a young diplomat, he may still have felt in need of. It was a rupture in their relationship that would not be easily repaired.

Victor had taken his tasks and appointments in his stride, disregarding the disappointments and hardships along the way. Beneath his apparently philosophical approach, however, there was always a concern for his future which was linked to the future of his country. He also worried over finances; the Foreign Office was often late in paying salaries. Yet he was in their hands and largely dependent on their goodwill.

He had done everything by the book in the hope of getting an early foreign posting. In 1931, at the end of the Moscow Conference, his efforts were rewarded. Victor was appointed delegate at the League of Nations in Geneva with special responsibility for narcotics. Geneva was to be their home for more than a decade.

CHAPTER TWO

Geneva

Sino-Japanese War- League Of Nations - Death Of Hoo Wei-Teh

In September 1931, following the Moscow Conference, Victor was asked to attend the League of Nations Advisory Committee on Dangerous Drugs in Geneva. He was expecting to return to China afterwards but whilst there an event occurred that was to have international repercussions and significantly influence his subsequent career.

On 18th September 1931 Japanese army leaders, apparently acting without orders from Tokyo, took advantage of the political confusion in China and the world generally to occupy part of Manchuria.

The sequence of events started with a bomb explosion on the South Manchurian railway line followed by the invasion of Mukden and other towns. It was the beginning of an unofficial war between China and Japan that was to change the complexion of affairs in the Far East completely.

In January 1932 the Japanese occupied Shanhaikwan and completed their military control of South Manchuria. In February Pu-Yi was installed as Regent in what was now Manchukuo, all important activities being under the control of Japanese advisors. In March the Chinese were driven back from Shanghai.

China decided to appeal to the League of Nations and Victor was appointed by the Waichiaopu, the Foreign Office, to assist Dr Koo in the task. The situation at the League was deadlocked by Japan's refusal to withdraw and China's refusal to negotiate unless it did so.

Both Victor and Dr Koo believed that most of Japan's leaders were in favour of negotiation but Japanese foreign policy in Tokyo was influenced by an increasingly powerful military group, encouraged in their aggression by the mild support given China by the US and other powers.

Victor's job in Geneva, representing China's interests, was made infinitely more difficult by the continuing disunity and rivalry within China itself. At that moment when, more than ever, a strong foreign policy was needed, China was struggling even to be a nation. In those days Victor and the cipher secretary would often stay up all night, cabling for instructions from the government. The replies, when they came, would sometimes contradict previous instructions. It was clear that in the power struggle that was ensuing the decisions would be made by people who had no idea of the international stage.

It was typical of the confused directions coming from Peking that at one moment the Government would order its delegates to promote the adoption of sanctions against Japan and then change its mind as the military situation in North China deteriorated.

During several crucial debates Chiang Kai Shek was either away, tending to the military situation in the North or fighting the Communists elsewhere. With no other Power acting against the Japanese military advance in China and with China unable to unify as a nation, Japan's progress was largely unimpeded.

Finally, the League decided to send a Commission of Inquiry to Manchuria headed by the Earl of Lytton, with Dr Koo as an "assessor" and later representative on the Council.

The Commission found in favour of China and the League consequently ordered that Japanese military pressure should case. However, the fact that the US was not a member handicapped joint action whilst the British were reluctant to betray their alliance with Japan, governed as it was by mutual colonial interests in the Far East. Instead of ordering the Japanese out of Manchuria a settlement was proposed, making it an autonomous state under Chinese sovereignty but under Japanese control. This proved no solution to either country.

Japan's response was to give notice of withdrawal from the League on 27th March 1933. The episode proved to be the first serious blow to the structure and authority of the League and Japan's example proved a stimulus to aggression elsewhere.

The conflict was made more bitter by the discovery that the Japanese were using opium and other drugs as a method of domination in Manchuria. This was a new military weapon which the European press was only just becoming aware of. Peddlers had been organised from Korea to sell drugs as cheap cigarettes to soldiers who would then flee or surrender without resistance. Over the next four years the production of opium in Manchuria would rise to thirty tons a year. Soldiers, the poor, the old, the despairing, the morally dispirited: all were victims.

The problem of drugs was to become a specialised field in which Victor became an authority. In 1932 he was appointed as China's Representative at the League's Advisory Committee on Opium and Other Dangerous Drugs and he continued his involvement after the War, when drugs became a social as well as a political issue.

In 1935 the League's attention was drawn to another act of aggression: the sending of Italian troops to East Africa. This was the beginning of the Ethiopian crisis.

As it became increasingly evident that Italy was bent on conquest, sanctions were put into effect, but there were loopholes and Italy continued to advance despite the almost complete unanimity of the League.

Dr Koo and Victor worked day and night in this debate with its obvious link to the Japanese aggression in Manchuria. It was the second occasion on which the League had been proved ineffective and it was a humiliation for all concerned. The imposition of sanctions clearly did not work and it was therefore pointless to invoke them for the Manchurian Question.

In July 1936 Chiang Kai Shek succeeded in gaining positive control of Kwangtung and Kwangsi but in September Japan presented seven secret demands to take over the Chinese Army.

Chiang's difficulty in consolidating and centralising the various factions in the face of this aggression culminated in 1936 with his kidnapping in Sian by Chang Hsueh Liang in an attempt to force him to declare war on Japan. It was one of the most bizarre episodes in Chinese history. He was eventually released unharmed after demonstrations of loyalty throughout China as the only leader of an anti-Japanese popular front, a fact admitted even by the Communists.

The event led to a temporary rapprochement between the government and the Communists as a rallying point against the Japanese, although various factions still prevented a unified policy, some favouring appeasement whilst others were in favour of intensified resistance.

At the time Victor made several speeches and broadcasts a week in favour of unity of effort to preserve peace since tensions in Asia affected Europe and vice versa. He saw Russia at this time as the only western country able and willing to help China and safeguard the Treaty of Washington which pledged the protection of China's independence and territorial integrity.

In August 1937 Victor gave a speech at The Maison Internationale des Etudiants on the Sino-Japanese crisis that was to be widely reported. The crux of it was that Japan needed China for its raw materials, as an outlet for its surplus population and as security against Chinese aggression in the event of a conflict between Japan and Russia. Its philosophy of "Be my friend or I will kill you" amounted to international gangsterism.

At this particularly difficult juncture in the history of the world, China did not expect very much of the League but she had hoped through the League at least to make her case widely known, to arouse attention and sympathy and perhaps gain some material or political benefit.

In July 1937 the Japanese seized Peking and Tientsin but Chinese resistance seemed to be consolidating. On 11th August Victor wrote in his diaries:

> There have been a number of small skirmishes with the Chinese resisting all along. One Japanese plane was shot down in Puoting. Jap raids on Puoting aren't very damaging which proves that our anti-aerial defence is improving.

> Nankem has resisted repeated Japanese attacks. The railway station was taken but the three 'passes' will be difficult to take, according to Japanese experts. At Ten Ho Techen, twenty kilometres north of Peking, Japanese troops were obliged to retreat about a hundred times before they regained their positions. They have now evacuated their concession in Nankem.

> In fact Japanese residents are being evacuated from all over China. They say it's so as not to aggravate the situation, or because they fear a repetition of the massacres of Tungtchem. The real reason was given in *Le Temps* on 9th August, however; namely that Japanese residents have been boycotted and they cannot bear it. It is happening everywhere in China, which suggests an awakening national conscience.

On 14th August the papers announced fighting in Shanghai. Victor wrote:

It is like 1932 but this time the Chinese are taking the offensive and are attacking Japanese factories and preventing navigation downstream of the Yangtse. They have also burned the bridges of Woosong. The papers say the war is costing the Japs a million pounds sterling a day.

By the end of August Chinese sources from the Waichiaopu confirmed that Chinese troops had reached the Whampoo and cut the Japanese forces in two.

Victor noted with satisfaction:

> For the first time in *L'Echo de Paris* there was an account of the heroism of Chinese soldiers in attempting to sabotage enemy lines. These acts normally go unrecorded, whereas the Japanese erect monuments to their soldiers who commit kamikaze.

The general trend towards a more sympathetic attitude to China was heartening. Victor wrote:

> In England *The Times* editorials are becoming more and more violently anti-Japanese. They consider the battle of Shanghai to be terrible and reminiscent of the Great War. They mention panic even amongst the foreigners. When Fen Yo Sian inspected our troops in Shanghai he said morale was excellent and they were going to their deaths as if going to their homes.

> All in all, the better we fight, the more sympathy we get. I am receiving a lot of offers from Swiss people who want to help China. The papers are full of the heroic, desperate efforts of Chinese soldiers to defend their territory every inch. If only we had enough war supplies.

The new spirit of unified resistance in China delighted him though he agonised over any incident that might show China in an unfavourable light. In August 1937 all the papers carried the story of a Chinese plane dropping bombs on the international concessions, causing hundreds of casualties. Victor lamented:

> They admit it was a mistake, but it will show China as wrong.

The balance was restored a week later with an unconfirmed report that the Japanese had used gas bombs from planes, then a few days later with the wounding of the British Ambassador through shots on his car from two Japanese planes. Victor wrote:

> There is an underlying anger in Britain despite the Japanese assertion that they thought Chiang was in the car. Since Japan hasn't declared war on China, the British don't regard this as a valid excuse. What is interesting is that the Americans are also moved. They are even blaming the British for being weak! *The Times* editorial says that Japan can choose her enemies but will not find friends so easily. The real difficulties will come when the war is finished.

Victor cabled Ambassador Quo Tai-chi in London:

> Now the psychological moment is favourable for you to make a declaration in the press regarding Japan's use of gas.

The growing feeling of optimism was temporarily shattered by reports on 27th August that Peiping, formerly Peking, had been evacuated without a fight, as a result of the defection of one of the Chinese leaders.

Victor had been due to attend a reception in Berne given by Assal, Egypt's Chargé d'Affaires. He records in his diary:

> Assal asked me to stay for dinner, but I refused as I was not in the mood to enjoy myself, despite the presence of charming friends. What makes one furious is that the loss of Peiping is said to be due to a defection and not to military defeat. This will simply confirm in the eyes of foreigners Japan's assertion that China is not unified. The papers announce the entry of 3-5,000 Japanese troops into Peiping, without music but with a harassed air. The Chinese population is staying indoors in an attitude of hostility.

Despite the general doom and gloom, however, Victor's public belief in the eventual victory of his country did not falter:

> That day I said to Stacki, Chief of Protocol, that we would beat the Japs. After the war I saw him again and reminded

him of my words which surprised him a great deal at the time. He admitted I was right.

On 30th August news came from Domei that China had concluded a non-aggression pact with the USSR. This was at first denied by China but then confirmed. He wrote:

> The following day *Le Jour* published a secret clause in the pact, to the effect that Russia would supply one hundred planes against gold deposited there.

In September the Japanese seized Kalgan and Paotung. By October Shihchiachuang and Cues had fallen and they were about to take Tai-Yuan.

Nevertheless, Victor wrote optimistically:

> The situation has developed in a better way than I could have hoped then, both from a diplomatic and military viewpoint. Diplomatically, the bombing of cities by Japanese planes had a diametrically opposite effect from the intended one. The civilian population was not terrorised. On the contrary they are more determined than ever to resist the aggressor. Furthermore, the bombings have provoked the indignation of the whole world and there is a movement to boycott Japanese products. Reports in the League are certainly more favourable to us than we could have hoped. At the beginning of the Assembly, I had the impression that the Powers were not prepared to do anything. At the end the situation changed completely and we think we have obtained the maximum in the present circumstances.

> Militarily, we have not suffered a real defeat. There have been some strategic retreats but the loss was foreseen. Chinese resistance was courageous everywhere and there were no defections as some Europeans predicted.

> Now on the eve of the Brussels Conference, we don't know exactly what we will do. Two things are certain: a serious attempt at mediation and a refusal to accept any arrangement contrary to the Washington Treaty. The US believes Japan is not averse to mediation by a Power that

has not shown hostility towards her. This is something new! It is also announced that British troops in Shanghai shot at Japanese planes overhead. I do not think this will have repercussions on the general situation, but we must wait and see. The important thing is to fight off defeatism and hold out, whatever it costs. A cable from Shanghai yesterday said that the movement in favour of breaking diplomatic relations with Japan is gaining ground and that we will accept no compromise.

At the Brussels Conference, both the League and the US condemned Japanese actions but failed to effect mediation. In November Shanghai and Soochow both fell. The capital moved from Nanking to Chungking on 20th November and a month later, amidst reports of terrible Japanese atrocities, Nanking also fell.

Ironically, the defeats led to the very thing the government had been unable to achieve - a demonstration of moral unity by the Chinese people, including the Communists. At this moment at least, Chiang Kai Shek enjoyed full support. Despite the fall of Tsingtao in January 1938 and the Japanese advance along the Hankow River, Victor wrote:

> Our resistance is surpassing all forecasts. We are now better armed and have more planes. We have taken the offensive on several fronts, regaining some important strategic points and making the Japs retreat. They haven't yet been able to cross the Yellow River. In China there is no longer talk of compromise.

> The only bad news is the fall of the Chinese dollar, but I believe it is a ploy by the financiers and that we will arrive at an agreement. Maurice Privat predicted in his book, *1938*, serious events in Europe for 11th March (Austria) and a Chinese victory at the end of March. Let us hope that it will be so because he predicts a final victory for China.

> The Powers, except Russia, do less and less for us. All they send is medicine. The international evolution is less satisfactory than our resistance.

China's failure to gain effective support in 1931 in the face of Japanese aggression had demonstrated not only the weaknesses inherent in the League but the hypocrisy of many of its member states. Japan was an important ally of Britain who hoped that, once installed in Manchuria, she would turn northwards against the Soviets and respect British interests in the Far East. Britain and France, anti-Soviet and mindful of their colonial interests in the Far East, had been reluctant to condemn Japan. Only the US was genuinely sympathetic to China but was unable to act in the League. Those were dark days in Victor's life, his pessimism expressed only in his letters to his brother Augustin.

In March 1938 a Reformed Government of the Republic of China was installed at Nanking, thus repeating the technique employed earlier in Manchukuo.

Whilst the world was distracted by the German annexation of Austria and the Anglo-Italian Pact, which the British hoped would free them of Italian hostility in the Mediterranean and the Near East, the Japanese resumed their advance.

In May they took Amoy and Soochow, Kaifeng and Anking followed in June.

In September a United Council for China in Peking was created under Japanese auspices with the intention of making China a Japanese protectorate as part of the projected "new order" in the Far East.

Whilst the German-Czech crisis dominated Europe, Canton and Hankow fell to the aggressor, finally provoking protest from western powers who saw their interests threatened. The protests made no impression on Tokyo.

With the Munich Agreement of September 1938, the League suffered the final blow to its existence and the world found itself at war.

During this difficult period in China's history, Peter and I had been largely unaware of the momentous events taking place around us, although from a very young age we became used to listening to the hourly news bulletins on the radio and knew to be quiet whenever a broadcast was in progress.

For Victor, despite the worrying international scene, these were the years when his own career was beginning to take off.

His appointment as Director of the Chinese Delegation to the League had been in addition to his post as Chargé d'Affaires at the Ministry in Berne. In 1933 he was promoted to the rank of Envoy Extraordinaire and Minister Plenipotentiary. Switzerland would be his home for the foreseeable future.

His new appointment not only involved him in a great deal of to-ing and fro-ing between Berne and Geneva but with a great deal of work and responsibility. Because the Foreign Office in China was not fully equipped to deal with the various international questions brought before the League, it was left largely to those members of the delegation such as Victor to take responsibility for defending China's position there.

At the age of thirty-eight he was now representing his country, co-ordinating the Chinese Delegation's activities at the League and in the Secretariat, playing host to Chinese diplomats converging on Geneva for meetings, and liaising with Chinese academics at the Bibliothèque Chinoise. The greater the demands on his time, energy and social skills, the happier he seemed to be. He made friends easily with the local society and intelligentsia and the members of other Chinese embassies in Europe often looked to him for help and advice.

In letters to his brother Augustin at that time he talks of his plans to add an "international flavour" to his commitment to China. His grasp of languages gave him great personal satisfaction and some delegates, particularly Litvinov, the Soviet Ambassador to the League of Nations, expressed incredulity that such perfect Russian - the Classical Russian spoken by aristocrats before the Revolution, could issue from the mouth of a Chinese.

The facility occasionally had its drawbacks, as when Victor and his friend W W Yen went to the theatre in Geneva and overheard a Russian lady behind them whisper to her companion: "I like Chinese men but these are two of the ugliest I have ever seen." Victor got his own back during the interval, when she pulled out a cigarette and, stepping forward to light it, Victor was able to make a comment in perfect Russian.

Switzerland was his natural habitat. His distinctive cosmopolitan nature had found its home. Later, when he had to have eight blood transfusions to save his life after an operation, he would jest that he had more Swiss blood in his veins than most Swiss! The country was indescribably beautiful and the people were honest and hard working. Within the League he was at the centre of European diplomatic activity, with easy access to other European capitals.

There were difficult moments, nonetheless. In May 1933 he wrote to his father lamenting the fact that holding two jobs concurrently had led to jokes about his earning two salaries. This was not the case. The only real advantage of the promotion was that of precedence in international diplomatic circles. Since fifty per cent of official business was conducted and settled at social gatherings, status was an important issue.

The Chinese community of diplomats in Europe was made up, for the most part, of a tightly knit group of able and eager individuals. They were mutually reliant upon each other not only in dealing with the problems facing them in a strange new country but with the common problem of an employer, the Waichiaopu, who paid badly and never on time and who gave them little moral support. Victor found it difficult to maintain the necessary facade of his position with only a fraction of the funds available to other foreign diplomats. Funds were not even made available for anti-Japanese propaganda and this was sorely needed.

Within the diplomatic community, as in a family, there were, of course, the black sheep, the jealousies, the gossip and the crises. On one occasion Victor had to assist the local authorities in putting a Chinese student in a mental institution. Some of the Chinese subjects, even amongst the diplomats, were financially irresponsible. Victor often had to juggle the budgets to help out and kept a scrupulous record of all transactions. When one diplomat, William Hsieh, was forced to borrow money destined for students, Victor had no choice but to be the hatchet man, incurring some unpopularity. To further aggravate matters, he had to assume his predecessor's debts, a fact which had not been made clear in advance and which seriously damaged his relations with his superior, Dr Alfred Sze.

As if his financial burdens were not sufficient, Victor heard from his father that year that he was himself experiencing financial disaster. What savings he had managed to accumulate had been invested in Russian roubles, French Francs and Chinese stocks, all of which had lost their value. He was looking to his eldest son for help. Fearing that the old man would be forced to serve in the Japanese government, Victor sent him a few hundred dollars for his fare to Switzerland in case he needed it. It was money he could ill afford and he hoped his father would appreciate it and not ask for more. Other men might well have felt discouraged but Victor's optimism generally remained intact.

His frenetic life was made busier by regular trips to Berne, even though his duties in Geneva often kept him working sixteen to eighteen hours a day. Whilst there he was expected to write, broadcast and make speeches on the Sino-Japanese conflict, in English, French and German, with the object of achieving future support for China's cause. Each day, he sifted through the European press to assess, analyse and report to the Waichiapu on media opinion of the conflict. Whenever possible he would himself contribute articles. He made appointments to see political editors and reporters in the hope of influencing them and often sought out those hostile to China in the hope of swaying them. He continued to plead the importance of propaganda and the need for funds to make it effective but the Government persisted in turning a deaf ear.

Throughout May 1933 he continued to meet with the Opium Committee which had been the reason for his coming to Geneva initially. The problem for the Committee was policing the production and distribution of opium, since China was a major producer and made it difficult for the Committee to monitor trafficking. Victor's involvement with the Advisory Committee gave him a lifelong interest in the problem. Whether or not he foresaw the explosion of drug abuse, he inculcated the fear of drugs in us to such an extent that we were never remotely tempted to try them, even in the sixties when it was very much the trendy thing to do.

His involvement continued after he had left the League and he kept up a correspondence on the subject with his friend, Harry Anslinger, who was the Head of the Drugs Commission of the US Government. As a result of their efforts, he and Dr Koo eventually succeeded in putting through the Council the prohibition of opium imports to Manchuria.

With so many commitments on his time, it was hardly surprising that in 1933 he could write to Augustin, albeit with tongue in cheek, lamenting the fact that he had not had a day's holiday in two years and never went to bed before one a.m., sometimes working all night. Nonetheless, he adds that he has found the time to continue his study of written Chinese and can now read official documents. He also mentions that he has been approached to go to Moscow but since he is now the expert in Sino-Japanese relations, he has to stay to instruct the new members of the delegation.

In his diaries, Victor often alluded to China's relations with Russia as one of his concerns. Russian culture was in his veins. He knew and understood the Russians better than he understood the Chinese and had devoted his doctorate thesis of 1918 to relations between the two countries.

His loyalty to China nonetheless left him deeply suspicious of Soviet leaders. He felt guilty about this suspicion but when the time came he was just as mistrustful of the Chinese Communists. His breeding had left him with a natural aversion to Communist doctrine.

Traditionally, China had welcomed Russia's influence in the North as guarantor against Japan's aggressive ambitions. Until 1920 Russia had enjoyed many benefits in China and, despite a fear in China of Communist propaganda, relations and privileges had been largely restored in 1924.

For the subsequent two years, the Soviet Government had actively supported the Nationalist Movement in China, but with the emergence of Chiang Kai-Shek, the party was purged of its Soviet influence. Russian agents were expelled and relations had rapidly degenerated.

Russia's attitude towards China depended largely on her relations with Japan and it was the threat of Japanese colonial objectives to both countries that led to a recognition of the need for a rapprochement. The news, in 1932, that China and Russia had resumed diplomatic relations, had been warmly welcomed by Victor.

Victor's diaries for the period reveal that he was "enjoying the advantage of Margie's absence to see certain people." To my mother, he wrote more reassuringly: "I'm being serious, you can rest assured … Cheap girls are diseased, good girls don't come out."

Whatever whimsical pursuits he might have indulged in at this time were shattered by the news, in November, that the father who had been an example and figurehead throughout his childhood, had died suddenly and unexpectedly.

During one of his periodical retreats in the countryside, Hoo Wei-Teh had felt a slight headache. When his wife came to fetch him back in the family car, they had called on Dr Tchou Kuang Siang who diagnosed a slight fever that would soon abate.

Three days later, however, his head was swollen and he was admitted to the French Hospital, still in the care of Dr Tchou, who continued to insist that the condition was not serious. By dawn the following day, he was dangerously ill and was returned to his family where he died later that morning, the 24th November.

There was no final diagnosis. One newspaper report suggested hair dye poison as the cause but Hoo Wei-Teh had never dyed his hair. Other reports suggested anthrax or an infected tooth. Despite Victor's insistence, later, on going to Dr Tchou's residence for first-hand information, a definitive diagnosis was never made.

On receiving the fatal news, Victor immediately offered to resign, in keeping with Chinese tradition, and cabled the Government for permission to return to China for the funeral. However, the Waichiaopu, realising that the League was in the midst of debating issues crucial to China ordered him to stay. A French-speaking delegate was essential in Cairo for the approaching Congress of the Postal Union. Victor was also the expert on the Opium question, which was due to be debated at the League on 1st May. Besides, the Manchukuo Question might come up at any time and again Victor was indispensable.

The Chinese funeral was very elaborate. A procession carried the coffin from Hoo Wei-Teh's home to a temple where it remained until burial. Dignitaries, including Chiang, all the retired Warlords and literati, such as Dr Hu Shih, sent scrolls as was the custom. For the rest of his life Victor continued to feel remorse at being absent from the final farewell to his father.

He wrote to Augustin that he did not believe he was irreplaceable. On the other hand he confided that this was in fact one of his great fears. His insecurity about the tenure of his post in Geneva, his fear of being left out in the cold and his obsession about his salary not being paid regularly, all conflicted with a deep sense of filial duty. His official excuse was that he was putting country before family and he quotes his father's advice to Lou Tseng-Tsiang not to return for his father's funeral in 1902, for the same official reasons.

Once in Cairo Victor's professionalism enabled him to rise above his personal grief. The Conference was one of the first where China was represented as a nation on an equal footing with other delegations. All the work was done in French and the foreign delegates were impressed by the brilliance of Victor's speeches. One of them remarked that he could speak French better than the Belgian delegate! A South African article congratulated him on making speeches with the agility of an acrobat. For the first time the Chinese delegation felt that it had made an impact. At social functions Victor made new contacts, in particular Sir Miles Lampson, the High Commissioner in Egypt, and was awarded the Order of the Nile by the King.

On the return voyage from Port Saïd to Istanbul, he had time for six days of sightseeing, taking in Jerusalem, Bethlehem, Nazareth and Beirut, meeting up with friends and accepting invitations: then to Ankara where he did some riding and attended a dinner party held for him by friends from the Berlin days. His irrepressible appetite for life would always win out in the end.

With the conclusion of the League Conferences, the Government gave Victor permission to return to China. In July 1934 he arrived in Shanghai to collect Marguerite and the children and to visit his stepmother. Our departure marked the beginning of an affectionate and in-depth correspondence between Victor and his stepmother that continued until her death a decade later. From this point on, Victor was, in effect, the head of the family, responsible not only for giving financial and educational advice to his stepmother and eleven brothers and sisters, but in looking for husbands and wives for them.

On the journey from Shanghai to Geneva, we were accompanied by two others. My grandfather Hoo had a cook, Chef Chu, who was an excellent chef. Chu wanted very much to work abroad, so we took him and his daughter, Ah-Wei, to be our Nanny. Ah-Wei was not as enthusiastic as her father about going abroad but they convinced her she was lucky to have been given this opportunity. The crossing by ship took us via India, through the Suez Canal. It took twenty-four days, during which Ah-Wei was seasick every day. We thought she would recover once we had landed but in Geneva Ah-Wei's seasickness turned to homesickness and I remember her in constant tears. We were patient for a few months but she was determined that she could not live outside China, even though returning meant another long sea voyage.

My parents therefore decided to look for another governess for us. We had some good friends, the Vigiers, who had a Swiss governess for their youngest son. They told us that she had a sister, Martha, who was available. We asked Martha to come for an interview and she immediately fell in love with us and from that day became a lifelong part of the family.

We settled in our house in Rue Charles Galland (recently the office of Merrill Lynch) in a quiet and dignified part of Geneva, next door to the Italian Consulate and a few hundred yards from the Russian Orthodox Church. The kitchens were in the basement and the two reception areas and dining/pantry on the main floor where there was a small garden.

The first floor contained the living quarters for the family, in one corner a large bedroom for myself, my brother and Martha, with an adjoining bathroom. At the other end of the extensive landing was Mother's large bedroom, with windows from floor to ceiling along one wall, a large adjoining bathroom and one the other side, a dressing room with a walk-in wardrobe. Mother had the best of the rooms available and she rarely stepped out of her quarters. My memories of those days were of her being constantly ill in bed whilst we tried to make as little noise as possible so as not to disturb her.

Next to the dressing room was a smallish room which Father used as a study and which also served as his bedroom. This personal space was laid out in a crescent shape around the dark landing.

The stairs going up to the second floor led to eight separate offices, crammed with old desks and worn equipment. The wider staircase going down in a semi-circular sweep was where we used to sit in the dark watching the cocktail and evening parties below. It was exciting to see the ladies in evening dress and the men in formal attire and ever since those days social functions have always afforded me great happiness.

Occasionally, we were shown off to visitors, having been washed and dressed up and taught the right way to bow or curtsy and address people. On very rare occasions we might even be allowed to join official cocktail parties and pass the snacks around. The Swiss and other Europeans seemed to adore Chinese snacks such as fried pork balls. Some of them would follow me around greedily. Father was the life and soul of any party - joking, teasing, flirting, always with a broad smile on his face.

On the floor above the offices there was accommodation for the chauffeur. We all lived very much cheek by jowl. There was no separate entrance for the office staff, we were not self-contained and there was no real privacy. On the first floor, between the children's bathroom and the toilet, was a small room occupied by two of Father's male staff. We often had to wait our turn to use the shared toilet and I imagine that our closeness was sometimes a nuisance to their working routine. With the worrying international scene leading up to World War Two, there were many important things to attend to and we children were strictly forbidden to be seen on the office floor.

Sometimes Peter and I would sneak up after everyone had gone and we knew Father was not in the house, in order to search the waste-baskets for stamps for our collection. We did this in fear and trembling of being found out. We were generally well-behaved as children and the ultimate sanction, the threat of telling Mother, kept us in line. Compared to today, there seemed to be no rebelliousness from anyone. Everybody exercised self-discipline and if there was any suffering it was borne in silence.

The only "problem" I can remember in the house in the Rue Charles Galland was that of lack of money. It was a constant, nagging issue and when I found Mother in tears it was always a question of finance. I was aware of similar hardships amongst those of Father's staff who had families. They were proud people who felt it a privilege to be in the Foreign Service but they had to make many sacrifices.

In some ways we benefited from the number of people around us. The secretaries always had a cheery word for us as they went in and out. I would get all the attention, being a little girl and looking the image of my father. Whereas we received very little warmth and closeness from our parents, we did receive a great deal of affection and love from Martha and from the secretaries, in particular Mlle Badan and Mlle Chazalon. They would sometimes look after us when Martha was away for an evening and it was always a treat because they were obviously very fond of us. The only other source of family affection came from Augustin, whose villa in St Jean de Luz we sometimes visited without our parents.

After a year, Chef Chu asked permission to leave in order to open the first Chinese Restaurant in Geneva. He did not really expect us to let him go as there was no replacement available and he was so obviously a great asset to us. Father, however, did not have a moment's hesitation in giving his blessing to Chu's venture and offered all the help he could give. This was typical of his egalitarian attitude, whereas Mother merely grumbled about the inconvenience to us of losing him.

Chu made a phenomenal success of his restaurant. There were two or three other Chinese restaurants in Europe but his was renowned, especially for his spring rolls with crisp, paper-thin pastry, for which only he had the secret.

Chu eventually "married" his Swiss mistress since his own wife in China was unwilling to live abroad. The Swiss Mme Chu contributed greatly to his success. She worked alongside her husband, doing all the necessary chores, making a little go a long way. When all their hard work brought them fame and riches, they were able to close the restaurant for six months of each year to rest in their home in the Alps. When Chu died in the 1960s, his son and family came out to help Madame Chu run the restaurant, now a big building on two floors.

Despite the fact that there are now almost forty Chinese restaurants in Geneva, the Chu Dynasty lives on and Mme Chu, now in her eighties, still works in the Restaurant Empire Celeste every day.

After Chef Chu left us the best replacement we could find was a crazy Swiss, Robert, who had wild tantrums whenever the mood took him. He once threw a hot pot of soup at Martha when she entered the kitchen at a bad moment. Luckily it fell short of her. We stayed very clear of him and put up with his erratic cooking.

The chambermaid, Julie, was a dirty-looking girl from Geneva who was rather ordinary and not inclined to work. When I was six years old I learnt that she had a boyfriend because she had an accident on his motorcycle. We often saw him hanging around the kitchen and Martha wondered why he was always here early in the morning. In her innocence she did not realise for a long time that he was living with Julie and taking advantage of everything the place could offer him.

After a few years Julie left to get married and we lost touch. Martha recommended an acquaintance, the Swiss-German Heddy, as Julie's successor. She was big and blond and very emotional. She was also extremely clumsy and spilt and broke things regularly. One of her duties was to take a tray to my mother's room at meal-times. It was unusual for her to complete the journey without bumping into walls and doors on the way, spilling things or breaking crockery. If she was not very efficient, however, she tried hard and was an honest and loveable person. Father complained about her clumsiness but we kept her and later took her to Berne when we moved.

The chauffeur, Max, was a suspicious-looking character who turned out to be a Nazi sympathiser, and who used to bring girls up to his room in the attic. He usually drove us to school and Martha often had to wake him up as we waited with our hats and coats on. It upset me to arrive at school in the official diplomatic car although it didn't seem to bother my brother. I finally persuaded Max to drop us round the corner so the other children would think we came by public transport. Still, Martha insisted on escorting us to the school door. I so much wanted to be like everyone else, without servants or with just a "bonne" (a cleaning lady). Since Martha refused to let go of my hand until we were in the school compound, I used to explain, shamefacedly, that she was our "bonne." When Martha heard this, she was quite upset. She wanted to be known as what she was, our "gouvernante" and did not appreciate being demoted in the social scale of domestic help.

My experience of life was completely bounded by the limited world of our domestic staff. Father would grumble about them, but he did not meddle. He was much too busy with his own concerns. As long as things ran smoothly, he showed no interest in household matters. Nor did he take part in teaching his children proper manners, though he was quick to remark on any lapses. One grumble would be enough to bring us to heel. We children saw him as a distant, authoritarian figure and believed that he was the most important man in the world. We lived in fear of his disapproval.

The question of education, however, did concern Father. His own education had been a privileged one, exclusive and elitist. It was surprising in many ways that he came out of it with such liberalism and egalitarianism. He had no class consciousness whatsoever. His philosophy was that we should take advantage of knowing the local people, wherever we happened to live. In Switzerland he wanted us to integrate into the Swiss education system, especially as it was such a good one. We started at the International School because they offered English as a language and because his colleagues sent their children there. After a year, however, he could no longer tolerate the progressive and liberal atmosphere of the American-type school and we were swiftly inducted into the Swiss State system with its characteristic emphasis on self-discipline and a Calvinist work ethic.

Victor's own obsession with work seemed to increase as Mother's health declined. To some extent the two were linked by the need for funds to support her in her illnesses. In his communications with the Foreign Office, Victor continually reminded them of arrears due to him since 1931.

Feeling the health issue to be important, Victor had got into the habit of hiring a villa by the lake where his family spent every summer. The house was always within reasonable driving distance of Geneva and Victor spent weekends and occasionally weekday evenings there, although cocktail and dinner parties often kept him in Geneva.

The villas - in Coppet, Hermance and Corsier - were also settings for social gatherings. Chinese and European friends enjoyed coming for the day, lying in hammocks, playing croquet, swimming or boating. There was a constant buzz of animated conversation, always dominated by Victor who with youthful exuberance would organise competitions even for the grown-ups. Mother often reminded us that we were fortunate and privileged to have such a place for the summer. She knew there would be hard times ahead.

In winter, because Peter was a sickly child, we always spent some weeks in the mountains. Peter and I learnt to ski and ice-skate at a very young age. Our education was often disrupted, but the sunshine, pure air and exercise turned Peter into a tall, athletic teenager. Access to the mountain resorts of Villars and Chesières was more difficult because of the mountain roads that were often covered with ice or fresh snow. Victor was not able to spend as much time with his family in the winter months but they spoke on the telephone every day and Mother invariably gave him a list of items to bring up on his next trip. They devised a number code for these, most of which were daily requirements not available in the small village. Because of the mood of impending war, the Swiss authorities had banned all telephone conversations in a foreign language. Normally, my parents spoke to each other in Chinese or English. Now they had to speak in French which was unnatural and gave rise to a lot of amusement.

In May 1936 Mother finally decided to go ahead with the operation on her goitre condition. She had never been strong and suffered chronically with nerves. The disorder in her thyroid had been diagnosed as a possible cause of her ailments.

The foremost specialist in Switzerland was engaged to carry out the operation, but it soon became apparent that the "simple" procedure promised by her doctors was going to be more complicated. For a start the operation would have to be conducted under local anaesthetic. The goitre was of a kind that required the knife to cut dangerously close to the vocal chords. She therefore had to be awake to try her voice throughout the operation.

Mother's courage was never her strong point. This traumatic experience and others affected her spirit and her physical health throughout her life. Her convalescence took many months, during which she lay semi-lifeless. There were complications with her blood count. She seemed unable to regain her energy. The doctors had no answer.

In January 1937, just as Mother was beginning to return to something like normality, Victor himself was rushed to hospital for an emergency operation on an intestinal obstruction. In later life Martha related the events of those days many times over, always with the same panic in her eyes. Having been trained as a nurse, she had been centre stage during Mother's illness and convalescence. One evening Father complained of severe abdominal pains and asked Martha for some castor oil to relieve them.

She was not accustomed to arguing with her employer but felt it might not be wise and declined to give it to him. The next day the pain was worse and his abdomen was very swollen. Martha called Dr

Honnefer, the family physician, who in turn suggested that a surgeon should be summoned. Martha recommended Dr Martin whom she knew by reputation. When he arrived in the afternoon, he ordered an immediate operation.

Martha accompanied Father to the hospital and later recalled how the jolting in the car aggravated his pain. She promised to telephone Mother as soon as the operation was over. It was to last five hours during which Mother rang several times but was given no information.

When Dr Martin finally emerged, he said there was little hope of survival and that Father's heart was no longer functioning. He went on to explain that the condition was so advanced that when he made the incision, the intestines exploded out of the abdominal cavity. He had repaired and cleaned as far as possible, but could not offer much hope.

Martha did not have the heart to tell Mother the truth but it became obvious during the next two weeks as Father lay between life and death. During that time Martha stayed at the hospital and witnessed the steady stream of Legation staff visiting and leaving with devastated expressions. She had never, she said, seen a person so well loved by his staff.

After the second week, miraculously, there was a slight improvement that continued in the days that followed. Father had begun to recuperate. Dr Martin was astounded. Only one in a million, he said, would have pulled through. From then on he remained a close friend of the family and Father always made a point of taking him to dinner on his visits to Switzerland. It was not the only time in his life that doctors were to marvel at his extraordinary energy and resilience.

The real victim of this episode was Mother, who had suffered a severe set-back and whose health declined from that point on.

Before long Victor was back at his desk, as indefatigable as ever. Between 1937 and 1939 he made more than a dozen speeches and broadcasts. Apart from the growing menace of Japan there were social issues, of which the fight against the use of drugs, was paramount. He raised the issue of the Protection of Women and Children at the League, contributed speeches at a drive to raise money for the Red Cross and attended meetings of former students of Paris, Oxford and Cambridge where he had made so many friends. Some of them were now, like him, representing their various countries.

It was with mixed feelings that in 1940 Victor received the news that the Geneva office was to close down. In retrospect war had been inevitable and was the ultimate proof that the League of Nations had failed in its *raison d'être* of keeping peace in the world. Born out of the Peace Treaty of 1919, the League had been dominated by France and Britain and was therefore predominantly a European institution. Its greatest mistake had been the insistence on heavy reparations from Germany. Another was the dismemberment of the Austrian Empire whilst the German Empire remained intact. The League had the impossible task of defending the status quo in a Balkanised Europe. Great Britain and France found it increasingly difficult to agree on any issue.

By the time the new palace for the Secretariat, the new Council Chamber and the new Assembly Hall had been ready for occupancy in 1937, the League was already decaying. The great powers had no enduring faith in it and were not prepared to relinquish any of their sovereignty or special interests.

The passage of events from the declaration of war in September 1939 is only too familiar. Hitler conquered Poland in less than a month and the Russians, who invaded Poland from the opposite side on 17th September, partitioned the country with Germany.

On 30th November Russia invaded Finland. Hitler had already made a decision to attack in the West through Holland and Belgium. The date of the offensive was set for 12th November but was subsequently postponed fourteen times and finally took place in May 1940, following the invasion of Norway and Denmark. The German armoured attack through the Ardennes reached the French coast on 20th May. The Belgian Army capitulated a week later. After the evacuation of Dunkirk at the end of May, the Germans attacked the new French line on the Somme and entered Paris on 14th June. With Mussolini's declaration on the 10th the world was at war.

CHAPTER THREE

Berne

*Uncertain And Sinister Times - Will Swiss Neutrality Hold? -
End Of An Era*

Given the passage of international events, it came as no surprise to
Victor when, in the summer of 1940, he was instructed to close the
Geneva office and move to Berne. He spent days classifying all the
documents in the office, making an inventory of those to be kept
and scrapping what needed to be destroyed. He was particularly
careful to keep a record of all accounts following his
misunderstanding with his superior, Alfred Sze. It was a monumental
task which he had to do himself since only he could decide what to
keep and what to throw away.

It was the end of an era and he admitted to Augustin that he was
sad to leave. But with his usual optimism he noted to friends that
Berne was a delightful capital to be working in and insisted that it
was all for the best. Ever the obedient servant, he made a virtue of
necessity and put his whole heart and mind behind his post of Envoy
Extraordinaire and Minister Plenipotentiary at Berne.

He arrived there on 13th November 1940, a month after the Italian
invasion of Greece. He wrote in his diaries:

> Thirteen has always been lucky for me. Let us hope it will
> be so again. I am starting a new life and will try to take on
> new habits - keeping a political diary, for example. Once
> I've received Pu's (the Waichiaopu's) authorisation, I will
> be able to look for a house for the Legation which is worthy
> of our country.

A location was soon found and the local papers came to take
pictures of the house and family of this exotic new envoy. When the

articles and the photographs were sent home to relatives in China, they expressed their wholehearted approval. Despite the rumblings of war, which everyone knew would involve Switzerland, Victor remained hopeful. Even the news from home seemed more promising, with rumours of a Japanese withdrawal.

The Legation was located in a quiet, upmarket residential area, away from the commercial centre. The house itself, stately, though not very big, was at the end of a leafy alley, the gravel forecourt shaded by a large oak tree. It was a quiet spot past a few distinguished houses. Beyond the Legation lay a rolling hill of green lawn, ideal for us to play games and with plenty of room to run wild. We never had such freedom in Geneva where our movements were restricted and cramped, limited by the small size of the garden and our location in a built-up neighbourhood.

The Legation staff included Y M Lee, who had joined the Geneva Office just before it closed down. A Canadian-born Cantonese, he was surprisingly traditional, with old-fashioned virtues of loyalty, respect and hard work. He had married a girl from Shanghai just before coming abroad and, once settled in Berne, he sent for her. She came out, leaving their daughter with her parents. Once in Berne, the couple proceeded to have three more children in rapid succession. Victor helped them out by allowing them to live in the Legation and so save on rent. This debt was later to be amply repaid.

The Lee children went to local schools and spoke only Swiss-German until they left the country. Mr and Mrs Lee, however, had difficulty in communicating with each other as she only spoke Shanghai dialect and he spoke Cantonese. They rarely understood what the other was saying, which was no doubt the secret of their long and happy marriage.

Mrs Lee became a close friend of my mother's, both being from Shanghai and having no other Chinese ladies to consort with. The Lees would join us in the mountains in winter. Poor Mrs Lee was prone to car sickness and the drives along the hairpin bends were torture to her, but she never complained.

The First Secretary in Berne, Mr Jen, was a very intense and nervous person who came out of China without his wife but lived with his Chinese housekeeper. They behaved as husband and wife when he entertained at his home but she never accompanied him outside or on official events. This kind of arrangement was accepted and not so unusual among Chinese diplomats abroad and somehow it seemed to solve problems of loneliness.

The junior member of the office staff was a young man called K K Tsien, at the time in his early twenties and fresh out of Manchester University. His father was Ambassador Tsien Tai, an old friend of the family's. He had been friends with my grandfather Hoo but his diplomatic career was of Victor's generation. This gave rise to problems of address. Victor felt obliged to call him Uncle and proffer him due respect in consequence of his friendship with Hoo Wei-Teh. Ambassador Tsien would refuse to accept the honour and there would be good humoured arguments about it. They finally solved the problem by calling each other Uncle.

KK started his career in Berne and continued to work in Victor's shadow from then on. After my father's death, he paid tribute to his capacity for hard work, his trust in his staff and his determination to treat everyone as equal.

KK was a brilliant and sensitive young man whose only shortcomings were his lack of personal ambition and his shyness. Being the only son of a successful diplomat, he was expected to follow on. Perhaps an academic or literary life would have suited him better, for he had a theoretical and idealistic mind that would have appealed to younger generations. In the event, he had no option but to deal with the real world which he must often have found distasteful.

As one of his duties, poor KK was asked to give Chinese lessons to Peter and me. It must have been unbearable for him since we had no interest in the subject and couldn't see the point of it. Luckily, KK was soft-hearted and we could usually persuade him to come out and kick a ball with us. He even took us for our first taste of Coca-Cola in a cafe. Later, when I was grown up, I apologised to him for the hard time I gave him. Typically, he apologised for being a bad teacher.

The Chef at our Berne home was a Chinese, Tan Swan-hoc. Mother reduced his name to Jack, which became Jacques, which was easier to remember. He was a good cook who did not appreciate the presence of children in the kitchen. Once, emboldened by curiosity and boredom, I ventured into the forbidden area. His response was a quick chop of the cleaver into the wooden board and a fierce glare. My curiosity evaporated. Peter was not as adventurous or rebellious as I was and had long since got the message.

Outside the kitchen, Jacques was very friendly and accepted his role as our playmate in his off-duty hours. His French was very poor and we soon acquired his pidgin-French and spoke it with him. It used to annoy him because he wanted to learn the proper way but we took the special lingo as a game and it was fun. He was lonely and often spoke of his wife and daughter whom he had left behind in China. Martha had a soft spot for him and would have welcomed a romance but he could not relate to her.

The other full-time member of the domestic staff was a German Jew called Hans Waldheim, a middle-aged, fussy man with a receding hairline. He had been recommended by another diplomat as someone worthy of help in view of the persecution of the Jews a few miles over the border.

It was immediately obvious that Hans was not born to be a servant. He had a natural bearing and self-assurance. Yet he was sincere in assuming his role as butler-cum-valet. He did not hide the fact that he was homosexual and he lived with an eminent and wealthy Swiss lawyer some years older than himself.

Hans particularly enjoyed flattering Victor and would always address him as "His Excellency" in the third person, which had the desired effect. Mother always felt threatened by Hans. It was almost as though he were challenging her as a woman.

One evening, Victor and Marguerite had gone to the only night-club in Berne with a group of visitors. Soon after they arrived, Hans walked into the club and, before taking his seat, walked over to Mother and gave her a deep bow. She was mortified, as she felt he was treating her as an equal, and demanded to leave the place in case he asked her to dance!

Martha did not get along with Hans either. They got on each other's nerves. She couldn't stand his "ways" and her overweening love for us children would irritate him.

After the war, Hans remained in Switzerland and eventually inherited a small fortune from his lawyer friend. He became a religious crusader, joined a faction of the Protestant Church and donated all his goods to the Church.

All in all they were a motley bunch and afforded us endless entertainment.

As soon as he was settled, Victor set about receiving and visiting his fellow diplomats. His judgement on some of them was merciless: the Romanian Minister, Bossy, was dismissed as "an adventurer, more interested in worldly vanities than anything else!", and as for the Chilean Minister, Bosta, Victor had "rarely come across anyone so slimy. He looks like a homosexual."

The new Swedish Minister, on the other hand, impressed Victor with his intellect and Kisseivanoff, the Bulgarian Minister, with whom he was to have many dealings in the next few years, he found frank and "sympa".

The main subject of discussion, inevitably, was the war. Victor's diaries, the bulk of which were written in these months, provide an almost day-by-day account of the fluctuations in the fortunes of those involved, or about to be involved, in the conflict.

The general feeling was that Switzerland itself would not be invaded since Germany needed to communicate with the outside world and send funds to the Fifth Columns abroad, and the majority of the Nazi leaders had left their fortunes in Swiss banks.

In November 1940 Molotov had visited Berlin, giving rise to speculation of an agreement between Russia and Germany. Molotov's behaviour on arriving to a guard of honour at Berlin station, however, had earned him the ridicule of most of Europe. Victor wrote:

> It was perfectly apparent that he didn't know what to do. Finally he gave a military salute whilst dressed in civilian clothes and with his hat on! The commentator described him as 'ein unbedentender Mann'.

Other speculation concerned whether the Japanese were indeed withdrawing from China and whether they intended to attack Burma, whether the Germans would help Italy in Greece and whether Germany still intended to invade Britain.

On the home front the news was improving:

> Tsi came today with Klein. He says that the military situation in China is very good, that we are prepared for any eventuality and that the only reason we have not invaded Indochina is because the US does not now want any change in the status quo. In a year's time we will be able to produce enough petrol to be self-sufficient. It is inconceivable that Japan could attack Burma by land, since the land is so mountainous. Chiang is in very good form and more optimistic than ever. Even if all our access routes are cut, we still have enough resources to last a year and a half.

> As far as the war in Europe goes, Kisseivanoff feels Germany can only do three things: attack Turkey to take the Suez

Canal, attack Russia, which is the least probable, or invade Britain. He thinks she will do the third and take advantage of the fog. He told me I was one of the best informed diplomats in Berne. The others aren't even interested in political questions.

Victor disagreed with many of his colleagues who feared that a German defeat would leave neutral countries vulnerable to Bolshevism.

Kisseivanoff says there are two currents in Bulgaria: the Russophones, grateful to Russia for deliverance from the Turkish yoke, and Germanophiles, particularly the leaders, who would be more Russophile if they did not fear the bolshevisation of Bulgaria. He agrees with me that the Soviets are no longer scheming to bolshevise other countries at any price but do not miss an opportunity if it presents itself.

I said, for my part, I preferred a Bolshevik but independent state, to a state like France which is a vassal of Germany. Fear of Bolshevism has done more harm to Europe than Bolshevism itself. Mistakes by the democrats are responsible for Hitler and Mussolini acquiring power and keeping it.

Harrison, the US Minister, remembers the Germans at the Versailles Conference already playing the Bolshevik ghost in order to obtain better conditions. The Germans maintain now that Hitler was so disgusted by the negative result of Molotov's visit, that he wants to attack Russia. He won't, in my opinion, although he could beat her. He will certainly attack later, when the situation is better. If Germany attacks now she'll gain that part of public opinion in Britain and America which always fears Bolshevism. It would be a clever move from the propaganda point of view but, from a political and military viewpoint, now is not the moment.

In December 1940 Victor was introduced to the representative of the Vichy Government in France, Comte de la Baume, whom he was surprised to find more pleasant than he had expected.

He told me the Germans would like to keep the League in Geneva. I spoke at length about the education of our children and the difficulty of finding a school in Berne and he recommended the school in Fribourg.

I have the feeling that the French, even those of Vichy, have not changed and only pretend to want to collaborate with Germany whilst waiting for better times. The fact that the official French press keeps repeating that they must collaborate with the Germans shows that the population is not of this opinion.

When he visited Vichy just before Christmas that year, his impression of the French was that:

> … they have become less exuberant, more silent. One feels that something is eating them up. It is a good sign for a proud nation like France. At Lyon, we had lunch at la Mère Brazier for forty francs: a unique course of Olivier Salad for hors d'oeuvres, then a very good hen in soup, then 'chardons' and fruit. No butter, no cheese, no meat, yet there was sugar with the coffee. The food was less copious than formerly but very good. Afterwards they asked if we had eaten enough. That shows how important the French consider food and indicates too that they are not yet used to restrictions.

> In Vichy I stayed at the Ambassadeur Hotel which is mostly full of diplomats. There is a certain animation as if we had come for a funeral or a birth. In the Lobby I met the 'insistance publique' who says that everything will be all right because a fortune teller predicted that Germany would be broken. I told him we still had to help break her whereupon he changed the subject.

> Apparently Pétain told Hitler he would be prepared to make concessions to Germany but not to Italy because they hadn't won any victories, and that he would refuse to turn against Britain, their former ally. Hitler is said to have replied that he understood.

In conversation with Wellington Koo, Victor was interested by the latter's comments on the Germans in occupation:

> In St Jean de Luz, he saw how the Germans behave. Much better than the Japs in the same situation. According to him, at the barber's, two German soldiers asked if they could smoke whilst waiting their turn. In the shops the Germans queue up like everyone else.

> Koo also believes that in the case of a German victory in Europe, the situation would not be so tragic for us. In such an event the Germans would not need Japan and therefore would have no reason to give away China, as Germany herself would need China's market.

> 12th December 1940. At noon, I had a beer and sandwiches in a crèmerie. The fat patronne expressed rejoicing that the Italians got a pasting in Egypt. In the evening the concierge of the Ambassadeur said the same thing. He said British radio announced that there were 50,000 Italian prisoners, that the Italian King was going to abdicate and it would then be the end of Mussolini. The Germans are said to have three army regiments in Italy to defend Italian ports against a British invasion. No-one believes now that Germany will attack Russia.

> At the hotel there is no butter, no sugar and the milk is skimmed. Tonight I dined with Ortrorog in a bistro for forty-six francs with a bottle of wine. He says the French collapse was mostly a moral collapse and agreed with me that the enthusiastic welcome given Daladier after Munich was a sign of this. I believe that he, like all the French, wishes for a German defeat, but not knowing how to achieve it, wants to stay on the fence. Even Laval can't say what he wants to. I have the impression that when the moment arrives, there will be a complete about-face.

On 14th December events took an alarming turn. Victor wrote:

> I came to Vichy to see what was happening and find myself in the middle of the biggest crisis. It seams that Pétain had

Laval arrested last night. Germany apparently asked for the right of passage for their troops, who have to prevent a revolution in Italy. The rumours are flying about madly: that Laval was fomenting a plot in Paris and that the Germans themselves, who are suspicious of his double-game, warned Vichy. They also say that Laval was arrested because he had accepted Germany's three demands - passage of the troops by train, passage of the troops by road, and delivery of the French fleet. Only the first demand is being executed. Already thirty trains are said to have passed through today. A fortnight ago two German divisions are said to have passed.

They say there are German troops on the Swiss frontier ready to go through the Simplon but the Swiss have threatened to explode it. I wonder if I will be able to return to Switzerland. There are no trains today.

Later in the day he was able to report:

At six this afternoon calm returned. I was told that forty trains full of German soldiers went through France to Italy. The ministerial crisis is solved. This is what Pétain said on the radio at 6.45 this evening:

'French people, I have just taken a decision which I deem to be in the best interest of our country. Mr Pierre Laval is no longer part of our government. This has nothing to do with our relations with Germany. I remain at the helm.'

So the 'heir presumptive' has been discarded. The Constitutional Act No 4 which had him as Pétain's successor is cancelled. Laval's political career is ended because it seems the Germans themselves don't trust him. There is even a rumour that he had links with de Gaulle. As Flandin now becomes France's Foreign Minister there will be no trouble with the Germans. They say Laval had insisted Pétain should be in Paris for the ceremony of the ashes of the Duke of Reichstag at the Invalides. Pétain would have been taken prisoner and forced to resign in favour of Laval.

The crisis was resolved rapidly. Trains, telegraph, telephones are working again and I returned to Berne none the worse for wear. Pétain has regained some prestige because it was Laval who was diminishing his power.

Voltaire once described the French as being like chameleons that can take on all sorts of colours and are capable of anything. I don't believe the French are as bad as that. All crowds can become hysterical, given the right circumstances, and the French are no exception.

When I had lunch with Holma, I told him France was being held by the testicles. That is why she dares not do anything, even though she has not lost any parts of her body. The testicles are the 1,800,000 young men held prisoner by the Germans. Secondly, Pétain's reference in his speech to 'strong domestic political reasons' probably referred to Laval's betrayal. Finally I questioned whether his assertion that the change in government had nothing to do with Franco-German relations meant that it could have a bearing on relations with Italy?

Later that evening, the volatile nature of wartime politics showed itself in an unexpected turn of events. Again, supposition and rumour were the main sources of information:

At 10.30 p.m., we learned that Otto Abetz, the German Ambassador in Paris, is arriving in Vichy tonight to save Laval. Hitler is supposed to have cabled Abetz that Laval is the only person who collaborated truly with Germany. They say it is Goering who is against Laval. We don't know what Abetz will require: Laval's release, his return to the government, or other concessions in exchange for Laval's imprisonment. We think it will be difficult for Pétain to re-accept Laval. They waited too long to arrest him. That allowed him to get too close to Germany. It would be bad for the French press to speak about changes in the Cabinet. Thus *Paris Soir* was censured for publishing what the morning papers had said on the subject.

In fact, everyone rejoiced at Laval's arrest but now a new complication is emerging. France is tied hand and foot.

One day they will lose patience. It will be the last straw and no-one can say what will happen then. British radio has presented Flandin as pro-British. The French fear this will further complicate matters.

16th December 1940: It is said that Abetz arrived with ten experts and 'symbols of collaboration' in the shape of German soldiers with machine guns on the *marche-pied* of his car! They say that Pétain will not give in, at least not as far as Laval is concerned.

But as always, nothing was certain. The following day he wrote:

Pétain was forced to give in. Laval is free. He remains the French negotiator for the Germans. It seems he was invited to return to the Cabinet but refused. The future will tell us whose prestige, Laval's or Pétain's, will suffer.

18th December 1940: Laval left for Paris with Abetz in his car. Thus he has justified the nickname 'traitor.' They reckon he is going to form a government in Paris similar to Wang Ching Wei's (the Chinese leader of the Japanese puppet government in Nanking).

———

31 December 1940: I have not had time to write for a fortnight. From Vichy I went on to Marseilles and then to Cannes. My impression of France was that the French are stunned by the shock of their defeat. Counting on a rapid British defeat, they are adopting a submissive stance vis-à-vis the victors, in the hope of saving what can be saved. British resistance is waking them up little by little, but they don't want to do anything to compromise an alliance with Germany in the event of the latter winning the war. Furthermore, the 1,800,000 French prisoners are hostages in German hands and the French do not want to jeopardise the safety of these prisoners. All France hopes for a British victory, or rather a German defeat, except for the few business men who would prefer to work with the Germans. In Africa, a French Army is coming together, hoping to fight either against Germany or England when the circumstances arise.

———

The beginning of 1941 was a tense time in Europe. Having survived the German bombers, Britain was hoping that the German economy would eventually collapse and America or Russia would enter the war on her side. The threat of invasion was still a very real one for it was not then known that, since the previous October, Hitler had been preoccupied with "Barbarossa", the invasion of Russia, which was to start on 15th May.

In January 1941 Victor went to Locarno to look at the furniture Haydt had offered to lend to the Legation:

> He has just returned from Germany and Holland. He says that in German trains everyone is well-dressed and good humoured. The food is better than a year ago and better than in Holland. One cannot see how Germany could be beaten militarily but the future from an economic viewpoint is sober. One foresees intense British bombing as soon as ice no longer weighs down the planes and he wonders if German morale will still be as high then. Only half of the workers are Nazis. Hitler's last speech to the workers did not please them. They say they can't be duped by words. Holland had reserves of food stuffs for three years for a population of twenty-one million. The Germans have taken all of it and it will only last three months. In Belgium there are no reserves. He says there is nothing to fear in Switzerland but that Swiss newspapers should be less happy about Axis defeats because that irritates the Germans. Schacht says that if Switzerland behaves herself nothing will happen to her.

> 27th January 1941. Today, on returning from Locarno, I dined in the train with an Italian pilot coming from Bardin to see his parents in Basel. He obtained leave because he had served for two years with distinction. He hopes the war will end and says he doesn't know why we are fighting. He probably thought I was Japanese.

Another month elapses before there are any further entries. During March, events led up to the almost simultaneous German attacks in the western Desert and on Yugoslavia and Greece. For most of the month Victor was away from Berne but on 4th April he records a number of developments:

There have been several Chinese victories, most notably at Kiangsi. Yugoslavia has seen a coup d'état, Italy has been defeated at sea and in Albania, and the British have advanced in Abyssinia.

The Yugoslavs, or rather the Serbs, are the only ones to have showed real courage. They confronted Germany without being invaded! If all countries had the same attitude, Germany would not be so successful. If the Czechs had had it in Munich, the history of the world might have been different.

On 10th April 1941 he recorded the Germans advance into North Africa and the fall of Salonika.

The political confusion of this period, the changes that took place from minute to minute and the difficulties of obtaining a clear picture of events, were demonstrated later that month. Victor had received confirmation from an informant that the much publicised meetings between the Japanese Matsuoka and Stalin, had no far-reaching political implications.

I drafted a telegram to this effect for the Pu, but two minutes after it was sent I learnt of the signing of the neutrality treaty between Russia and Japan. Thank God I was able to stop the cable.

It is generally believed that it was Russia who proposed the treaty with Japan, to scare the Germans. Japan has been so weakened that even after the signature of the treaty she would not attempt anything. Russia knows that too; I doubt that Germany will attack Russia now as she wants to spread towards Suez.

The British have suffered their worse air raids so far. This war is costing a lot more than the last one and Europe will be in an even greater state of exhaustion afterwards. Then it will be China's turn to play a big role because the Chinese market will give work to all the European workers who no longer manufacture armaments.

In May, Victor, like the rest of the world, was intrigued by an extraordinary turn of events:

Rudolf Hess has taken flight alone from Germany and landed near Glasgow. The German press treats him like a madman and maintains he has been ill for several years. If that is true, one can't understand why Hitler named him as successor to Goering in the event of something happening to him. Kelly, the British Minister, who is always a bit simplistic, thinks this flight means Hess knows Germany will lose the war. Now that he has fled, he won't be able to return unless the Nazi regime is overthrown. Therefore he has the greatest interest in divulging to the British all the secrets he knows.

I believe Hess must be in discord with Hitler and has left him in order not to be mixed up in his decisions and to save his life, but he must be rather courageous and patriotic not to divulge anything, unless he believes that Hitler's downfall would be Germany's salvation.

I am inclined to think that in the end it will be the economic situation that determines the outcome of the war. If the people in the German occupied territories starve, they will have an uprising and risk being shot rather than die slowly of hunger. If Britain can hold out until November she will have won the war. Even if the Germans go to Africa, the British will harass them there. Germany is getting further from her bases and therefore her difficulties increase.

On 14th May 1941 Victor gave his first dinner party in the new house in Berne. It was very successful. He recorded:

After dinner we spoke politics and Masson said bitterly that irresponsible Swiss journalists will drag the country into war by showing hostility to the Germans and thereby giving them a pretext. If there is war the Swiss should rally and fight together. They mustn't start a war on an issue where they are wrong. Radziwill remarked that Germans can always find a pretext and if the Swiss give in all the time, so as not to provide one, they will never be able to justify themselves.

I took on the discussion, giving an example of two raped women: one, before being raped, slaps her aggressor and is blamed for having provoked the rape by the slap. The other gives in to all the pressures until she cannot avoid the rape, nor give a slap.

20th May 1941. Dr Ting, from our Berlin Embassy, came to dinner. He says there is less food in Germany than in Switzerland. They have 500 grams of meat, including charcuteries and eggs, per week. He says Germany will attack Russia by June. It is the Yugoslav Campaign that postponed it. Germany will want to go on to the Urals and Bakou. Then she will attack Gibraltar. Suez will be for next year.

He believes that Hess had to leave Germany because his life was in danger, not in order to try to arrange a peace treaty. Hitler is playing up to him to stop him revealing secrets. This is why the German press is so soft on Hess.

By the middle of June he was writing:

It seems less and less likely that Germany will attack Russia, despite what Ting said.

But on 2nd July 1941 he wrote:

Germany has done just that! So much for my predictions, though most diplomats shared my view. Apparently it was the Wehrmacht who wanted to wage war against Russia, to crush Communism.

In the same entry he recorded that the Axis and its associates had finally recognised Wang Ching Wei. Victor wrote:

The fact that they have done it now must signify that the German war against Russia has released Germany from the obligation of sparing the latter who was against such recognition.

The outcome of the Russo-German war will almost certainly depend on whether Russia is able to conserve its armies and do what we have done in our war against Japan: retreat without giving in. The Germans admit that the Russians fight very well and do not capitulate.

15th July 1941. Our Embassy and our two Consulates in Germany have been here a few days, in order to go to China. Amongst the members of the Embassy there are a variety of opinions on perspectives of the war.

Chen Chieh, our Ambassador in Berlin, wants to show that Wang Ching Wei's recognition by Germany could not have been avoided, in spite of all his efforts. Japan demanded it. Chen had notified the Wilhelmstrasse that there would be a breaking off of diplomatic relations in the event of recognition and that the good relations between China and Germany, established after so many years of effort, would be affected for at least a generation.

Ninety-seven per cent of the Germans deplore our rupture. Many came to the station for the Embassy's departure and some were even crying. We broke with Germany and not vice versa.

Some members of the Embassy like General Kwei, believe the Germans will soon come to Switzerland. Mrs Beue Tan says that a well-informed German told her not to stay too long in Switzerland. But perhaps he meant she would no longer be able to pass through Spain and Portugal. Chen Chieh does not believe in an invasion of Switzerland before the end of the war, especially a victorious one for the Germans. They say in Berlin that it will only become dangerous for Switzerland when Germany attacks Italy.

On 16th July Victor obtained strong confirmation that Germany was running out of provisions and was hoping to find raw materials in Russia. He noted laconically:

They will be disappointed, since the Russians destroy everything and the war could finish very quickly if the Germans don't succeed in Russia.

The Russian soldiers are fighting so well that the Germans try to find absurd explanations, like the Japs and Hankow,

61

who maintained we had orang-utan reserves. Some believe that the Russian soldiers fight because they have no choice as they are machine-gunned from the rear.

One German soldier who had been on all the fronts had never seen anything as ruthless as the Russian campaign. They use any method to kill as many of the enemy as possible. Today the German press says the Russians are unfairly accusing them of using gas, in order to use it themselves. We will see who uses it first. It will be a total war of destruction in which the Russians will follow our policy of scorched earth.

Klein and Ting say that food is getting scarcer in Germany than it was in 1918. Rations are more generous but they can't be bought in the shops. Now, the people get 400 grams of meat a week, compared to 350 grams then. In 1918 one could still buy food in the countryside, but now even they have none. In the first war the German people only suffered hardships after 1914, whereas now they have been rationed since 1933.

Japan has again changed her Cabinet. My opinion is that, because there is an admiral in foreign affairs, it indicates their intention towards the south, Indochina. Matsuoka really wanted to avoid confrontation with the US and his resignation suggests that the new Japanese cabinet has a more 'positive' policy.

On 5th August 1941 he wrote:

My forecast was right; Japan had obtained new concessions in Indochina from France. In order to justify it the French gave a truly unworthy explanation: that Japan has declared it will recognise Indochina's integrity and French sovereignty and that they trust Japan with the protection of Indochina. They also invoke the British and Chinese threat to the area.

Yesterday I saw Klein in Lucerne. He told me confidentially that Chi Tsun returned to Chungking with a report proclaiming an agreement between China, Britain and US not to conclude a separate peace. Schacht is supposed to have given a personal letter to Chiang. Chiang could make proposals for a just and lasting peace which everyone would be prepared to accept. In such an event Hitler would go and we would avoid the continuation of the war and eventual German defeat. Klein asked me to take charge of the link if the proposals come to fruition! Schacht's idea is surely to use us to prevent a German defeat and achieve power for themselves.

I have been negotiating with the Political Department on the protection by Switzerland of our interests in Germany, Italy and Romania, but Kocher says that as Germany has recognised the government of Wang Ching Wei as the national government of China, they cannot agree that a third power should represent the interests of the 'Chiang Kai-Shek Regime.' The Germans are therefore going farther than at the beginning, when they only recognised Wang as a local authority.

29th August 1941. For a week the talk is that Germany is preparing a winter campaign. The papers here mention it openly. The Germans have ordered portable barracks from Switzerland, 600,000 pairs of skis in Sweden, sleighs from France and furs, etc.

The day before yesterday I dined with Politis, President of the League of Nations, who has returned from France. He thinks it will take until 1943 to crush Germany. I told him I thought the war would end in the autumn of 1942, that the Reichswehr would not wait to be crushed in order to overthrow Hitler and make an honourable peace. I said that if statesmen remain as stupid as before the war, we will have another one in twenty-five years, even if Britain is victorious.

The news coming out of Germany had begun to take a sinister turn. On 15th August 1941 Victor wrote:

Mme Clavel yesterday told me that certain sources are absolutely sure the Germans are killing their own disabled and sick people so as not to have to feed them, and their fat is then used for lubricants! There are surely barbarians who emerge during times of war.

Hans, the butler, underscored the rumour passed on by Mme Clavel by declaring that he had heard from a person coming from Germany that doctors in hospitals were being forced to give injections to kill the old and incurable and those with hereditary illnesses.

In 1942 an article in the *New York Times* confirmed the rumour.

Despite the often sombre news recorded in the diaries and the continuing uncertainty of Switzerland's position, Victor was, by and large, happier in Berne than he had been in Geneva. The air was better and his staff were more compatible. Other ambassadors often asked his advice and help in transferring their wives, getting jobs for their children, etc. More crucially, in 1941, he was able to save the lives of some Jewish friends, Mr and Mrs Walbaum, by asking his friend, Ambassador Frank Lee in Lisbon to secure passage for them to the US.

In the second half of 1941, however, just as he was beginning to feel thoroughly at home in Berne, he received some disturbing news:

> At the beginning of September I received a cable from Tsien warning me that I was about to be recalled by Chiang. Besides, Quo believes it would be better for me to serve for a time in the Pu. The following day I received an official cable from them. I don't know the real reason for their decision. When I get to China I will certainly find out.

————

Although he was unhappy about leaving, Victor was not in a position to argue against his recall and in any case, it wasn't in his nature to be downhearted. He was soon turning the decision to advantage:

> For myself it would really be better that I return to Chungking to renew contact with the leaders. Life and work will be more interesting there. Everyone in Switzerland has expressed real regret at my departure.

> Sometime after receiving these cables, I was informed that General Kwei Yun Ching had been appointed Conseiller

of the Legation and Chargé d'Affaires in my place. The Swiss Government will not be pleased to have Kwei in Berne, since he was not accepted as attaché militaire.

At the end of September 1941 Victor left for Lisbon, travelling by car via France and Spain. He took Mother and Peter but allowed me to do the trip by train with the Tsien family because I suffered badly from car sickness. The plan was to leave us with his brother, Augustin. In our own time, we could then arrange our passage to the US to await the end of the war.

Victor himself left Lisbon by ship for the US The journey was not a pleasant one and on 2nd November he wrote:

> I am grounded in my cabin on the *Exeter* by a ridiculous rheumatism in my left shoulder. I don't know where I caught it. It could be the beginning of a rheumatism which will plague me for the rest of my life but I don't think so.
>
> I left Margie and the children in Lisbon with Augustin and Lou Che Ngan. It is better, I'm told, for them not to stay in Shanghai and under the circumstances, Lisbon is the best place, since it is less expensive than elsewhere, the climate is mild and Augustin is there. The children will not waste time, as there is a good French school. In such times I don't know when I will see them again, or where, or under what circumstances. If I am sent abroad within two years, their stay in Lisbon will have cost me nothing, as I shall have saved the cost of their trip to China which would have been around $5,000, whereas $200 a month is enough for them in Lisbon.

Victor eventually arrived in New York on 19th November 1941, in time for one of the most significant events of the war. The Japanese attack on Pearl Harbour on 11th December, which finally brought America into the war, was a great relief to everyone, but especially to the Chinese, who had been fighting longer and more desperately than any of the other Allies ...

CHAPTER FOUR

Washington

Working with T V Soong - The United States At War

Although Victor had been bewildered as to the reasons for his recall and unhappy about leaving Berne, fate was about to throw the dice in his favour again.

On his way to China, he went, via the US, to meet with T V Soong, the newly appointed Foreign Minister.

Soong had been sent to Washington on a special mission to obtain war supplies and aid from the US under the Lend Lease. Although America had traditionally been generous in its attitude to China, the feeling now was that the primary task was to overcome the enemy in Europe. This was underscored by Marshall and Stimpson in their foreign policy, by Roosevelt's friendship with Churchill and by the special relationship with Britain.

Soong's job was to sway the US into giving equal importance to defeating Japan. His close advisors were mostly non-Chinese and all were US specialists. The great advantage of Victor's presence was that, unlike them, he had a thorough knowledge of Europe, the Far East and Russia. Soong, by appointing him as one of two Vice Foreign Ministers, was able to use him both for his languages and for his European contacts.

Throughout the latter part of 1941, Victor's diaries record the vacillations in America's attitude. Kurusu, the Japanese envoy, had come from Japan on a special mission to try for an eleventh hour agreement. The Chinese, particularly Hu Shih, our Ambassador in Washington, did not believe that negotiations between the US and Japan would succeed or that America would ultimately sacrifice China to an agreement. Nevertheless, the Japanese bombing of Pearl Harbour came as a relief.

Victor wrote in his diary:

Militarily it is very logical. From the political viewpoint the entire blame lies with Japan and this excludes the possibility of even the most die-hard isolationist opposing the war. In the street faces are grim. There has been no manifestation of patriotism, nationalism or enthusiasm. However, the Japanese aggression has at least united all Americans. They now know they will have to enter a war. I'm sure they will wage it with the firm determination to win and will not retreat in the face of any sacrifice. There will be no defeatism.

On a personal level he noted:

This is the first time since 1931 that we have found ourselves in an international situation favourable to us.

Nicaragua, Costa Rica and Canada followed by declaring war on Japan and Japan in return declared war on the US and Britain after the bombing of Pearl Harbour. War between the US and Germany was now imminent. The only unknown factor was Russia. Victor mused:

What will she do, enter the dance or allow Vladivostok to be used as an air base. Litvinov arrives in Washington today.

At a dinner in honour of the Litvinovs Victor was able to pick up some interesting information about the war:

Litvinov says the Germans are calling their last reserves from everywhere, to send to Russia. If the British could land with two divisions in France it would change the course of the war, but the British are afraid of another Dunkerque. He reckons if the Japs take the Dutch Indies, they will only need to stay on the defensive and will attack Russia in the spring with a million soldiers mobilised from Manchuria and Mongolia. It would be disastrous. He says the authorities in Hawaii were warned thirty-six hours before the attack but did nothing.

The early stages of the War brought little comfort. The Japanese made remarkable gains and inflicted great destruction at Pearl

Harbour. The American habit of publicising everything resulted, Victor noted, dryly, in some regrettable indiscretions.

As it became apparent that the war would last some time, Victor's concern turned to his family:

> I don't know what I ought to do with them. They will be isolated and unable to come to the US. And even if they did come I might have to leave. Not that this is very likely, for where could I go?

In January 1942, however, his own situation is clarified:

> The war carries on with more vexations than satisfactions for the Allies. What has changed is my personal situation. TV Soong had been appointed Minister for Foreign Affairs and will probably stay in Washington. The day after his appointment, the 24th December, Rajchman (Soong's political advisor) called me in New York, where I was staying at the Gladstone Hotel, to tell me Soong wanted to see me with a view to my serving as liaison with the Soviet Embassy. I was unfortunately bed-bound after an internal haemorrhage from a duodenal ulcer. I replied that I would go as soon as I was able and finally arrived there on 11th January. It is a great honour for me. None of the unemployed diplomats in the US were called, although they all asked Soong what they could do. It was Rajchman and Hu Shih who recommended me to Soong. Perhaps he would have asked me anyway. He was very well disposed towards me at our last meeting. When he called for me, we thought there would be meetings of a Supreme Council amongst the Allies, as Churchill had arrived in Washington. Luckily for me, who could not come at the beginning, there were no meetings. Therefore I did not lose anything by coming later.

Despite his satisfaction with his new role, Victor was uncomfortably aware of his ambiguous position in relation to other diplomats:

> On my first meeting with Soong he asked me to draft a telegram to Chiang about myself and my wish to remain in Washington. He insisted on my doing it myself, to see if I

made a mess of it! Next day I went to see London, the Dutch Minister, with Soong's credentials. He immediately asked where Hu Shih was. I replied that he would be the liaison with the State Department. I am afraid to usurp Hu Shih's prerogative by seeing accredited diplomats in Washington but what can I do when I am ordered by Soong?

Soong was not an easy man to work for, although Victor's relationship with him benefited from their common western grounding. Exceptionally brilliant and with a razor-sharp mind, Soong stood intellectually head and shoulders above his two brothers and, for his sisters, he boasted the three most influential women of the first half of the twentieth century: Mme Chiang Kai Shek, Mme Sun Yat Sen and Mme H H Kung. After graduating from Harvard he had been appointed Manager of the Central Bank of Canton, achieving instant success and becoming Minister of Finance at the age of thirty-one. From 1927 onwards he simultaneously held the three top positions of Premier, Foreign Minister and Finance Minister, although he and Chiang often disagreed violently and Soong was widely regarded as the only man prepared to stand up to Chiang. The fact that Soong remained on the scene was unquestionably due to his family connections.

It was undoubtedly to China' benefit, however, that with his considerable financial abilities, he had been in a position to negotiate a US loan of $50 million in 1933 for the purchase of wheat and cotton. In 1940 he had secured military supplies and credit of $50 million and later obtained further loans of $125 million, topping this up in 1941 with further loans of $500 million each from the US and British treasuries. He had proved his monetary prowess as acting Premier back in 1932, when he became the first man to balance the national budget. Dr Wellington Koo's impression was "of a man of few words, but very practically minded." With Soong, there was no beating about the bush. His one defect, according to Joe Alsop, one of his friends and a CDS man, was his vanity.

He certainly expected a great deal from his employees. His official base in Washington was China Defence Supplies Inc on Massachusetts Avenue but he liked to work from home and would call on his subordinates at any time of the day or night and expect them to be available.

He and Victor were extremely different in temperament - Soong very reserved and socially inhibited, was never really happy as a politician, whereas Victor's outgoing, sociable nature fitted him perfectly for the job. Some of Victor's more old-fashioned colleagues and possibly Soong too, with his Methodist breeding, did not feel a strong affinity with Victor's ebullience but they shared a deep mutual respect in their working relationship and a common commitment to their country. They also had in common the fact that their knowledge of Chinese, particularly written Chinese, was less than perfect. Soong conversed more naturally in English, which made it easier for him to deal with the non-Chinese.

On 19th January Soong's brother married. Victor was unable to attend the wedding in New York, because he was waiting for an answer from Chiang on the subject of the Anglo-American contribution to China' military expenses. Chiang's response was to ask for $500 million. In February agreement for the loan went through Congress "like a letter in the post." Victor noted:

> The general feeling is that the Allies could not win the War without China and Russia. If the Pacific situation had been better, we would certainly not have obtained this loan so easily. There is a terrible fear here that we might sue for a separate peace. After Koo's speech declaring the Pacific was less important than the Atlantic, Sun Fo made a speech asking why China was still fighting. This had an effect on people. Besides, the loan will be repaid in blood since we shall now take the offensive at the first opportunity.

In the same communication Victor was relieved to get Chiang's assent to his remaining in Washington:

> Now I can go ahead and rent a house and buy a car. Little by little, I am starting to obtain the kind of work which suits me. I don't have a general responsibility but I accomplish the work I am given. It is always important, confidential and often urgent. Thus I am in charge of liaising with the Dutch. I saw London again and accompanied Soong when he want to see Van Mook, Lt Governor General of the Dutch Indies. Afterwards I wrote an official report which he sent to Chiang. I am doing some translating and writing memoranda on international questions. Soong wants me to devise a project of speeches for him. These days he is interested in the formation of a

Council of War amongst the Allies in Washington, at least for the Pacific operations. Churchill wanted the Council in London but in his Commons speech today he decided on Washington. Russia is against it on principle because she is not at war with Japan and wants a free hand. All the others - China, Holland, New Zealand, Australia - are in favour of a Council in Washington. It would be very interesting and would certainly give me something to do. It is, after all, for this kind of work that Soong sent for me.

By February 1942 things were not going well for Britain. With Singapore about to fall and the German fleet gaining the upper hand in the Atlantic, confidence was very low. Singapore's surrender, along with 60,000 British, Australian and Indian troops, resulted in a wave of discontent against Churchill.

In America, however, Pearl Harbour had so shaken the American public that they were prepared to wage war for twenty years if necessary. Victor, who had been asked to give an interview on American radio, commented on the simplicity of the American mind:

The questions are all very elementary and personal. That's what the ordinary American likes. For Europeans it would be too childish.

In March the Korean Government in exile, led principally by Syngman Rhee, requested help from the US in a revolution against Japan, which had occupied Korea since 1910. From 1919 onwards, Rhee had campaigned relentlessly for the recognition of the Provisional Government by Western Powers. As the war progressed, Japanese oppression in Korea had increased, the country was used as a supply base, Korean rice went to feed Japanese cattle and their metal was taken for munitions factories.

Roosevelt asked China's advice and Soong in turn asked Victor to study the Korean Question and the case for aid. In conversation with Rilso Haan, Rhee's political rival, Soong had suggested that Haan was very good at assassinations. Haan had replied that he himself had killed more than three hundred Japanese. Given Japanese atrocities in the areas they conquered and the disorganised state of the British in 1942, such enthusiasm could have been a deciding factor. In April 1942 Victor wrote:

Yesterday I visited Hsuing She Hui. He said the British are in a chaotic state and their lack of combativeness is terrible. Mandalay was bombed on the 4th. On the 7th Chiang went there and none of the debris had been swept up, nor the wounded hospitalised. In Hong Kong, when the British heard the Japanese were willing to make a truce, they started dancing in the streets. The Japanese are now no longer raping the Chinese women, but inciting the Indians to rape the English women. Some English priests were forced to witness the rapes and one who refused to look, had his eyes put out by the Japs. However, it seems Roosevelt has decided he doesn't want to do anything for the Koreans at the moment, so Soong has lost interest in them as well.

In June 1942 Victor was interviewed on the subject of Korea and China after the War. His personal opinion, he said, was that Korea had a strategic position in Asia, like the Balkans in Europe, and should not be under Japanese, or Russian, or indeed Chinese influence. Its fate, however, would depend first on whether it had a government that commanded the respect of the population and united them, and second, on the world collective security organisation. Korea could be the place where an international police force might be stationed. However, there was no point in recognising a government that risked being overthrown soon after being installed. The problem with Korea was its internal disunity and the inability of its leaders to agree a common programme.

On 14th June 1942 Rhee had an interview with Soong during which he accused him of telling the Pacific War Council that the Koreans weren't united. Soong replied that it was no use not telling the truth. Rhee answered that the Koreans were united. Later, he said that the Koreans were united now, whereupon Soong replied: "Since you say they are united now, it proves they weren't united previously."

In his diaries, Victor wrote:

Rhee accuses Haan and his crowd of being Communist. That has yet to be proven. My impression is that Rhee wants people to think the only dissident is Haan. Yesterday, Haan asked me to say that to counter this objection, he will now be quiet. For a month he has been making advances to Rhee and offering to collaborate. Is Rhee simply being obstinate, is it patriotism, or has Haan really been boycotted by the majority of Koreans? Hopkins of the State Department asked me on the phone yesterday if we would recognise the Provisional Government as soon as the Koreans are united. I told him that lack of unity would delay recognition but that unity would not mean immediate recognition, it would only facilitate it. He suggested that was also his viewpoint.

There were other territorial questions connected with Korea which would prove problematic after the war. Victor wrote:

I am told that Rhee expects Chingtao to be Korean after the war, as there is a considerable Korean population there and the region was part of Korea in the past. But even the Japs never occupied it as part of Korea and, as for the Korean population, it was artificially introduced by Japan. Such minority problems exist all over the world and we must find solutions for them.

It was always Victor's feeling that, as far as possible, countries should be self-determining. It was this belief that made his later appointment to the Trusteeship Department of the United Nations such a felicitous one. Even Formosa, he argued, although logically it should be returned to China after the war, might have to be relinquished for the good of international security. If other Powers were prepared to make sacrifices, so should China.

Chiang, who had recently returned from India, gave his opinion that the Allies could not win the war without the help of the Hindus and that Britain must be pressured by the US and China into giving them political rights. Mme Chiang's outspoken comments on British colonialism in India had not endeared them to Churchill, who gave Soong a cool reception when he visited London in 1943.

The War had its ludicrous moments, as when Eden complained in the Commons that the Japanese did not make any racial distinctions when they committed atrocities. Victor wrote mockingly:

As if the Japs could have been forgiven if they had not attacked the whites. This way at least there is less likelihood of their compromising at our expense.

73

It was interesting, nonetheless, to note how defeats suffered by the British, Dutch and Americans, seemed to spur them on. The demand was increasing for offensive rather than defensive policy. From the Polish Sikorski, they learnt that the Germans had lost an estimated two million men.

In March, following a request, the Pope agreed to admit a Chinese representative to the Vatican and Victor's name was mooted. He wrote:

> For me it is like choosing between the Alps and the Riviera for my New Year's holiday. Both alternatives are attractive, remaining here or going to Rome, but here my work is more varied and Marguerite would prefer me to stay. Besides, the War Council for the Pacific is meeting tomorrow. I'm not sure how useful I'll be. The sessions are ultra secret. Only Roosevelt, Hopkins and one representative from each country are present.

By May he was complaining that, contrary to expectations, he seemed to have nothing to do, although he was heartened by the response given to his speech for Russian War Relief.

On the political and military front, the news was going from bad to worse. Burma was now cut off; Corregidor had fallen and in America rationing had been introduced.

Victor's attitude towards the American public was softening in the face of their response to misfortune:

> They accept rationing without a murmur. There is a lot of goodwill, but they don't know what to do. They are a peace-loving people taken by surprise, who have to learn everything. I am slowly beginning to understand them. They have two great qualities, their general good humour and a love of their work. They always want to do their best and don't hesitate in the face of sacrifice if they think it is to their advantage in the end.

Even their indiscretions now appeared as a disarming honesty:

> This is truly a democracy. Roosevelt is criticised for contradicting himself. Nowhere are leaders criticised so openly, even in Switzerland.

He added that the Chinese could also learn from their methods of propaganda:

> In the cinema and on the radio there is always a little film on the necessity to produce more and give money to the State. Walt Disney has made some very good ones, funny and patriotic at the same time. This is a great people in its infancy, full of goodwill and vitality.

Amongst the interesting Americans he has met he singles out:

> Williams in Philadelphia, who admitted that he was angry at himself for being vexed when the Negro Robeson refused his invitation to dinner at the Racket Club, after he'd done everything to have him accepted.

Then there was Masaryk and Lord Marley in Philadelphia:

> They are considered a little mad. And I was put in their company! The next day I made the acquaintance of a delightful American family, the Watson-Spellissys. Apparently the wife was a student in the same class as Mme Chiang.

His life story to date, had been sufficiently interesting to inspire one of his contacts, the Yugoslav Petrovich, to advise him to write a book. Victor reflected:

> I am not at all tempted. I don't feel interesting enough to write about myself. I have never taken notes on what I've done; I am too Russian in character to be systematic and to prepare the material for a future book as some diplomats do. I must look up the Schiller verse on the 'edle Menschen' who are known for what they are and not by what they do. Here amongst our compatriots there is not enough to do and this is always a bad thing.

In September 1942 Victor was sent a propaganda brochure which the Americans intended dropping on the occupied regions of China. It depicted the Chinese chasing The Japanese and traitors into the sea, with a text in Chinese detailing their deceit, American aid and UN principles.

75

Victor was not in favour. If Chinese children were caught with the brochure they risked being massacred by the Japanese. If the Americans were prepared to go to such lengths with so many attendant risks, he argued, why not include words which would incite the population to action, or at least be more meaningful to the peasants. His feeling was that it would be more advantageous for the Americans to drop bombs on Japan than brochures on China. If they wanted to go ahead with it, he urged them to contact propaganda organisations in China who would be able to advise them on the wording of the text. He concluded:

> If we do a job, it ought to be done properly.

In the same month Victor attended a dinner party at Soong's where he met Manuel Guzon. Amongst other things, Guzon had revealed that Roosevelt was responsible for the loyalty and resistance of the Philippines, who had refused to surrender and had enough supplies at Windanao for another five years' resistance. Churchill, he implied, was responsible for persuading Roosevelt to concentrate American forces in Europe after Pearl Harbour.

Picking up Chiang's cable earlier in the year, regarding Britain's reluctance to enlist the help of Hindus in India by giving them political rights, Victor noted in his diary after the party:

> Guzon says Churchill will not make concessions to the Hindus. He even says the Cripps Mission was only for the benefit of American public opinion.

It was not the only occasion on which the Chinese were led to conclude that the British had showed bad faith. Later Chiang was to warn Soong about the British tendency to duplicity and Victor himself was moved to wonder whether his faith in the British regard for fair play and gentlemen's agreements had not been misplaced.

CHAPTER FIVE

Chungking

Vice Foreign Minister - Wartime Sacrifices - Life With The Chiangs

The meeting with Guzon was destined to be the last occasion recorded by Victor in the diaries for several months. In November 1942 he was recalled suddenly to Chungking to report to the Waichiaopu.

The Government seat had moved there from Nanking in November 1937 after Japanese troops had seized Peking and Tientsin. By November Shanghai and Soochow had fallen after merciless bombing and the capital, Nanking, was under threat. Chungking had been chosen as a temporary capital on account of its rugged terrain which it was hoped would prove a handicap to Japanese bombing. The only possible attack was by air and the weather, unpleasant as it was with its chill, damp winters and oppressively hot summers, at least favoured Chinese defences. At night a heavy white sulphurous mist descended on the river and in winter it was surrounded by morning fog. The rock base made a good shelter and aid from the West could be obtained along the Burma Road between China and the Indian Ocean.

At the time of the move, China's answer to the Japanese take-over was a "scorched earth" policy, destroying anything that might be of use to the enemy, including food and crops. This meant that Japanese troops had to be sustained from home which depleted their economy. China was also "trading space for time" in the hope of bringing the major powers to the rescue in defence of their treaty and trade rights in China. To this end Wang Ching Wei had been sent to negotiate a peace but had instead turned traitor and formulated an agreement with the Japanese who installed him as Head of Government in Nanking in 1940. A number of the leading embassies subsequently moved their offices from Nanking to Chungking, as they were accredited to the National Government

77

and not the puppet administration established by the Japanese in conquered areas.

China, at this time, was divided between three separate governments: the National Government in exile in Chungking, the Chinese Communist Government in Yennan, and the Japanese sponsored puppet government in the coastal areas. Each anticipated eventual control of China.

Although the War had succeeded, temporarily at least, in uniting the factions, the Communist problem persisted. Even amongst conservative Britons and Americans, many felt that Chinese Communist claims to raise the life of the peasants should be heeded. The difficulty lay in deciding whether the Communists were sincere in their belief or merely looking to increase their own influence. Victor's feeling was that the Communist problem was a Russian rather than an international one and would be easily solved after the War. The way to deal with the Communists, he felt, was to take the wind out of their sails by taking from them, in the form of social reforms, what was attractive for the masses.

The Government in Chungking was nonetheless faced with severe difficulties, which would eventually prove insurmountable. It was unable to conquer the warlords and landlords of Szechuan, an area as big as France, and it lacked the faith in revolution that might have enabled it to mobilise the populace and lead them. In 1937 the Kuomingtang, with its large proportion of academics and students, and the Chinese Communist Party had agreed a united front against the Japanese. But, as the war progressed and the KMT itself splintered, it failed to learn to live off the countryside, as the CCP was doing, and its handling of the wartime economy had resulted in soaring inflation. Clerks and workers were underpaid and undernourished, giving rise to the belief that, "No-one ever saw a fat Chinese below the rank of Minister of Finance." Officials were making fortunes whilst the Government issued bank notes without controls or any underlying plan.

Corruption was inevitable under such conditions. Rich refugees built luxurious villas for themselves in the hills around Chungking. The underpaid officers squeezed the soldiers' inadequate pay and the soldiers in turn took it out on the peasants. Chinese companies smuggled goods from the occupied areas as well as up the Burma Road.

According to Robert Payne in his *Chungking Diary*, despite the humble surroundings and privations of many of the diplomats, the house of the American Attaché was something of an oasis. There one could find servants in uniform, good butter, books, whisky, the choicest wines. In some parts of the city, contrasting with the flimsy facades of bombed out shops and dwellings, there were tall buildings with lifts and black, shiny limousines. There were even areas reminiscent of England:

> ...small country cottages smelling of wetness, tobacco and hemp, the smell of fresh pinewood and charcoal down by the river and on the outskirts of the city loads of rice hay reminiscent of Cornwall. Conversely the motor buses smell like French buses, perhaps because they both use wood oil. People sleep under mat sheds, thin crusts of bamboo ten inches high. In the shelter of the rock, beggars and small children huddle. In the village barn, ancient Chinese plays are performed to the beating of drums and cymbals.

The locally accredited international press corps was housed in straw thatched round huts in a compound under the aegis of a Dr Hollington Tong, who became Chinese Ambassador to Moscow after the War. It looked like an African village, but within its perimeters were lodged some of the most distinguished correspondents of the press: Brooks Atkinson, former Theatre Critic of the *New York Times*, Colin MacDonald, the Australian-born correspondent of the London *Times* and Spencer Moosa of Reuters.

The Secret Police were everywhere in Chungking. They formed an essential component of the so-called Blue-Shirts, an organisation with fascist leaning which also embraced the Whangpoo young officers' clique. It was a measure of how strongly influenced the latter were by the German Nazis, that each officer carried with him a copy of Hitler's *Mein Kamp*.

Amongst their other functions, the secret police took it upon themselves to stop all forms of amusement. This included arresting anyone found playing mahjong. They had their uses, however. Soong's personal assistant, Dr Sze, gave an interesting account of the Chungking Secret Police in his memoirs:

> When T V Soong first arrived in Chungking, he had great difficulty finding housing in the congested wartime capital. He appealed to Tai Lee, the head of the Secret Police and

a political friend of his and, in no time at all, an excellent, even palatial house was found for him.

Short of stature and somehow rather unimpressive, Tai Lee was nevertheless one of the most powerful men in the power structure around Chiang Kai Shek. He knew his power and was surrounded by fawning subordinates who indulged his every whim. One characteristic born of power was his impatience which could assume such unreasonable proportions as bucking the elements. He was to die in 1946 in a plane crash in bad weather, having forced his pilot to fly despite the forbidding weather reports.

Throughout this period with its despair, deprivation and corruption, the Communists managed to present an image of integrity, of concern for the people's interest in the areas controlled by their armies. Red guerrilla activity against the Japanese in the Northern Provinces, when compared with the inactivity of the Nationalist Armies, also gained friends and won influence for them.

The regime was haunted by a sense of insecurity. Concrete machine gun emplacements on street corners in Chungking and Kunming were not designed for use against the Japanese. The great patriotic surge of 1937-38 that had frustrated the enemy, had petered out in fatigue, oppression and profiteering. Chiang Kai Shek held things together by his aura, but he ignored spreading sores and sheltered in escapism.

Beaten by circumstance, long since helpless to accomplish its original purpose, the Kuomingtang, like the last Manchus, had settled for one thing, retention of power, without the strength or capacity to cope with multiplying troubles.

In *The Long March*, Dick Wilson described Chiang as a man of action whose personal integrity was undisputed, but whose judgement of character was poor. Wealth did not appeal to him, nor did cheap popularity. His lifestyle was unpretentious and simple and he concentrated all his energies on the main task. Yet he had built up around him an army of lieutenants, too many of whom were corrupt, sycophantic and incompetent.

His private secretary, Wu Juo-Cheng, described him as a military man with no liberal education. He had patriotic determination, personal leadership, decisiveness and foresight but his methods were often crude. He used the Shanghai underworld gangs to kill his opponents and, once established, his revolutionary idealism became watered down. Wherever the Chinese Communist Party were a "bloc within" the Kuomingtang they were expelled in the power struggle. Eventually the profound social revolution was abandoned: students and peasants were not mobilised to contribute, there was no literacy promotion or public health system and whilst continuing to pay lip service to Sun Yat Sen's ideals, Chiang never tried wholeheartedly to put them into practice. Having consolidated his own power, he had become more or less a dictator even by 1938. No congress of the Kuomingtang was held after 1925 and in 1938, when one was convened, nearly all the Party representatives were Chiang's men. He was elected supreme leader with no obligation to abide by the decisions of the Central Executive Committee. If he wished he could even veto its decision and do exactly the opposite.

Chennault's 1943 analysis of Chinese politics described two factions: the Traditionalists, who were reactionary, anti-Communist, anti-foreign, frequently corrupt and inefficient and embraced H H Kung, Soong's brother-in-law, and the Modernists, like Soong, Chen Cheng of the Army and Sun Fo, who knew the outside world and recognised the need to rebuild China as a modern nation.

Whilst the Modernists refused to subordinate themselves, Kung and the Traditionalists were prepared to serve virtually as eunuchs in exchange for the protection of their vested interests. Chiang Kai-Shek, in his desire for absolute power, would not allow freedom of judgement, hence the many conflicts with Soong.

A lack of enlightened leadership went hand in hand with his reluctance to share power in a democratic way. Even Victor was moved to comment that a truly great man would have listened to all views, even dissenting ones. Chiang rarely listened to any views opposed to his own. Therefore, the only advice given him was what he wanted to hear. Power, not wealth, was his great weakness and, as Victor had foreseen in the diaries, it was eventually to cost him the support of his only great ally, the United States.

There had been differences of opinion between the two countries since 1941, when a joint Chinese, US and British Military Council was set up in China. Stilwell, the Commander-in-Chief of US Forces in China, Burma and India, had been infuriated after the fall of Burma, by Chiang's preoccupation with the Communists. A conceited and quarrelsome man, he deeply resented Chiang's wish to store Lend Lease material against the day of civil reckoning rather than using it at once against the Japanese. As far as Stilwell was concerned, Chiang was letting the US win the war for them. He had a low opinion of Chiang's military staff and regarded Mme Chiang as a meddler who merely wanted credit and to demonstrate her power. In fact the only power she had was in bringing issues before Chiang, not in influencing his decisions.

Eventually Stilwell was relieved, having refused to give up Lend Lease money or his control over it. Chiang wanted both, but by this time Victor was sufficiently conscious of the Chinese leader's frailties to confide the belief that, had he gained access to it, the money would simply have gone into the family pockets.

By 1942, after three seasons of relentless bombing and with no airforce of its own, Chungking had become something of a legend. All the people had were bomb shelters dug in rock caves and the warning system relayed by watchers stationed along the edges of Free China.

A great friend of Victor's, Berkeley (later Sir) Gage, who was in Chungking between 1942-44 as First Secretary of the British Embassy, found the "Bamboo" warning system surprisingly efficient, with alerts always relayed several hours in advance of the bombers. Poles had been erected high up in conspicuous positions, so that at least one was visible from any part of the city. "On the first alerts one red ball was hoisted, on the second two red balls, and on the final alert a green sock, known to the bawdy as the "French letter".

In spite of the bad conditions in Chungking, Gage had a strong loyalty to China and acted principally as a catalyst between the British and Chinese. When a transfer to Teheran came through in 1944, he asked to be allowed to stay in Chungking where he remained until the end of the war.

It was a loyalty not shared by many of the other diplomats. Victor wrote later:

> According to Stein all the foreign journalists and diplomats who stay any length of time in Chungking turn against the regime. It seems we are not liberal enough for them but that has yet to be proved. It is true that there are people in power who lack an understanding of the European mentality. We insist on unimportant details which irritates them. On the other hand, on great issues of principle, we are prepared to give ground because, being of a more abstract character, these issues do not hit our weak points. As Kung said, we would not give fifty dollars in cash but we would easily sign a cheque for a lot more.

82

The final weeks in Chungking, as described by Gage, were a fearful mixture of terror and exhilaration. There was a threat of bubonic plague advancing from another part of China which in view of the five million or so resident rats, was no small cause for concern. Rats outnumbered the human content of the city by five to one. "Moreover," wrote Gage, "they ate soap, which was already in short supply, as were sex and a decent drink."

Gigantic thunder and electrical storms shot off sparks that not only burnt small holes in the furniture but in the body as well and there was no air conditioning to combat the heat and humidity. Whilst they awaited death or final victory there was considerable scope for social life, however. Since public dancing was still forbidden, a Club, the North-South, was formed where dancing could take place "in the privacy of the house of a charming Chinese lady."

The house, as described by Gage, was separated from the Embassy compound "by an easily surmountable wall which was my usual route of entry and exit." In the Pa-Tai-Tai, "the Hen-Pecked Husbands Club", only Chinese were admitted. The PTT was a drinking club where "the members talked yearningly about submissive Japanese women, who, once an amorous bout was over, would remove themselves from the bed and lie across its end until the next call for action came."

Despite its dubious pleasures Chungking was not a city generally considered as "desirable". Victor's experience there was to prove very different from his experience of America and Switzerland and the journey from Washington served as an omen of things to come.

The flight followed the Trans-Atlantic route from Brazil to West Africa as the more direct crossing through the Mediterranean was no longer safe due to Rommel's activities in Libya and Egypt. The trip was endless as well as dangerous, with stops in Miami, Puerto Rico and Trinidad. Even in November crossing Africa was unbearably hot.

The airport at Chungking was a mud bank perched on a rocky island between the Yangtse and a tributary. Everything was temporary, including the airport buildings on the mud bank. These were constructed out of straw matting on bamboo poles and removed one by one as the river rose, the rest of the straw matting, which served as the landing strip, being the last to go.

On his arrival, his old friend and predecessor, Dr Tsien Tai, gave a dinner in his honour. Victor was touched but he was already noting the tendency of Chungking to draw those within it into a bond of shared desperation, reminiscent of former prisoners of war. Describing it later to his children, Victor said that nobody who hadn't been there could imagine the conditions and torments they had to endure.

Chungking was a modern city, but traces of the ancient city founded 2,000 years earlier, still remained in its crumbling walls. In *Chungking Diary* Payne described old houses which had escaped the bombing, still with the remains of golden intaglios of hinds, serpents and tortoises cut out of white marble on their facades. Even in their scorched and splintered state they provided a moving testament to the beauty of line that characterised the early carvings of the Ch'ing Dynasty.

There was rubble everywhere, the broken walls suggesting a flimsiness that was not merely physical but the signs of a great nation being brought to its knees. With its extra wartime population crowded into meagre, overstrained facilities, it was the most uncomfortable and unsanitary capital in the world. Dead dogs, rats, refuse pits and gutters streaming with filth sent up a constant stench from the streets. There was little improvement inside. Victor recalled:

> At night they were woken by rats pulling their hair. Even in the hotels there were rats nesting in the bathrooms. Cats were imported to deal with the situation but the cats fled with fright! Malaria and dysentery were rife, medicine in short supply or unobtainable. Flies, mosquitoes, bed bugs infested every room. No matter how many were eliminated there was always a fresh supply.

People accustomed to a decent western life, found the conditions in Chungking filthy and lacking in the most basic requirements. There were no sophistications, life was dull and the men missed their wives and families. People tried hard to avoid going to Chungking and, once there, would use any excuse to get out.

Victor was given two rooms in a hostel reserved for high officials of the Foreign Ministry who were there without their families. The hostel, a two-storey brick dwelling with a small courtyard and an air raid shelter nearby, was at the top of a hill. Twice a day Victor had to walk more than 100 steps to reach it.

Inside were five rooms on each floor and a dining room on the ground floor. Various Ministers and Vice-Ministers, such as Henry Chang, Liang Lone and Wu Nan Ju, lived in the hostel and Victor was able to renew his friendship with Tan Beue, whose Russian wife and daughter Tatiana were close friends of Marguerite and the children in Washington.

A manservant was assigned to him on his arrival but Victor quickly began to suspect him of being a government spy and always stopped talking when the man entered.

There were a few occasions for social activities and he soon got into a regular bridge playing routine, so much so that after the war he became known in the US as an expert. There was also chess and Chinese chess and, on occasions, an opportunity for dancing which he took up gratefully as a means of passing the time. As there were no tennis courts, he organised and ran an ongoing Ping-Pong tournament. His humour and his philosophy of making a virtue out of necessity sustained him and in spite of the intolerable conditions he discovered an interesting mix of old friends in Chungking.

These included Dr Han Li-Wu, the Chairman of the Sino-British Cultural Mission to Britain in 1944 and Dr K C Wu, Mayor of Chungking. Amongst his European friends were Sir Horace Seymour, the British Ambassador and Jean Paul-Boncour, French Ambassador. British visitors to Chungking included General Alexander, Lord Mountbatten and Sir Stafford Cripps whose dislike of Mme Chiang was common knowledge.

At the weekends Victor soon got into the habit of going for long walks with Berkeley Gage in the Szechuanese mountain ranges on the south side of the Yangtse. There were two striking ranges of mountains within view of Chungking, both of them very steep and dramatic, as portrayed in Chinese painting. The walk to the house of a European friend on the second range took at least two hours each way in the hot, humid climate, up terrace after terrace of cultivated and then barren, rocky mountainside - an exhausting experience compensated by the promise of lunch when they arrived.

Victor also took the time to improve his oral and written Chinese both of which were put to the test in the many lectures and broadcasts he was now required to make. After a month in Chungking he had made more speeches in Chinese than in the whole of his life to date. Topics ranged from his impressions of the US to the diplomatic history of France. One fifteen-minute speech outlined the qualities necessary for a diplomat on graduation day.

He initiated a course for young diplomats on "Western Culture and Manners", feeling that it wasn't sufficient for Chinese diplomats to know a foreign language. They should know the ways of the West so they could feel at home in western company and not disgrace their own country by their ignorance of social customs. He gave them an historical and diplomatic background of western countries and taught them western table manners: the proper way to use knives and forks for example, how to eat cheese, asparagus, artichokes, what to do when your host proposes to drink a toast to you: in China the person must stand up, in the West he must remain seated. What should the uninitiated do with the cheese course, most Chinese having an aversion to cheese and other dairy products. Do you tackle it with a knife and fork? That would be the height of bad manners at a French table just as using a knife with a salad course would be taboo.

In Chungking there were no complicated negotiations to deal with and his work consisted mainly of correspondence between Ministries and Legations, often on issues unrelated to foreign affairs. More delicate issues required him to ask for instructions and he was often bored by the lack of scope for initiative.

He wrote:

> In fact our work here consists solely of presenting the issues, though naturally the manner in which they are put can influence decisions. The most important questions are those arising from treaties such as the abolition of extra-territorial rights.

A century before, unequal treaties had been imposed on China which gave special rights and privileges to foreign nationals there. These included restrictions on China's right to regulate her own tariffs without the consent of all interested powers, the right of foreign nationals to remain subject to their own laws, not those of China, the continuing legality of old treaties giving privileged rights to foreign merchants, and the possession by foreign nations of areas of certainties. None of these rights and privileges were reciprocal.

These humiliating conditions, which contravened China's sovereignty, had not been changed at the 1919 Peace Conference and were impediments to China's growth as a modern state. All Chinese deeply resented them and Victor in particular asked to address groups of young people on the need for change.

Other issues were the retreat of the Russians from Sinkiang and the more complicated problem of relations with France and their joint interest in Indochina. In order to maintain contact with

Indochina, the Chinese were reluctant to break with the Vichy Government. They had also decided against seizing the Yunnan section of the railway to Indochina, for fear of giving the Japanese a pretext to pressure Indochina.

The Vichy Government's accordance of special rights to the puppet regime in Nanking had put a severe strain on diplomatic relations, however, and the last straw came with the restoring of the French concession in Shanghai in late July 1943, in favour of Nanking.

China decided in consequence to break with Vichy and take control of the Yunnan Railway. The moment seemed right since the French Liberation Committee had not yet been recognised and there was no longer a Vichy representative in China.

However, Coiffard, who represented de Gaulle and the Liberation Committee and regarded himself as the protector of French interests in China, had protested so violently and sarcastically that the Chinese refused to see him any more. Victor noted:

> All of which will probably do us more harm than the railway
> is worth - always in deficit and not much use to us, at least
> for the time being.

Victor's arrival in Chungking had coincided with a visit by Dr Koo whose main concern at the time was to improve China's relations with Britain. As always, the collaboration between the two was based on trust, respect and friendship. Victor was flattered to discover that Koo had spoken highly of him to Chiang. Despite any private reservations about the National Government Victor remained its loyal servant. In Chungking it was the custom to eulogise the Generalissimo, the tendency in adversity being to cling on to any hope to avoid despair.

The Government in Chungking, and Koo in particular, relied on Victor's advice on Soviet matters. He was the Russian expert, although some believed that this very fact made him too subjective and blind to Russian motives. He understood the Slav soul so well that he mistakenly believed Stalin to be of that mould.

Dr Koo wrote in his memoirs:

> ... attached importance to Dr Hoo's views on Russia. He
> had studied there since childhood and spoke the language
> fluently. I advised him to pay particular attention to Russian
> questions in the Foreign Ministry and expressed the hope

that he would give some time to studying Russian periodicals and newspapers for the Generalissimo's benefit. I said I and many others looked to him to handle relations with Russia in the near future.

Chungking was speculating over the ambivalent situation between Russia and Japan. Victor believed that if Russia were dissatisfied with the US and Britain she might get closer to Japan and this would affect China. China's relations with Britain would play an important part.

When asked officially in 1943 what his opinion on the subject was, he said he did not think Japan would attack Russia. He thought there might even exist a secret pact between the two countries. For China, he said, it was a question of whether a Soviet-Japanese war would or would not benefit her. He thought that if Russia won, she would occupy Manchuria anyway. Nor would defeat weaken Russia much on the European front since she could easily retreat and fight against Japan in Siberia.

In an entry in his diary in May 1943 Victor recorded a conversation with Gunther Stein who had suggested that the Allies would be so preoccupied after the war with guaranteeing European order that they would be militarily unable to make a full effort in the Far East. This could well make it worthwhile for Japan to occupy the whole of China, to prevent the Allies establishing bases.

Stein reckons they could do it, given our lack of food and poor economic conditions. Certainly Japanese bombing is getting worse.

Anxious about Russia's attitude, Chiang wanted to improve relations with Britain. It was suggested that Mme Chiang make a visit to the UK. Her personal beauty, intelligence and charm made her by far the best ambassador the government could send. Mme Chiang hesitated for a long time. She felt that she and the Generalissimo had not been treated as important leaders of a country on their tour of India and despite an invitation from the King and Queen, she felt that she was not well-liked by the British and was too sensitive to open herself to criticism. Furthermore, Roosevelt advised her not to go. This might have been because he wanted a free hand with Britain in settling colonial issues in Asia after the war.

The trip to America by the Generalissimo and his wife in March 1943 had gone well and Madame Chiang had made a good impression on Roosevelt with her skill in conciliating the divergent viewpoints. Britain was a different matter, however. Churchill, in his statements about the post-war situation, made a point of not including China. He was still irate that Mme Chiang had spoken publicly on the issue of India's independence. The British press was affronted at what they considered interference in their domestic affairs and some were openly hostile to China.

Afraid of a bad reception, in the end Mme Chiang declined to visit Britain on the pretext of ill-health. Had she gone, she might have charmed the British into better relations and could have won a higher regard from them for China. She might have influenced Britain into giving higher priority to the war against Japan. In the event Soong went to London in the summer of 1943. Churchill was not very forthcoming and the two had sharp exchanges in Washington at the Pacific War Council on the subject of Burma and Tibet.

It was not until July 1944 that Victor was finally allowed to leave Chungking. Soong had asked him to accompany him to Washington in preparation for his visit to London but after two months Victor was recalled to Chungking. In the latter part of 1943 the Great Powers were busy at international conferences to end the war and plan the peace. The signing of the Declaration of the Four in Moscow and the Conference of the Two in Cairo, later the same month, represented a diplomatic victory for China. In the Cairo Declaration, previously approved by Stalin, China was mentioned for the first time as one of the three Great Powers.

Despite the euphoria over the Cairo Conference, Chiang remained wary of the British. At the start of their parliamentary mission to England, he had advised Soong to be very careful of everything we say, as the British always have an ulterior motive and when they ask a question it is often difficult to know what that motive is.

In Cairo the British had been opposed to the restoration of Manchuria and Formosa to China and it was Roosevelt who obtained British approval of the communiqué. Privately Churchill revealed to Soong that he was glad France had surrendered in 1940, instead of moving their government to North Africa, since if they had, Germany would have occupied North Africa instead of attacking Russia and the whole course of the War would have changed.

The British way of dealing with issues was often at variance with the Chinese way, a fact which Victor frequently commented upon.

He tended to agree with Sir John Pratt's conclusion in *War and Politics in China* that "Chinese political thought, by its purity, moral elevation and harmony with nature, provides a sounder basis for action than the systems of the West." The Japanese, with their "narrow, tribalistic outlook" were equally at odds with Chinese humanism and tolerance.

As a result of a quarrel with Chiang, following the Chinese leader's visit to the United States, T V Soong had had to resign as Chairman of the Bank of China and took no part in the conferences. He was succeeded by H H Kung, his brother-in-law and perpetual rival. Soong thenceforth attended to Waichiaopu matters only, working closely with his two Vice-Ministers. Victor was pleased to have his definitive offices and functions. In Washington, where Soong worked from his home, there were periods of frustrating inactivity and ambiguity of functions.

Chungking was rife with rumours, gossip and jealousies. Victor's counterpart, K C Wu was an ambitious man, as his later behaviour indicated. Victor was not at first aware of any animosity, though some of his friends had warned him of it. To the end, he was unwilling to accuse Wu of malice. One incident, however, seemed suspect, and was related by several people including Dr Koo in his memoirs. At a lunch given by the Generalissimo Wu was present but Victor had mysteriously not received his invitation. Both were meant to submit a joint memo on the subject of policy towards Vichy France which was offering to return the French concessions to China. If accepted, it would be tantamount to *de facto* recognition of the puppet government in Nanking. But to break off diplomatic relations with Vichy could provoke retaliation. It was a difficult question and Victor felt he should have been there.

There were two other incidents in August which dealt a blow to Victor's sense of morality and idealism. One involved a Ministry Councillor who, having promised to leave the room when Wu Nan Ju arrived, subsequently changed his mind. Victor wrote:

> This is the first time that a person I trusted has not kept his word.

The second instance centred on a letter from Harry Anslinger asking Victor to investigate a case of drug smuggling.

> Soong tells me that I am an idealist like himself, but that I have not been scorched as he has and that if one is going

to lose one's life, idealism will not save one! A sacrificed life, he maintains, would not change the situation one iota.

In the winter of 1943, whilst Victor languished in bed with bronchitis, his brother Raymond and sister-in-law Grace arrived in Chungking, together with his youngest sister, Clementine, whose university had been transferred to the interior from Peking. His brother Edward, twenty-two, had arrived a few months earlier, having been stranded on the way from Peking to Free China. He had run out of money in Paochi and it was there in the small town that he learned from the newspapers of Victor's presence in Chungking.

The family were thus together when they received the news of the death of Victor's stepmother. The relationship between Victor and his stepmother had undergone many permutations over the years, from the filial respect that had forced him to relinquish his first love, to a warm sympathy for a woman who had tried to hold the family together in difficult circumstances.

In the years following the death of her husband and the outbreak of war, the family's fortunes had declined and she had been forced to rent out portions of the house, to sell the car and dispense with the servants, with the exception of the old gatekeeper and amah, who served as both cook and maidservant.

Her letters to Victor during the difficult period since her husband had died shine with genuine affection and gratitude. Apart from his role as advisor Victor had also assumed some responsibility for the family. Augustin, in particular, had become a source of great anxiety to the whole family and something of a liability to Victor.

Of all his brothers, Victor felt closest to Augustin. Margot Walbaum, who had known Victor since his school days, told me that she had been unaware that Victor had any other brothers. But she knew that Augustin was named as a result of Victor's efforts to master *Ach! Du Liebe Augustin* on the piano.

The bond between the two was to last through life, despite Augustin's reckless lifestyle. Perhaps, being so much older, Victor's interest was paternal, perhaps it arose from a recognition that Augustin merely represented a more extreme and less controlled version of himself. Both men were *bon viveurs* at heart but a natural self-discipline and moral sense held Victor's inclinations in check, whereas Augustin's marriage to a woman whose instinct for gambling surpassed his own marked them for a life of continuous debt and dishonour.

Victor had bailed him out on a number of occasions. In a final, agonised letter, his stepmother expressed her distress at hearing about Augustin and his wife:

> Victor, you must tell them to clear their debts and if they don't listen to you, you must never help them again.

She is similarly protective of him with regard to the importuning of other members of the family. In 1939 she had written:

> My income has been reduced by half, though others of my family have lost everything and are in a desperate position.

Although Victor appears to have given generously and there are numerous assertions of gratitude:

> .... am so happy you are going to help the family and will forward the $120 ...

> ... how sweet of you to offer to help with Ray's PhD, tears of appreciation run down my cheeks...

She nevertheless counsels circumspection:

> Of the $550 you sent, I gave 100 to Aunt, 100 to Ta-Saw and 200 to the family, leaving 100 for next year. I told them all your situation and they must not count on it every year or bother you with letters. One can't be so helpless if one has some spirit of independence. Not enough Chinese have it.

With the death of her eldest daughter, Emma, from typhoid in 1939, however, and the additional burden of caring for Emma's two small children until their father could remarry, her own spirit began to break. She confesses to Victor in her letters that she is very tired and smoking heavily "which is a bad habit". Her hand shakes and her memory is failing.

Her anxiety over Augustin reaches new heights in 1941:

> We have not heard from Augustin for nearly a year. Tell
> him to think a little of his worrying mother. Even if he
> cannot help financially, a few words of comfort will soften
> his mother's heart.

In 1943 she died suddenly, closer perhaps to Victor than at any
other time in the history of their life together.

CHAPTER SIX

The War Ends

*Bretton Woods - Dumbarton Oaks - Yalta & the Sino-Soviet Conference -
San Francisco Conference and the Birth of the UN - Death of Roosevelt -
Chiang's Retreat to Formosa*

In June 1944, after two years in the war-torn Chungking, Victor was
notified of his appointment as a delegate to the Monetary and
Financial Conference at Bretton Woods, New Hampshire, described
by Roosevelt as "the cornerstone for international economic co-
operation." Victor was delighted. The appointment meant that he
could at last join his family in the US, in a relatively comfortable and
peaceful environment. It also meant a return to the kind of life he
most enjoyed, representing his country abroad and mingling with
other delegations. Moreover, the world was now looking forward to
the end of the War and a rebuilding of the peace. It was an exciting
time and Victor's colleagues, still trapped in Chungking, envied him.

The Bretton Woods Conference attracted delegates of forty-four
nations the most distinguished of whom was the British Chancellor
of the Exchequer, John Meynard Keynes upon whose theories all
post-war modern economies were subsequently based. This
Conference established the International Monetary Fund, set up the
World Bank and created other means to foster international financial
co-operation on the premise that international trade and
development are essential to the economic welfare of the world.

To begin with, Soong had declined to let him go to Bretton Woods
and, in the event, the Conference provided him with little opportunity
to contribute but it led directly to his appointment, in the late summer
of 1944, to the Dumbarton Oaks Conference. This was the first
concrete step towards the creation of an international security
organisation that would evolve as the United Nations. It also marked
the beginning of the decline of Sino-American relations.

The setting for the Dumbarton Oaks Conference was a stately mansion, ten minutes' drive from the White House, on an estate called "America's most civilised square mile". A man-made Garden of Eden, with flowers, fountains, bridges, woods and streams, no finer site could have been chosen for a conference which it was hoped would mark the beginning of a new world of peace. The motto above the door read: "Quod Severis Metes" - "As you sow, so shall you reap."

The Conference had to take place in two parts, as the Soviet delegation refused to sit at the same table as the Chinese delegation, on the pretext of their neutrality in the Sino-Japanese War. A more likely explanation was their reluctance to see China given an equal standing with the other powers, as well as a reluctance to antagonise Japan.

The Moscow Conference of 1943, which included ministers from the US, Britain, the USSR and China, had contemplated the establishment, at the earliest opportunity, of a general international organisation based on the principle of the sovereign equality of all peace-loving states.

At that time the American Secretary of State, Cordell Hull, had insisted on China being invited to sign the joint declaration. This time he said he would arrange to have two conferences going on a the same time. Later it was decided to hold two separate conferences, one after the other.

In mid-August Dr Koo was asked to represent China, along with Victor and Wei Tao-Ming. Victor warned Koo that the start of the Conference might be delayed because the Russians had to refer to Moscow for instructions on every single point. It was important, he felt, for China to set out its views on the formulation of the UN Charter before any agreements were published by the others, since there was a danger of Russia ignoring China's views once she had reached agreement with Britain and America.

The resulting document had to be rushed out so hurriedly that the so-called Chinese proposals pre-empted Dr Koo's arrival and had not even secured the approval of the government in Chungking. The go-ahead had been given by the Waichiaopu and Chiang himself.

Whilst waiting for Dr Koo to arrive, Victor witnessed the manoeuvres of Kung and Wei to get themselves appointed as head of the delegation. During the Bretton Woods Conference Roosevelt had told Kung of his idea of holding a conference to promote international peace and security. Kung subsequently told Chiang that he would be willing to be China's chief delegate to such a conference.

When he did not get a favourable answer, Kung had suggested Victor as Vice-Minister of Foreign Affairs because Britain and the US were both appointing Under Secretaries of State. Victor was duly appointed.

As usual, personalities and personal rivalries threatened to jeopardise the proper working of the delegation. Wei Tao Ming, appointed by Chiang to be in charge of propaganda and not someone for whom Victor felt any great respect, was another candidate. He had already published a list with himself at the top. In the event, Koo headed the delegation. Victor wrote:

> We don't know who is supposed to be second. According to Chungking it's me but, according to Wei, it's him. I don't really care.

After further protests, Wei sent in his resignation on the pretext of illness, an outcome with which Victor was more than happy. Even then, after the problem of who headed the delegation was officially settled, Kung gave a breakfast inviting the main protagonists and declared that he was to be the real chief of the delegation, in terms of directing and supervising.

Dr Koo, rising above the petty squabbles, called a meeting to discuss the essential points outlined in the Chinese proposals. He felt that the original documents could be made less rigid to facilitate the carrying on of negotiations. The topics covered included a definition of the term "aggression". Kung and Victor took opposite views on whether to enumerate acts constituting aggression. Victor favoured it as he had been much impressed by the arguments in the League of Nations regarding the definition of international aggression.

Russia wanted nothing to do with the old League which had expelled her from membership. Koo favoured contacting the Soviet Ambassador and giving him a copy of the proposals to show that China did not wish to ignore him but Wei was against it, fearing a rebuff.

On 31st August Koo and his associates, Hsia, Liang and Miss Kwan, left for Blue Ridge Mountains to spend three days with Victor's family in their rented summer house. There, Koo worked on the speech he was to deliver at the opening ceremony and on the memo setting out China's case. I remember being allowed to bring food and cold drinks into the meetings. It was a very hot summer, even in the mountains of Pennsylvania. At times, I sensed that I had intruded at the wrong moment, but they were all very kind and appreciative, especially Dr Koo. Without really understanding the meaning of the talks, I knew these were important times. These people were rebuilding and shaping the future.

The first phase of Dumbarton Oaks, which included Britain, US and the USSR, met from 21st August to 27th September, although they had been due to finish before 5th September. As predicted by Victor, the Chinese delegation had to sit through long delays during which they made an effort to keep in touch with the other delegations.

The sticking point was the question of voting and veto. The US and Britain insisted that no nation involved in a dispute affecting peace and security should be allowed to vote on the matter. Russia insisted that they should and Gromyko declared that each of the sixteen Soviet Republics should have a vote in the General Assembly. It was eventually agreed to postpone this particular item until the meeting of the Big Four.

In the meantime, a conference was taking place in Quebec between Britain and the US, to discuss how to expedite the war against Japan and to plan a new strategy to that end. Kung wanted China to participate in the conference and approached Roosevelt with a request to be included. Kung had addressed the US Senate on 24th August, although US press coverage at the time was unfairly critical of China and he was given very little publicity.

On 28th September Victor was asked to return to Chungking immediately to report to Chiang. The meeting lasted twenty minutes. Victor noted:

Those before me only got five minutes.

Chiang's main concern was American hostility. Victor wrote:

I explained the criticism in the US press since the fall of Changsha, as a natural response to the upturn in their own fortunes when things were going badly for the Americans, they exalted us. Now that they are winning on the other hand, they can afford to criticise us. In the US, everything follows the pattern of the movies: there are highs, lows, climaxes and anti-climaxes and, of course, the indispensable happy ending. An article by Freda Utley 'Why Pick on China?' was not even published, it being fashionable at present only to criticise.

Although he remained fundamentally faithful to China, Roosevelt's attitude was undoubtedly cooling. This was due partly to Chiang's controversy with Stilwell over the appointment of an American to command their troops, partly to Britain and America's wish to enlist Russia in the fight against Japan, thus saving casualties and bringing the war to a more rapid end. The US in particular seemed prepared to do anything to please the Russians, being convinced by this time that they could beat Japan without China's help.

At the Moscow Conference China had achieved recognition as one of the four major powers. Dumbarton Oaks was a step backwards in this respect. It was obvious that the second phase of the conference was a mere gesture and that the important features of the future international organisation were already a *fait accompli*. Appeasement towards the Russians had been the US policy throughout Phase I.

At the start of Phase II Koo was handed a set of proposals which had been worked out between the other three. The Chinese delegation went over these proposals and also discussed the Chinese proposals not covered by Phase I, particularly those questions of interest to China.

Koo was ready with fourteen questions at the plenary session on 2nd October which was presided over by Secretary of State, Stettinius. The US delegation expressed its appreciation of China's penetrating questions and thorough understanding of the subject, given the brief period of time they had been given to study the document.

The Chinese delegation had undoubtedly benefited from its experience of the peace conference in Paris. There, Koo had represented China on the Commission which drafted the Covenant of the League of Nations. There were many similar issues under discussion here. Furthermore, the failure of the League pointed up some of the unsolved problems and difficulties which would be encountered in the operation of an international organisation. The Chinese delegation's participation in the Conference had therefore resulted in at least some contribution to the common cause and this was recognised.

Despite his growing differences with Chiang, Roosevelt had continued to back China as the biggest nation in terms of population and the biggest Asian country in terms of territory. Moreover, it had been a peace-loving nation throughout its history and he was determined to make China one of the four powers responsible for the maintenance of world peace. With China as a strong ally, he could maintain peace in Asia and the Pacific whilst devoting his full attention to the maintenance of peace in Europe.

However, it soon became obvious to the Chinese delegation that the US and Britain had backed down on some issues under Soviet insistence, for example, the veto in the Security Council and the additional votes awarded to the Soviet Republics. The overriding desire of Britain and America was to retain Soviet co-operation in the war against the Axis at any price. The result was to weaken and diminish the Chinese contribution. Not only was the Chinese delegation downgraded and virtually disregarded by the uncompromising Soviet attitude but the start of Phase II finally opened on 29th September, giving China barely a week of negotiations.

The Americans told the Chinese delegation to make Phase II as short as possible because the conference had already taken too long and because any radical change in the agreed proposals of Phase I would require new negotiations with Russia. After their tug of war with the Soviets during Phase I it was felt that Phase II was more to "uphold China's prestige" than to listen to any serious contribution. At heart, Britain, like Russia, did not recognise China as a major power. The Americans ended up agreeing with the other two, perhaps in consequence of the general swing in public opinion away from China at the time.

Within the Chinese delegation there was much debate and some disagreement as to how they could assert themselves. Dr Koo took the realistic view of showing a practical and serious desire to make a substantial contribution to the plans of the new organisation. He relied to a great extent on Victor's familiarity with the international situation and with Soviet policy and attitude. The final decision was not to present all the prepared proposals but only the most important ones, which they would then defend as essential for a Charter of the new international organisation, regardless of whether or not the US and Britain concurred.

The proposals, which were agreed between China, the UK and the US and sponsored by the USSR for presentation to the San Francisco Conference, were:

1   That the Charter should provide for the settlement
       of international disputes with due regard for the
       principles of justice and international law.

2   That the Assembly should be responsible for
       initiating studies and making recommendations with
       respect to the development and revision of the rules
       and principles of international law.

3   The Economic and Social Council should
       specifically provide for the promotion of education
       and other forms of cultural co-operation.

It had been agreed that no public announcement would be made
of the results of Phase I. At the end of Phase II a document was
published simultaneously in the four capitals. The 5,000 word
statement set out the bare bones of the UN and gave hope to the
whole world. Some countries were still at war. They all approved of
the structure worked out by the thirty-nine delegates at Dumbarton
Oaks. The organisation would comprise a General Assembly, a
Security Council, an International Court of Justice and a Secretariat.
Membership was open to all peace-loving states.

The significant decisions taken at Dumbarton Oaks were mindful
of the failures of the League of Nations. The Security Council would
be more powerful and effective than the League Council, internal
police would implement decisions, old treaties would be revised,
political independence and territorial integrity against external
aggression would be guaranteed. The promotion of educational,
cultural, economic and social matters would be high on the agenda.
The unanimity rule of the League was abandoned: this was a great
advance.

Whilst in Chungking, Victor had delivered a four-hour lecture to
students of diplomacy and then read thirty essays comparing the
League proposals with those of Dumbarton Oaks. He was impressed
by their understanding of his message:

> The striking thing was that all of them without exception
> attached great importance to the absence of the US from
> the League and felt that this was why it failed. It
> demonstrates the faith they have in the US whom they not
> only consider the most powerful nation but also the most
> equitable power with good influence on other countries.

Positive steps had been taken for the building of peace. In spite
of opposition by Britain, the Chinese delegation proposed certain

criteria for the settlement of international disputes, in accordance with the principles of justice and law. These were to become part of the United Nations Charter.

Dr Koo and his delegation, despite enormous difficulties and setbacks, had made their voice heard through skilful diplomacy and steadfast determination and were congratulated for their contribution. Undoubtedly the excellence of the Chinese team contributed towards China's ultimate acceptance as one of the Four Powers. Invitations to the San Francisco Conference, the result of the Dumbarton Oaks Conference, included China as one of the four sponsoring countries. China had achieved equal status with Britain, the Soviet Union and the United States.

It was ironic that such a hard-won achievement should coincide with the deterioration of China's relations with the US, its only true supporter amongst the Big Powers. Although relations between the two delegations were based on mutual respect and cordiality, the rapport between Roosevelt and Chiang was plummeting and the divergences were getting wider and more acrimonious. In spite of his explanation to Chiang, Victor was disheartened by the bad press in the American papers.

The Chinese Army had exhausted its supply of equipment and arms. American policy was to arm the Chinese Army as long as the Nationalists and Communists could form a coalition to fight Japan. This was unacceptable to Chiang who, in desperation, made direct representation to Roosevelt through Stilwell, thus keeping the Chinese delegation in the dark. When Chiang and Stilwell had their final disagreement and parted company it brought about the virtual end of American support for Chiang's regime, in spite of America's deep-rooted mistrust of Communism. By November 1944 they saw power shifting to the Chinese Communist Party. These events occurred at the most delicate period of the war, when China was on the verge of collapse.

Despite Chiang's and to some extent Kung's intransigence, Dr Koo, with the support of Victor and others, pleaded a softer line. The rationale was that the US was our only true ally. We needed her in order to win the war and to reconstruct the country afterwards. If friction between the US and China's leaders were allowed to escalate, we might well be left out of the fight against Japan and lose our position after the war.

Chiang, however, continued to ignore advice, missing military opportunities and selecting his commanders on the basis of their personal loyalty rather than their ability. He was not accustomed to giving in and he could not understand the western mind.

On the evening of 5th December 1944, whilst he was still in Chungking, Victor went to a dinner party given by Chiang in honour of Soong's birthday. Amongst those present were Hurley, Wedemeyer, Stilwell's successor and Chiang's eldest son. The mood was sombre. Victor described the occasion as:

> One of the most historically depressing moments in our history. Yesterday we lost, without resistance, a place easily defended. One wonders if the Japs will come to Chungking. Chiang declared this morning that he is confident of holding Chungking and Kunming and we are taking urgent measures to reinforce the places we must hold. Already two battalions of Americans are at Kunming. It is a dangerous time and everyone is aware of it. There is no spontaneous gaiety. Only Hurley can tell a joke: that he eats like his parents, as slowly as his mother and as much as his father. When Chiang offers him a cigarette he says he is too young to smoke. These were the only jokes. No-one is beaten but we are in a serious mood.

> TV is back in favour as the favourite boy of the hour but one wonders how much power he will have in decision making. As I told him one day when he was out of favour he is always indispensable in critical times.

> The dinner was good without being lavish and for dessert we had melons from Hani. Will they still come in the future, now that there is a revolt in Sinkiang? Perhaps the present crisis will open the eyes of the old man and bring a fresh approach to our government.

> These days I am reading many articles about Russian heroism and their wish to sacrifice themselves to their country. Here the civilians only think of getting out. Our soldiers are dying of hunger and cold and are fighting reluctantly. What a shame it is, to be upheld by foreign troops in our own country whilst we had all the necessary time to train our own troops. Where has the money for their provisions gone? We need to be hit over the head with a club to wake us up.

Only three days later, however, Victor wrote optimistically:

Everyone is cheered up today. The measures we adopted
are bearing fruit. The enemy is encircled between Tushan
and Tuyan and we will probably be able to retake Tushan,
which will allow us to better resist future enemy advances in
that direction. In Kweiyang and Kunming the population is
full of confidence, because they see the growing number of
troops and armaments arriving. Our soldiers are better fed,
all the trucks are requisitioned for their transport and the
number of planes used for this is considerable. It is said that
part of our best troop from Burma is already near Tushan.

Yet he adds laconically:

Mme Sun Yat Sen is still pessimistic. At dinner I had a bet
with her that the Japs will not come back to Chungking.
She is influenced by a certain group who happily spread
bad news to prove everything is rotten in our government
and that we need reforms and a coalition. To this end their
newspaper did not announce the regaining of Tushan,
though its fall had been blazoned in large letters across
the front page!

On an international level Victor noted that everywhere in Europe
Communists were entering the political arena. In France, they seemed
more powerful than the Gaullists, although de Gaulle had the support
of Britain and France.

He observed:

Europe is recovering rapidly and the European factor will
have to be taken into account. US-Russian relations are
better than those between Britain and Russia, but everyone
fears Russia. There are two trends, either to beat Russia,
but this would be a risky undertaking in view of the
Communists in all countries, or to follow Roosevelt and
Churchill in trying to prove to Russia that she can co-
operate with the others.

America was waiting for the Soviets to enter the war. However, the
Chinese were aware that they would certainly require some payment

in return and were anxious to prevent this by coming to an agreement with Roosevelt on the conditions of Soviet participation in the war against Japan. If the Soviets got in first, the fear at home was that the UK would be prepared to accept anything, whilst the US might be persuaded to recognise Russian rights in Manchuria.

———————

Even without the hindsight of history, the Yalta Three-Power Conference in February 1945 was deemed to be an unmitigated disaster for China who had been excluded from it. The professed aim of the Conference was to maintain peace and security along the lines laid down at Dumbarton Oaks. Although Roosevelt continued to treat China as an equal ally, he was close to death and remained naive about Stalin's intentions. This was evident from the Yalta proposals. These were:

1   That sovereignty over Outer Mongolia would be left to China.

2   That the Chinese Eastern Railway would be under Chinese ownership but under a joint Sino-Soviet-American Committee to improve efficiency.

3   That Port Arthur would be leased to the Soviet Union to guarantee them an ice-free sea port in the Far East.

Roosevelt indicated that Russia and China should negotiate directly to agree these terms and he urged that the differences between the Kuomingtang and the Chinese Communist Party be settled. Unable to see Soviet designs in the Far East, he was blind to everything except the expedition of the war and Russia's participation in the world peace organisation. He ascribed his own inspiration to his allies and believed that, because democracy was the highest form of government, all nations aspired to it. Yet, as Disraeli noted, democracy is the most difficult form of government because it requires a high average level of public and individual intelligence and morality to make it succeed. It is also dependent upon the development of a public spirit amongst the people who are guaranteed the basic necessities of life.

———————

In 1945 liberal elements in the US were beginning to believe that the CCP was a real party and were starting to support it. Roosevelt had recommended that China should work with the CCP. Dr Koo advised his government that all parties should be represented in the Chinese delegation. Chiang, however, continued to oppose sharing anything with the CCP and the latter would only take orders from its government in Yennan.

In March 1945 Victor left Chungking for the San Francisco Conference which had been arranged at Yalta in order to prepare the United Nations Charter. The term had first been suggested by Roosevelt and was unanimously adopted at San Francisco. China and France had been asked to act as sponsoring nations though France declined.

Accompanying Victor on the mission were Dr Koo and C H Wang. Before leaving, the three met with Chiang who expressed his refusal to let the CCP into the delegation. Roosevelt's cable on the subject put him in a state of agitation and he queried why Roosevelt should feel so strongly about it.

Dr Koo explained that the question of China's national unity might become a thorny international issue working to our disadvantage. Leaders of the China Youth Party were invited to participate but did not respond. In the final analysis, the delegation included one Communist member, Tung Pi-Wu.

The preparations for the San Francisco Conference started in April in Washington. There were logistical problems about how many chairmen there should be and in what rotation. The Chinese delegation was instructed to give support to the American proposals without irritating the British and the Soviets. At the time Chiang was directing the country's foreign policy. Dr Koo, for his part, was eager to promote national unity and to be seen to promote it in the eyes of China's critics.

Next to maintaining peace, the most challenging task for the new United Nations was to deal with an even greater enemy to mankind: poverty, illness, illiteracy, hunger and early mortality. In drawing up the Charter at San Francisco, the delegates recognised a basic need for extensive international, economic and social co-operation. The resulting document contained six full articles on such co-operation alone.

In the meantime Victor was assigned to the Committee of Jurists to draft a statute for the proposed new World Court to be sited at The

Hague. China's vote for a Fifteen Judge Court rather than a small one was decisive. Britain, France and Russia were in favour of a smaller court. The US was not represented on the Committee.

On 12th April news came from Warm Springs, Georgia, that Roosevelt had died suddenly from a brain haemorrhage. It was a great blow to everyone, particularly China. Had he lived to see the end of the war with Japan four months later, he would have realised that he had overestimated Japan's war-making capacity. Roosevelt had based his entire foreign policy on conciliation and co-operation - some would say appeasement - with the Soviets, even complying with their unreasonable demands at the expense of another ally, in order to secure Russia's participation in the war against Japan. In the event, the Russians finally entered the war just one week before the Japanese surrender. Dependent on public opinion, Roosevelt had promised a war-weary nation that the boys would soon be home from the wars. Thus pressure was put on Chungking to start negotiations with Russia to secure her entrance into the war.

In June 1945 Victor and Soong arrived in Moscow for the Sino-Soviet Conference. This had been instigated by Soong on the pretext of tightening the bonds of friendship with Russia and discussing any questions either country might wish to raise. It was hoped thereby to establish an agreement not only with Russia but with the Communist Chinese. Victor's official role as a member of the delegation was Technical Expert and Official Interpreter.

The first meeting between Stalin and Soong, with Victor present, took place on 30th June 1945. Nothing was discussed but the atmosphere was one of apparent geniality and co-operation, with a wish expressed on both sides that the traditional understanding between Russia and China should continue.

Stalin was at pains to emphasise that new people were now in power in Russia. In the past Russia had wanted an alliance with Japan in order to break up China. Now it wanted an alliance with China to curb Japan.

By the time of the second meeting two days later, however, Stalin's attitudes were already hardening. The first shock to Victor and Soong came with Stalin's insistence on China granting independence to Outer Mongolia.

At the Yalta Conference in February, the three Powers had shown sympathy and understanding of the difficulty China would have following a long war in giving up any of its territories, particularly one as vast as this. It had been agreed to resolve the issue by not discussing it at all. The question would be put into abeyance. The Powers agreed simply to maintain the "status quo" in Outer Mongolia.

Now Stalin was claiming that his understanding of "status quo" meant giving independence to a country that did not want to remain a part of China anyway. His principal argument was that Outer Mongolia's geographical position jeopardised the Soviet Union's position in the Far East. Japan would be crushed now but in twenty to thirty years she would recover. The Russians should have the right to defend themselves in that event. They had been fighting for four years and had shed much blood. Now Russia was expected to attack Japan. An attack could only be justified if they were to be strengthened by it.

He rejected Soong's plea that, regarding Outer Mongolia, Russia should "let sleeping dogs lie." The passage of Russian troops in time of war was not contested, said Soong, but the Chinese people had been brought up since the time of Sun Yat Sen on the integrity of Chinese territory.

Stalin's "solution" was to sign the treaty for Mongolian independence now but not make it public until after Japan's defeat, when China would regain her other territories.

The lease of Port Arthur, and the construction of a free port at Dairen as an outlet for the Soviet Union were other issues over which a struggle for supremacy between Russia and China now seemed inevitable.

As Soong pressed Stalin to be more specific in defining his intentions, Stalin repeated, as he was to do several times over the ensuing days, that he was not interested in profit or financial privilege, simply with safeguarding Russia's position.

On 7th July Victor and Soong returned to the Conference table after reporting to Chiang the content of the first meeting. In terms as diplomatic as possible, Soong reiterated to Stalin Chiang's decision that they could not recognise the independence of Mongolia as this would bring about the downfall of the Chinese Government. They would, however, agree to maintain the "status quo" as had been determined at Yalta.

Stalin continued to bully Soong on the issue, hinting that China's failure to recognise the independence of Outer Mongolia would "hamper and spoil" Sino-Soviet relations. The threat was in the air. An alliance with Russia, Stalin insinuated, depended on "all causes of conflict being eliminated."

The argument raged on, with neither side prepared to give ground. It would be thirty to forty years, Stalin suggested, before Russia's ports and railways would be adequate to sustain their defence against Japan. Therefore an alliance with China was vital. Mongolia was part of this plan.

When he realised that Soong was not going to be beaten into submission Stalin abruptly terminated the meeting.

Two days later Soong announced that he had reported to Chiang that the meeting was deadlocked. Again he emphasised the strength of Chinese feeling for her sovereign territory, an instinct that had prompted its refusal to give up Manchuria even in the face of superior Japanese might. It was an instinct that transcended the safety and security of the Government.

Soong then read a telegram from Chiang, prefacing it by saying he hoped Stalin appreciated the sacrifice the Chinese Government was ready to make on the altar of perpetual friendship between China and the USSR.

In essence, China was prepared to give ground on Dairen and Port Arthur, provided the sovereignty of Mongolia was maintained. In return, because of the disunity within China, Chiang requested that all moral and material assistance from the Soviets be confined to the Chinese Central Government. Russia's help was requested particularly in eliminating trouble in Sinkiang, so that trade and commerce could resume. Last came the question of Outer Mongolia: since this was such a sticking point to progress, Chiang agreed to grant independence to Outer Mongolia after the defeat of Japan and following a plebiscite to avoid any future dispute.

Still Stalin resisted. Soong pleaded in vain that, for Chiang to agree on Outer Mongolia, he must show something to the Chinese people who had suffered so long and made such sacrifices.

Stalin remained obdurate. During the following days, as draft after draft was picked through, often late into the night, Soong had repeatedly to refer back to Chiang for instructions as the Soviets pushed forward their own demands and interpretations of previous agreements.

Finally, on 12th July, Soong suggested he should report back personally to Chiang, even though this would delay a settlement until after Stalin was due to leave for Berlin. Meanwhile both sides agreed to maintain silence and publish nothing in the press.

The meeting ended, somewhat ironically, with Soong thanking Stalin for his frankness and expressing the gratitude of Chiang and himself over Stalin's desire for friendly relations with the National Government.

Stalin repeated that Russia no longer wanted to break up China but wanted her to be a prospering and powerful state. Not all Chinese believed him but the time would come when they did …

All Stalin's victories at the Conference table had been secured with the pretext of Japanese aggression - both current and in the future. If there were no Japan, he insisted, there would be no need to ask for concessions. Russia was after all about to fight and shed blood for the sovereignty of China.

Soong assured Stalin they were anxious to reach agreement. The Chinese had yielded on Outer Mongolia, they had conceded to Russia on Port Arthur, they were giving ground on Dairen …

On 10th August 1945 Stalin announced that the Japanese wanted to capitulate. If they did not surrender, they would collapse within a week, being poorly armed, with no fighting spirit and apparently fearful of the Russians.

Soong expressed their anxiety to sign the treaties before the Japanese capitulation, as it would be easier to present the terms to their people.

Stalin replied that certain problems remained concerning Dairen and the Railway. Soong again referred to the enormous Chinese sacrifice on the question of Outer Mongolia - "almost half of China."

"It's a desert," Stalin replied.

"Yes, but it doesn't look so on the map," Soong protested. "School children will judge by the size, not the value of the land."

Presenting to the Chinese people the considerable compromises they had had to make before Stalin was a great difficulty. Repeatedly Soong used his diplomatic powers to bring about a more discreet phrasing of a formula that, whilst giving Stalin what he wanted, would make the proposal more acceptable to the people.

In the final instance, the Russians achieved their objectives in almost every case. The Treaty of Friendship and Alliance with Russia had secured Soviet recognition of the Nationalists as the Central Government of China. In return the Chinese had had to agree to the independence of Outer Mongolia, to a thirty-year joint ownership with the Russians of the Manchurian Railway and the Port of Dairen, and the conversion of Port Arthur into an exclusively Chinese/Soviet naval base.

The gentle, scholarly Soong had been no match for the aggressive single-mindedness of Stalin, though in the event it was Wang Shih-

Chieh, the Foreign Minister, who finally put his signature to the Treaty. Wang and his colleague, Chiang Ching Kuo, had joined the talks a week earlier and were present at the final debate.

Even Chiang Ching Kuo, who was a friend of Wang's, wondered why he had assumed the foreign affairs portfolio at that particular time and affixed his signature to a Treaty which was bound to be condemned by posterity. An explanation was put forward by Wang's former close associate, Chang Chung-Fu. Wang had told him that the signing of the Sino-Soviet Treaty corresponded to a brave man cutting off his arm to save his life, since the Treaty would allow thirty years of peace between the two countries.

Nevertheless, it was unbelievable that as one of the major Powers to win victory over Japan, China had to surrender territories and economic concessions to the Soviet Union as if she had lost the war. The Treaty was one of the harshest and most unequal ever concluded with a foreign power. China had paid heavily for her wish to tighten the bonds of friendship with the Russian bear.

The Treaty seemed to mark a downturn in the fortunes of the Nationalist Government. At the time of the Bretton Woods, Dumbarton Oaks and San Francisco Conferences, Nationalist China's prestige as one of the Big Five had reached a high.

In December 1945, however, following the Sino-Soviet Treaty and in line with America's feeling that some sort of compromise between the opposing parties was a priority, Truman announced the need to broaden the base in China, end the Civil War and create a unified democracy. Marshall subsequently went to China with the intention of mediating between the Nationalists and the Communists.

The move was initially successful. In January 1946 he arranged a cease-fire and created an executive headquarters in Peking to monitor the truce whilst the Political Consultative Conference (PCC) convened in Peking.

By February agreement had been reached between the Nationalists and the Communists to integrate the two armies. In London, Vishinsky, Dr Koo and Stettinius met to discuss the Security Council.

In March Marshall flew back to the US to report to Truman but in April the CCP violated the cease-fire and he was forced to return.

The Civil War continued throughout May and June, whilst the Nationalist capital returned to Nanking and the Manchurian truce began. In July two members of the Democratic League were assassinated in Kunming, the CCP ambushed a US Marine Convoy, and the Democratic League boycotted the National Assembly. Any optimism now seemed premature.

John Leighton Stuart, who had lived in China half a century and was better qualified than anyone to deal with the present situation, was appointed US Ambassador. By the end of August, however, both he and Marshall were becoming increasingly frustrated by their inability to end the dispute between Nationalists and Communists. A backlog of missed opportunities and rejected counsel on the part of the Nationalists was coming to a head. Wedemeyer, who had replaced Stilwell in 1944, had urged Chiang, through the Supreme Chief of Staff, Cheng Chen, to inaugurate political reforms, take steps to eliminate corruption and improve the livelihood of the people through philanthropic activities.

Chiang was never one to take advice, nor was he, even at this eleventh hour, seriously prepared to compromise with the CCP. The US, for its part, was willing to mediate but not to involve itself in the Chinese Civil War, despite having sold $900 million of war surplus to the Nationalists.

In January 1947 Marshall was recalled to Washington and the US ended its efforts at mediation. Chiang was to pay heavily for his intransigence.

During the next six months, amidst student protests at the Civil War and economic conditions, both the CCP and the Democratic League were outlawed. In November National Assembly Elections were held in Kuomingtang-controlled areas and won most seats in the Assembly.

By September, however, the CCP had made serious advances and in December Mme Chiang Kai Shek went to Washington for more aid.

It was too late. By the end of 1948 inflation in China had reached staggering heights and the staunchest supporters of the Nationalists had given way to defeatism and disillusion.

Though criticised on all fronts, there was still no real alternative to Chiang Kai Shek, however, and perhaps the greatest tribute to his personal qualities came during those waning months in 1948, from John Leighton Stuart himself:

> During the last weeks, when his world was cracking up around him, Chiang Kai-Shek was superb in his serene courage and indomitable will. It was not always easy for

111

him to distinguish between his personal and his country's advantages but he acted nobly and faithfully for what he believed to be his country's best interests. For eight years of the war, he was the inspiring embodiment of the popular will, ruling by the united support of all classes. He had none of the venality, avarice, indolence and cowardice of the traditional mandarin and his nobility of character stands out as exceptional.

It was a moving tribute to a man more sinned against than sinning.

In January 1949 Tientsin fell to the Communists and the national capital moved to Canton. On 21st January Chiang retired and Li Tsung-Jen stepped in as acting President. It was the beginning of the end. In the same month, the Communists took Peking and in April CCP soldiers entered the US Embassy in Nanking, occupying Hangchow, Hankow and Shanghai in May. In June Chiang took control of the Kuomingtang but there was nothing more to be done.

In August Stuart left China and a US White Paper announced the cessation of all aid to Nationalist China. The latter's collapse was attributed to the military, political and economic incapacity of the Kuomingtang leaders, who had come to rely on US help to win the war and keep them in power.

On 1st October 1949 the People's Republic of China was officially proclaimed at Peking and in December 1950 the Nationalist Government withdrew to Taiwan.

Victor was to have several meetings with Chiang in the 1950s and in 1954, proffered his advice to Cheng Chen on plans to invade the mainland:

I told him he must outline a political plan prior to the invasion, rally all the non-Red Chinese in the world and get the necessary funds for effective propaganda. Finally, an ally must be made of the Taiwanese, in case of a plebiscite.

One of Victor's greatest battles in later life was to prevent Peking's admission to the United Nations. When the People's Republic was admitted in October 1971, he described it as "the unhappiest day of my life."

CHAPTER SEVEN

Trusteeship Department

The Job For An Idealist - One Of Trygve Lie's Deputies - Ralph Bunche Joins The UN

The Atlantic Charter had undertaken to respect the right of all people to choose the form of government under which they lived and to act to see sovereign rights and self-government restored to those who had been forcibly deprived of them. Freedom and self-government for peoples everywhere in the world was the declared aim.

It was therefore agreed that the United Nations Charter must contain a section on Trusteeship - for military as well as humanitarian reasons. Unless dependent peoples were assisted towards ultimate self-government they would provide the kernel of future conflicts.

Although the matter had been discussed at Yalta, it had been decided at Dumbarton Oaks that there would be no mention of Trusteeship areas. One man who was determined that Trusteeship would form a large part of the new United Nations, however, was Ralph Bunche, soon to be wrenched from the State Department by Victor to direct its Trusteeship Division.

Bunche, an American Negro, was fervently committed to the idealism of the Trusteeship concept. Born in an era of segregation and prejudice, he was plagued all his life by the colour of his skin, endlessly labelled during his rising career as "the first Negro", "the first black man", "the first coloured man to ..." The badge often obscured his more extraordinary qualities of intellect and humanity.

The idea of international accountability for colonies was not easily accepted by the Big Powers, particularly Britain and France, who preferred to keep their possessions without interference. Although officially they had to support the theory of self-determination, they were sensitive about the UN's involvement. The British view was that one could not legislate equality and that it would take a long time to achieve a necessary awareness and maturity in all fields. Churchill had approved the Atlantic Charter but had refused to preside over the liquidation of the British Empire. It was clear that Stalin intended to deprive Eastern Europe of its freedom. France and China were still occupied. It was up to the United States to back Trusteeship. But even Roosevelt, who was fervently committed to it on idealistic grounds and had proclaimed that the US should derive no territorial benefits from the war, recognised as a Navy man that America needed bases in the Pacific and elsewhere.

Bunche worked non-stop on Trusteeship proposals to be presented by the US delegate at the San Francisco Conference in April 1945. They not only had to meet the deadline for the Conference but to obtain Roosevelt's approval, as he was clearly very ill.

On 10th April Roosevelt approved the idea of international Trusteeship in principle. He died two days later but Truman went along with Roosevelt's approval and out of deference to the late and much revered President, so did the Navy.

Bunche and his team worked on sixteen drafts of the US Trusteeship proposals for San Francisco. France and England continued to defend their colonial privileges whilst China and Russia supported colonial liberation. In the meantime, the war in Europe ended.

Once established, the Trusteeship Council rated equally with the five other arms of the United Nations. It had begun with fifteen people and grew to 120. Bunche, more than any other man, was responsible for this. Within fifteen years the Trusteeship section would pave the way to freedom for thirty-three nations with a combined population of almost one billion people.

The Trusteeship Division was an entirely new concept which had not existed in the League of Nations Charter. The interests of the peoples of the trust territories were, for the first time, of paramount importance. They were given many new rights, including the right of petition. Indeed, Trusteeship was the only unit in the UN which could deal with individual complaints. Those petitions that merited consideration were taken up by the Committee. The individual could even appear before them himself. If necessary, a UN mission was then sent to the spot to investigate and make recommendations. Most of the issues were political, social and economic, and affected the lives of thousands of human beings whose voices had never been heard before in the international arena.

Victor, for his part, believed passionately in the right of colonies to self-determination. In March 1946 he was appointed Assistant

Above Victor's mother
ght Victor's father, Hoo Wei Teh, in the
service of the Manchu Dynasty
elow The engagement is announced of
liss Marguerite Chen to Dr Victor Hoo,
January 1927, Shanghai

China's Victor Hoo, UNO Assistant Secretary-General for Trusteeships, Makes a Point With His Countryman, Dr. Quo Tai-chi, President of the Current Security Council Sessions.

Left Caricature in a New York newspa[...]
1946
Below Marguerite at Lake Geneva,
September 1931
Top Right Some members of the Chin[...]
Delegation at the League of Nations, 1[...]
Bottom right During a weekend brea[...]
Nice, 1931
Bottom far right The Envoy Extraordin[...]
and Minister Plenipotentiary at Berne [...]
his family

*Left Family outing in Switzerland
Below left Marguerite in Geneva
Below right With Nehru at the United
Nations*

*Opposite top One of the reception rooms
the Chinese Legation in Berne
Opposite below Chiang Kai Shek with
two Vice Foreign Ministers, in Chunghn
1944*

Above Dumbarton Oaks Conference. Lord Halifax on left of table, Edward Stettinius right of table, Andrei Gromyko to his left, then Wellington Koo, Victor third from rig Below Chinese Delegation at the San Francisco Conference. Front row left to right, Vic Wellington Koo, H H Kung, Wei Tao Ming

Above Secretary General Trygve Lie and his Assistants, 1946
low The first session of the United Nations Commission in Korea, January 12, 1948

Above The Trusteeship
Visiting Mission to Camer
November 1949
Below   Secretary General o
United Nations, U Tha

Secretary General of the United Nations, in charge of Trusteeship and Non-Self-Governing Territories.

The appointment had been made by Secretary General Trygve Lie, partly, as he wrote in his autobiography, "because Mr Hoo had the decided advantage of being in London at the time and on the spot, so to speak." Victor's background in foreign affairs, as delegate to the Preparatory Commission and member of the Chinese Delegation to the London Assembly, had all prepared him ably for his new post, however. Apart from the years he had been a delegate to meetings of the League of Nations, he had recently played an active part in the Bretton Woods, Dumbarton Oaks and San Francisco Conferences leading directly to the creation of the United Nations. In addition he spoke four of the five official languages (subsequently adding the fifth to his repertoire). Later, as China underwent revolution, Victor's views and those of Trygve Lie came to differ regarding UN policy towards China but he paid tribute in his autobiography to Victor's "wise and objective counsel" and the continuing cordiality of their relations.

The Big Five had asked Lie to appoint a national from each of them as ASGs. The others were Andrew Cordier, Henri Laugier, who was succeeded in 1951 by Guillaume Georges-Picot, John Hutson, who resigned in 1947 and was succeeded by Byron Price, Adrian Pelt, succeeded by Shamaldharee Lall and Arkady Sobolev, who was replaced in 1949 by Constantin Zinchenko.

These men were the Secretary General's official "cabinet" available for advice on all matters, particularly those relating to their home areas. They were also the heads of their departments.

Although, had he been given the choice, Victor might have preferred the Social Department, having been involved in economic and social problems since his League of Nations days, he was happy to make a virtue out of necessity. In his diaries he admitted the satisfaction the appointment had brought to his self-esteem:

> All the work is diplomatic, and demands the daring reflections of imagination. I need not waste time trying to please and curry favour with politicians. In fact I find Trusteeship more exciting than the Social Department. It is more concentrated and the Secretariat has greater impact than on social questions. We could have a really positive influence on the policies of the Powers, to the benefit of the non-self-governing territories ...

Victor had already met Bunche at Dumbarton Oaks in 1944 and had been impressed by his arguments in favour of Trusteeship in the face of his own government's determination to retain islands in the South Pacific. In January 1946 the two men met again at a Soviet Embassy reception in London. On returning home, Victor offered him the job of Director of the Trusteeship Division. He wrote in his diary:

> I have already found two good collaborators: Bunche and Benson, both of them liberal and independent. I might also have Beeley, very competent though less liberal. The three 'B's will make a strong combination. With the experience I've gained to date in handling my compatriots I think I can get along with my foreign collaborators.

The position was a particularly challenging one in the immediate post-war era when dozens of small protectorates that had fought in the war on the allied side were demanding independence.

The entire world at this time focused its hopes on the United Nations. Until now Victor's career had centred solely on the government of his country. The idea of becoming an international official delighted him. He had always welcomed challenges and always proved well up to them, savouring his achievements as naively as a school boy.

If the atmosphere of 1946 was euphoric for most people, it was exhilarating for him. The international diplomatic scene, inhabited by world leaders, was his natural habitat and one in which he came to feel completely at home.

His initial fear that his government might refuse to release him for the post had proved unfounded. The appointment, made him the highest ranking Chinese in the Secretariat and prompted a flood of congratulatory messages from all over the world.

Only ten days previously, he had had an operation to remove a duodenal ulcer which necessitated the removal of two-thirds of his stomach. On 24th April 1946 he wrote in his diary:

> I can finally write here after so many months of interruption. I came in this afternoon to have the polyp removed from my stomach. They tell me I have three polyps which makes a Tripolype! I have so much to write since I last did so that I won't be able to do it all today. In truth I am lazy and

116

uninterested. If I wrote my impressions every day I could publish my memoirs to earn money when I am too old to have a job, and am poor. If fate wishes me to participate in important events, my memoirs will be no worse than anyone else's and less naive than certain American memoirs which have become best sellers. Furthermore, by writing every day, I could maintain my French, which I am starting to forget.

But, although he was an avid reader, writing was not his first love and he was very frustrated at having to stay in hospital and convalesce just at the moment when his social life would have been at its most rewarding. The dinner jacket was the diplomat's battle dress. Some countries celebrated several quasi-national days each year and most embassies held receptions whenever their cabinet ministers or other VIPs paid a visit. Victor could expect to be invited to several cocktail parties every night of the week. Instead of the usual lobbying that was a pleasant by-product of these occasions, he was forced to rely on the telephone. Luckily his natural resilience had enabled him to withstand the surgery exceptionally well and his spirits remained undaunted.

In spite of his own euphoria and optimism, however, the choice of a Chinese to head the Trusteeship Department had its sceptics. China had always encouraged independence for colonies, which did not ingratiate them with those Powers who were trying to hang on to theirs.

Furthermore, as more and more Third World countries became members of the UN and Mao Tse-tung's regime overtook China, Victor's pro-Nationalist connection made him increasingly unpopular among the members of the United Nations.

Although he undoubtedly preferred to be well liked, Victor did not brood over the political aspects of his unpopularity. His first mission as an international official was in September 1946, when he went to Paris as an observer, representing the Secretary General at the Peace Conference.

Whilst there, he planned to meet with French officials on Trusteeship matters. There was much work to be done on trust agreements to be submitted to the General Assembly in October and a wealth of documents and information to be obtained. He decided to contact his former secretary, Nanette Badan, who had been his right arm during his mission in Geneva. She was now retired and married to a prominent Swiss dentist, but she accepted the challenge and came to Paris to work with Victor leaving him free to concentrate his attention on the delegates whilst she dealt with the journalists.

The flight from New York to Paris in the days before the jet took twenty-two hours including three hours of stopover. Victor had to spend the night sitting up and on arrival immediately started the round of visits which he had arranged from New York.

He wrote in his diary on 18th September:

> I arrived in Paris rather tired, having slept badly. Here I found a room at the Hotel Georges V, thanks to Tsien Tai and our delegation. The UN was unable to do anything. It is always your own country that will help you out.

On 21st September he wrote:

> The day after my arrival I went to visit Fouges Duparc, Secretary General of the Conference. I gave him an Eversharp pen, the *dernier cri*, which he had never seen and he was sincerely delighted. He was, as usual, very kind to me and promised all facilities. I did not ask for a car to be put at my disposal as was done to Lie, Sobolev and Laugier but I asked P N Chu to arrange this for me. Fouges Duparc thinks the Conference will end before the Assembly 'touch wood'. In the afternoon I went to visit Chauvel, Secretary General of Foreign Affairs, who seemed less optimistic.

> These days it is the Wallace-Truman Affair which interests everyone more than the Conference. Truman proved himself totally incompetent. I don't remember ever seeing a statesman making himself so ridiculous. First, he approved Wallace's speech on relations with Russia, then he announced that he only approved of Wallace's right to make a speech, then he agreed with Wallace that he would not make a speech before the end of the Conference, then he forced Wallace to resign.

> I increasingly have the impression that the Conference will not end before the Assembly, especially because of the question of Trieste. After the Wallace Affair the Russians

will be more intransigent and Byrnes more firm. Molotov is of the opinion that we could continue to discuss Trieste in New York during the Assembly.

And in passing:

I finally obtained a car today. I was annoyed yesterday because they led me to believe that there would be no hope of getting one. I said I wasn't asking as a personal favour but as a courtesy vis-à-vis the United Nations. Luckily, Fouges was on my side.

The Conference, with its meeting of four Foreign Ministers, was big news. The headlines spoke of compromises on Trieste, the Danube, the Spanish Question, Germany and the Straits of Iran, though in effect the first meeting was, according to Victor, "a storm in a tea cup".
On 24th September he reported:

A journalist told me that the Four made mutual concessions - the Russians on Trieste and the Anglo-Americans on the Danube. The Spanish Communists accuse the Russians of ditching them by postponing the Assembly, where the Spanish Question is to be discussed.

By 27th September he could write:

Mlle Badan arrived yesterday from Switzerland and will certainly be a great help to me. Tomorrow I see Bidault. I spoke to Molotov yesterday in the lobby and expressed my desire to see him. He said he would let me know. Pavlov tells me that my driver in Moscow often speaks about me in the most praiseworthy terms. All drivers are fond of me. Those in London also spoke well of me.

Next day, outside the Conference Chambers, Victor met with the French Foreign Minister, Bidault, an old friend from his student days. The meeting did much for his self-esteem:

When I left Bidault, he said, 'My wife likes you very much and admires your virtuosity and qualities of statesmanship.'

Yesterday, Quo apparently invited Molotov and the Soviet delegation to lunch and said: 'We have given the best man to the UN as we consider it important.'

He also had a meeting with the Chef de Cabinet in colonial matters, Montet, whose father had been an old friend. With Montet he discussed, amongst other things, the appointment of the liaison officer between the French government and the Trusteeship Department. On 2nd October he met with Monnerville, the French Deputy, who was an expert on questions of Trusteeship and later went on to become leader of the Senate. Their talk was frank and open, both men augmenting their respect for each other. They agreed that the trust territories could be part of the French Union. Some of the dependent territories wished to become French departments. "At first he was quite reserved," wrote Victor, "but he relaxed after I paid him a compliment: that he was the best informed person and the most authoritative amongst the Députés from the colonies."

From Nemanov, a journalist, he gained several significant pieces of information:

Nemanov says the Russian policy is to support everything accepted by the Four. As to the rest, it will be negotiated with the Four later on. In Europe, it is Germany and the Straits of Iran which interest the Soviets. On the Straits, all the Russians agree and the Soviet Government seeks a diplomatic victory that will be popular with all Russians. They will not give in on the Straits and will link it with the navigation on the Danube. For Iran, the Soviets would like a sharing of the zone of influence, as under the Tsars.

A war could occur over the Straits if the Soviets believe that the British would not wage war to defend them. I lunched with Posnanski in a bistro where the cooking is very good: 22 rue St Dominique. He said the Conference is not important. Molotov is not going to settle vital issues here because he can bargain in New York where he has promised to discuss Germany with the other three.

Posnanski was much more worried about the Soviet note to the Turks about the Straits. That could cause a war as it did for Poland in 1939. He is convinced that sooner or later there will be a war between Russia and America. I told him I did not feel there would be a war in the near future, that perhaps the sending of the note was decided before the Stalin meeting, that it would be interesting to know if the questions at that meeting were posed before or after Wallace's resignation. He said that de Gaulle's speech against the French Constitution was motivated by his belief that there would be a war in six months. France would be invaded and the French Government would have to be exiled, which is difficult with the present constitution which demands the consent of the candidate of the Council President before he forms his cabinet. De Gaulle risks his position if the Constitution is still adopted with a large majority. Now there will in any case be twenty per cent who vote against the Constitution. Everything above twenty per cent will be the measure of de Gaulle's influence.

It was at dinner at the home of Kaeckenbeeck, Victor's oldest and closest friend, that he met Loridan. The latter was the Chef de Cabinet in the Belgian government dealing with Trusteeship questions. "Over dinner" was certainly the best way to deal with official matters and time and again Victor's European education proved to be a useful and pleasant means of forging contacts:

Spaak says that the Belgian position and that of Laurency of the Ministry of France's *Outre Mer*, is that Trusteeship accords should not have the Assembly on their side. It is an agreement between the States directly involved and not with the organisation, as was the case with the League of Nations.

All in all, it is going better with the Trusteeship than I had imagined.

On 10th November he wrote:

All the mandatory Powers except South Africa have submitted Trusteeship accords for their former mandates, except Palestine. They have naturally tried to commit themselves as little as possible, but are afraid of public opinion and that of other UN members. Whilst touchy

121

about anything that might reduce their privileges and prestige with the natives, they nevertheless feel on shaky ground, like a thief who's hidden his loot. It is particularly the Russian presence which makes them feel this way because for once Russia could have the game in her hands and use these very arguments to justify her critical attitude towards the others.

However, his general feeling was that, "all the countries involved wanted to show their loyalty to the Charter," and to that extent he remained optimistic.

––––––––––

The question of where the United Nations should be located was a vexed one and there were many heated discussions about permanent headquarters and groundless fears of rivalry between UN and Pan American systems.

One of these early discussions was considerably enlivened by Victor's explanation of his late arrival. A message had been left for him to come to the meeting at 610 Fifth Avenue, the UNIO address. But Victor had misunderstood the venue as Room 610 at the Waldorf Astoria, the hotel where members often worked together in the early days. He had arrived at the appointed time and knocked at the door. An elderly lady answered and when she saw Victor with his oriental features, promptly told him: "Oh, no there's no laundry today." In Trygve Lie's autobiography, he paid tribute to Victor's keen sense of humour in enlivening "cabinet meetings", a humour which appeared at its best when he told stories against himself.

––––––––––

The Bronx campus of Hunter College in New York City was used as temporary UN accommodation for the first few months of its existence, when there were still anti-UN outbursts by the isolationist press. Later it moved to Sperry Plant at Lake Success on Long Island. The plant was owned by the War Assets Administration of the Federal Government and had been built for war production. Half of the plant was no longer needed for this purpose and all of it was air-conditioned unlike Hunter College. It was an ideal location, some miles from New York City, in an attractive area close to the small town of Great Neck on the North Shore. That was where I was sent to High School, together with several other UN children. We were made to feel very special and welcome, and discovered at an early age the generous spirit of Americans.

For the General Assembly Hall, the Mayor of New York City offered the former Municipal Auditorium built on the World Fair's grounds in Flushing Meadows, provided the Secretariat moved to the Sperry Plant. The city would provide it rent-free, plus $1,200,000 in repairs and remodelling costs. The UN signed the lease for half of Sperry Plant for three years from 1st July with an option to renew for two more years.

The question of the permanent seat of the UN increasingly became a political football, with arguments divided along the lines of the Cold War. The heated discussions about accommodation were a reflection of the power struggle.

For Victor it was no more than a base from which he constantly took off. Visits abroad were always a pleasure bordering on a passion. He did not mind living in hotels, packing and unpacking constantly, but he was always meticulous about not having to pay for excess baggage and on occasions I helped him cheat by holding heavy items whilst he put his luggage on the scales and then slipping them into his hand luggage out of sight. He would have with him a small, portable scale, which fitted into a plastic *étui*, so that throughout his trips - which often took in more than a dozen countries - he could check that his luggage remained within the limit.

During 1947, quite apart from his usual duties and overseas travel, Victor made over a dozen speeches. He enjoyed the media coverage, which gave him credibility as an expert on Trusteeship matters. The press at the time was very respectful of the UN. The latter did not allow its speakers to accept payment but they were allowed to accept VIP treatment which was just as good. I remember going with Father to Tarrytown during UN week. We sat in a limousine and were ushered through the small town with a police escort, the sirens blaring. We were treated to a sumptuous lunch and Father received the same treatment as a visiting Head of State.

There were broadcasts on Trusteeship matters, the UN in general or world events in various languages, speeches at Council lunches and addresses at various universities. Victor found it all very exciting. He never appeared nervous and always appreciated the fact that people were nice to him. Throughout his life, he was prepared to see the best intentions in everyone.

Working for the UN Secretariat mean dealing politically with the governments of the various countries involved. Good personal relationships helped. When Victor went to have talks with officials in the State Department to discuss Trusteeship matters early in 1947, he was treated to an elegant lunch at Blaire Lee House where he found out the policies and thoughts of the American administration. The people involved were from the African section of the Political Department and Victor mentioned in his diary that they were surprisingly well-versed in Trusteeship matters. They had their ideas about abuses by the colonial powers and told Victor that they put great importance on the questions of trust territories and would support him in obtaining the best personnel in his department.

He received the same treatment in London. In France, however, he found the officials less well-informed and although he was well received at the Ministère d'Outre Mer, they did not extend an unreserved welcome. Victor was piqued at their coolness for these were personal friends with whom he had been at university. Clearly the French resented any interference in their colonial matters.

At the beginning of March he went to Canada for twelve days, attending nine meetings in Quebec, Montreal, Ottawa, Kingston and Windsor and speaking on behalf of the UN at various colleges and institutes. He came back very disappointed. He had found the Canadians "revoltingly niggardly". He was never invited to dinner, nor to visit the town; they did not cover his travelling expenses and, with only one exception, his audience consisted of no more than ten to fifteen people.

On 27th March 1947 the Secretary General left New York on a trip and Victor was asked to deputise. He expressed his concern in his diary because it meant he would have to neglect the Trusteeship Council meetings. Aside from that there was not too much work to do as, "No-one wishes me to take too much initiative." Only in a crisis would he be asked to act. His routine duties were signing letters for Lie and representing him outside the UN.

On 1st April, as Acting Secretary General, he called a meeting of the ASGs. He made two recommendations which were both well received: one, to meet twice a week at a fixed hour and day, the other, to have each make an oral report on the workings of their department so that these meetings would not consist only of complaints.

The following day, Victor faced his first press conference as Acting Secretary General. He used all his experience and diplomatic skill to put the journalists on his side, with some success. Lie had the reputation of being rather dry and stodgy, typical of the trade union

124

leader he had been at home. On this level at least, there was no competition. "I answered all the questions," Victor wrote, "including two embarrassing ones and I think I gave a good impression. Several people congratulated me afterwards and a journalist said they found me charming and witty."

His diplomatic skills were about to be tested to the limit by the United Nation's mission to Palestine.

CHAPTER EIGHT

Israel

Dangerous Assignment - A Secret Meeting With Terrorists - The Partition Of Palestine

The problem of a Homeland for the Jews was not new. Since the Balfour Declaration of 1917, the Jews, particularly the Zionists, had fought for the restitution of Palestine. Indeed the Zionists had fought on the Allied side in the Great War with this in mind.

In 1922 the League of Nations had placed Palestine in British control under a mandate incorporating the Balfour Declaration. The promise to facilitate the establishment of a Jewish Homeland in Palestine was complicated, however, by traditional links between the British and the Arabs. The issue continued to fester until the aftermath of the Second World War brought it sharply into focus with the massive exodus of Jews from Russia and Germany.

There was no doubt that guilt and sympathy played a large part in the changes of attitude towards the Jews in 1946. During the War Britain and the US had done little to help the Jews and the American policy of making public promises to the Zionists led to increasing violence in the latter's pursuit of their demands. In 1946 this culminated in the blowing up of the British Embassy and the British Government & Army HQ at the King David Hotel.

By this time all Jewish dissidents were regarded by the British as outlaws and even the distribution of pamphlets by young girls and boys was forbidden under penalty of death. Members of the two militant groups, Irgun and Stern, were shot on sight.

Palestine had become a Police State and the entire Jewish population, even those opposed to terrorism, were engaged in passive resistance. Twenty-five years of British rule had culminated in chaos.

Finally Britain appealed to the UN Trusteeship Department for advice on how to carry out the mandate.

In May 1947 an inquiry commission, the United Nations Special Committee on Palestine (UNSCOP), was recruited from eleven delegates of smaller nations whose objectivity could be presumed: Guatemala, Uruguay, Peru, Iran, Australia, Canada, Sweden, India, Holland, Czechoslovakia, Yugoslavia. Victor was appointed to represent the Secretary General, who was determined that the Committee's Secretariat should be above reproach, not only technically but politically. The plan was to hold the inquiry in Palestine whilst Britain sought American co-operation in an "agreed policy".

Given American consent to continue British rule, the British Foreign Secretary, Bevan, indicated that he would make concessions on Jewish immigration thereby eliminating in one stroke the pressures of the Jewish Agency, quieting the doubts of President Truman and appeasing public opinion and conscience in US and Britain.

The moderate Jewish Agency indicated that it would be prepared to concur with this plan, although it did suggest the alternative of a partition state. It seemed at this stage that in spite of everything that had gone before a compromise was still possible.

Victor, appreciating the delicacy of the task ahead and given responsibility for electing a Chairman for the Inquiry Committee, was anxious to keep out the South American contingent whom he regarded as undisciplined, ambitious and inexperienced. He and his close friend Nazrollah Entezam of Iran, agreed the choice of Emil Sandstrom, a former Justice of the Swedish Supreme Court, a man of great wisdom and experience whose suave courtesy and apparent impassivity concealed a strong will. It was a good choice but the suspicion amongst other delegates that this election had been stitched up did not make for an auspicious start to the proceedings.

Within the Secretariat, other major problems had arisen, particularly over the appointment of Jewish members. Victor had a conversation with the Secretary General, the gist of which was that Epstein could join the Commission in Geneva at the drafting stage of the report; but that there should be no Jew or Arab of the Secretariat in Palestine who could be in contact with Jews or Arabs outside.

There were other internal problems. As leader of a Secretariat of around fifty-five people, Victor headed a virtual army of aides, typists, translators, interpreters, administrative, finance and press officers - a microcosm of the UN. On 22nd May 1947 he wrote in his diary:

We want to reduce the numbers in the Secretariat but are unable to have fewer than fifty-five. The Peruvian delegate insisted on taking a Peruvian member of the Secretariat who can't do anything. Not to antagonise him, we took him.

The Committee was blessed, however, with several men of outstanding ability, not least Ralph Bunche, now its Principal Secretary. With his intelligence and energy, Bunche was quickly to become the driving force that kept UNSCOP going. Not surprisingly, the Jews cultivated him steadily.

Victor's own appointment as the Secretariat's Representative on the Commission had been made by Lie without consulting Victor. Nonetheless, it was a post he took on readily.

Victor wrote:

Everyone is congratulating me and saying they could not have made a better choice. The Chinese papers say it is a guarantee of impartiality. Other papers say it shows the importance attached to the Commission if an ASG is appointed. My task will naturally be delicate but interesting too. It's a question of luck: if relations are good I will be praised. If not, I'll get the stick with the others.

Trygve Lie opened the first meeting of the Committee. No-one underestimated the difficulties of the task before them, fraught with so much emotion and passion, surrounded by so many appeals for humanity and justice.

The Commission left for Palestine on 10th June 1947. There was a stop-over in London where, according to one of the delegates, Garcia-Granados, the officials were treated with contempt. It seemed the British were out to show that the UN had no international or diplomatic status to deal with the Palestine problem. From the outset UNSCOP was treated with cold indifference by the British Foreign Office.

At the airport, conversely, the Palestine Administration received the UNSCOP members with courtesy. No Arab dignitaries or newsmen were present. The ride from Lydda airport to Jerusalem, about twenty-five miles, took the Commission through a series of Arab villages, reminiscent of biblical landscapes. The houses were rude, square, one storey huts of whitewashed clay and concrete. Arab men in white and brown robes wearing skull caps, stared after them. The countryside was a barren wasteland of untilled, arid soil, bald rock hills and small herds of goats.

The approach to Jerusalem led through a poor section of dilapidated one-storey buildings and tiny shops. The centre of Jerusalem, however, exhibited an exciting mixture of antiquity and modernity. A majestic forty-foot-high wall surrounded the old city. People in modern European dress mingled with Arab water-carriers bearing huge pig-skins filled with water, donkeys carrying heavy loads with cars sounding horns behind them, and British soldiers with machine guns and armoured cars.

Overlooking Jerusalem was Mount Scopus with its towers and turrets where Titus had assembled his legions for the final assault on the Temple of the Jews. On its summit they found the Hebrew University and Hadassah Hospital and from that vantage point they could see the cupolas of the Mosque of Omar, the Church of the Holy Sepulchre and the dome of the Great Synagogue. The Chapel of the Ascension, where Christ is said to have ascended to Heaven, stood next to the small tower of a Moslem mosque. At seven a.m. the Muezzin standing on the minaret sent forth his melodious call.

Kadimah House, some distance from the centre of Jerusalem, was entered through a grilled gate in a low wall, guarded day and night by three watchful Arab policemen.

The delegates had been warned by Lie not to expect much in the way of amenities but they found Kadimah House to be comfortable and well served and Victor, particularly, was gratified to discover that the hotels of Tel Aviv, Haifa and the Dead Sea compared very favourably with those in the West.

The Committee members were dazzled by the spirit of Jerusalem and agreed privately that the only unfortunate thing about Palestine was the political situation.

From a secret transmitter, a woman's voice relayed a message of welcome from the Irgun:

"This is the voice of Fighting Zion. Gentlemen of the United Nations, we greet you on arriving in our occupied country. We assure you that no harm will come to you whilst you are here. All stories to the contrary are British insinuations and untrue. We have no false illusions as to your work or what you will accomplish. Nevertheless, we extend our co-operation to you. Welcome to Palestine!" This, from one of the most militant and ruthless of the terrorist groups, one that had publicly committed itself to bombing, kidnapping and bloodshed as a necessary tactic in driving out the British.

There was no doubt that the underground was everywhere. Scarcely a day passed, Victor noted, without the Committee receiving up to a dozen letters signed by Irgun or Stern, containing demands or accusations against the British or reports of police mistreatment of Jews which had been censored by the press. There were hundreds of letters pleading for deliverance.

––––––––––

The first session of the Committee opened on the very day the Jerusalem Military Court sentenced three youths to death by hanging for their part in a terrorist attack. Anywhere else they would have received a prison sentence, having killed no-one.

This flaunting of the humanitarian law made the UNSCOP members intensely anti-British. The Chairman received a petition from the parents of the three condemned men to intervene to halt the executions and obtain a commutation of the death sentences. Some members of the Committee, like Garcia-Granados, who had himself suffered prison and exile in the cause of his country's liberation, were deeply and emotionally involved.

After heated deliberation the Committee decided to intervene to prevent the executions. A carefully worded resolution suggested that the death sentences would have unfavourable repercussions on the day when the Commission held its first meeting.

The British were outraged by this unwarranted interference but the stand UNSCOP had taken immeasurably increased its credibility in the eyes of the Jews who showered them with thanks and congratulations.

Victor wrote:

> At Tel-Aviv there were ovations for me everywhere which were pleasant and embarrassing because the Arabs will think I am anti-Arab or pro-Jew and I want to be impartial. My colleagues are already teasing me by saying they will create a Hoo Square in Tel Aviv and my name should be Ben Hoorion! I told them I would like to be called Jamel el Ben al Hoorion.

From the start the two sides had gone about achieving their ends in characteristically opposite ways: the Jews endeavouring to give the

Committee the best possible impression, whilst the Arabs refused to co-operate on any level.

In his diaries, Victor wrote:

> We have had several excursions which were supposed to provide an opportunity to listen to testimonies, but were simply sightseeing tours. It is difficult to speak to people as we are surrounded by journalists who write down the questions and answers.

> On one of the excursions I took my shoes off in front of the Omar Mosque and then went into another mosque. They brought my shoes to the second mosque while I thought they were where I had left them. I thus went fruitlessly towards the first mosque with no shoes on. The journalists then made up a story about me losing my shoes. On another day, the Peruvian delegate, Salagar, took my Panama, which was too big for him, but he didn't notice.

There were plenty of opportunities for socialising:

> These days I am the most popular man in Palestine for the Jews. In every cafe they treat me to drinks. In Tel Aviv the owner of the Pilz invited me after midnight to drink champagne in his apartment and had brought some interesting women, one of whom sang about the adventures of a woman. I added the last verse!

It was a heady time and by October Victor was lamenting the fact that the pages of his diary, which he was supposed to fill during the Palestinian Mission, remained largely blank.

> I am too lazy to spend a few minutes each day jotting down my thoughts. Perhaps one day I will fill in the pages which should have been filled in earlier but I don't think so.

Given the choice, Victor preferred more gregarious pursuits. On 23rd June 1947 he wrote:

> Today I lunched with Weizmann and his wife, who are of Russian origin. Rarely have I had such an interesting and

131

perfect lunch: the weather, the scenery, the historical sites, the house in brand new German style, the furniture, the menu, the cooking, and especially Weizman's conversation. His wife kept encouraging him to tell interesting stories which also served his cause. He has a lot of personal charisma and his seventy-four years appear sixty. Bunche took notes of the conversation. I only find that his explanation of certain events is, *post facto*, very witty but not always very realistic. He said that only in Palestine do the Jews give themselves up as prisoners, that each ship bringing Jews is a *Mayflower* and that Zionism means the rehabilitation of the Jews in the eyes of the world. Hostility to the Jews is due to the fact that they do well in their professions.

Whilst politics was endlessly discussed over the dinner table, however, Victor saw the dangers of allowing himself to be courted by the Jews and often turned down invitations which he suspected of being politically motivated.

There were historical claims from both sides. For two thousand years, the Jews had looked to Palestine as their Homeland. A member of the Arab Higher Committee was quick to point out that if national issues were settled on the basis of biblical promises the entire map of the world would have to be redrawn.

Nevertheless the Arabs had benefited in many ways from the Jewish presence. The Jews had transformed barren soil into flourishing farmlands. They had taught the Arabs new methods of irrigation, crop rotation and fertilisation. They had introduced free medical clinics open to Arabs. From 1920-39 the Arab population in Palestine had doubled, not only because of increasing health standards but also as a result of Arabs being drawn from neighbouring countries by the promise of new jobs in developing cities and an ever rising standard of living.

But, above all, the Jews had the undisputed weight of the Balfour Declaration with its promise of a Jewish Homeland in Palestine. Over the years it seemed that with Arab oil pressure, successive British governments had lost track of the purpose of the original mandate and were ruling Palestine virtually as a British colony.

The British insistence that they weren't surrendering the Mandate but merely asking the UN for advice on how to administer it did not smack of conciliation. Neither did Sir Henry Gurney, Chief Secretary of the Palestine Administration - an archetypal British civil servant whose strong sense of superiority was concealed under an icy courtesy.

The Arab case, fuelled by the fact that Palestine was an Arab land, was underscored by the revelation that over the years numerous unofficial as well as official promises had been made to the Arabs by the British.

The alternatives facing the Committee were:

i) An all-Arab state.
ii) An all-Jewish state.
iii) A bi-national state.
iv) Partition.

A turning point in the Committee's inquiry occurred with the setting up by the Associated Press Correspondent, Carter Davidson, of a secret meeting with the Irgun High Command.

Had the British known of the meeting, the Irgun leaders would undoubtedly have been sentenced to death and therefore Sandstrom, fearing his colleagues in the Committee might not maintain the necessary secrecy, decided not to inform them until afterwards.

A major problem was how to avoid British agents and news correspondents covering the Committee's hour by hour timetable. Sandstrom and Davidson had to take great care even in talking to each other, meeting on one occasion in the washroom of the British Sporting Club in Jaffa.

Victor and Bunche were the only other members of UNSCOP to attend the secret meeting. Victor had always suspected that rooms occupied by members of the Committee were bugged and a loose electric socket in his bathroom, although it became a topic of humour, leant credence to the suspicion.

When the scheduled afternoon tour of Jaffa was over, the three took rooms at the Park Hotel in nearby Tel Aviv. They rested, had a leisurely dinner and at eight o'clock, as darkness fell, strolled out of the hotel. A car was waiting to pick them up a few yards away (only Sandstrom knew this). The car took a weaving path through the city and finally stopped at the mouth of an alley.

A girl stepped from the shadows and the driver instructed them to follow her. At the end of an alley another car waited, containing a young woman whose face was concealed under a veil and a burly driver with a revolver. After driving for half an hour through twisted streets, they stopped at an apartment and the girl led them up a dark flight of stairs, pausing on the landing to whisper a few words of Hebrew through a door. She took her leave, announcing that she would return for them at 11.30 p.m.

The door opened and a young man led them into a brightly lit room. The apartment, they discovered, belonged to the poet Yaacov Cahan. Seated at a table with two others, was Menachem Begin, the leader of Irgun, a man denounced by the British as a murderous desperado, a fanatic responsible for the death of scores of British soldiers and the destruction of millions of pounds' worth of property. He had been in British hands half a dozen times and always managed to slip out of the net before they realised their catch.

To Victor and the others he looked like a mild schoolmaster whose fanaticism was suggested only in the mystic gleam of his eyes. He shook their hands cordially and thanked them for coming. Wine, fruit and biscuits were produced.

In a measured, carefully rehearsed tone, Begin spoke of the present situation in Palestine, of the bloodshed and suffering of Jews who were treated by the British like colonial natives.

He discussed the various alternatives which the Committee might recommend as a solution for this troubled land. Bunche had come to favour partition. Begin spoke strongly against it. "Do not forget, gentlemen," he declared, "the Biblical land of Palestine has already been partitioned by the British. In 1922 they had a mandate from the League of Nations to govern the country. But not to give three-quarters of it away to Jordan without consulting anyone. The land that was left was still called Palestine but it is only one quarter of the original Jewish homeland. The Irgun is against a further partition of that one quarter."

"Do I understand," Sandstrom asked, "that the Irgun demands all the land that is now called Palestine? This would be your new Jewish State?"

"No," said Begin, "we want our Biblical homeland: all of Palestine. The Arabs, after all, have seven nations with a territory almost 300 times that of Palestine. Much of that territory is vastly under-populated. The Arabs would scarcely be displaced in the Middle East. Whereas if the Jews had had a homeland in 1933, six million lives would have been saved."

He had spoken for three hours. Finally Sandstrom said: "We have heard what you want. Will you hear what we want? An end to terrorism in Palestine. We are working towards a peaceful solution to terrible problems. But terrorism and violence can only damage what we are trying to achieve."

Begin answered: "We will respect the UN's request for an end to violence, if the government halts its violence, if Britain carries out the immigration clauses in the mandate and if she stops imprisoning the Jews who come to this country. But if the government continues to halt our ships, to send refugees who arrive here back to Europe or to concentration camps in Cyprus, then we shall carry on our struggle."

The girl returned to say the car was waiting. Begin asked that the meeting remain confidential until UNSCOP had left the country. It was agreed that Bunche would take notes for an official report of the meeting and an Irgun member would come to his room in Kadimah House in a few days to collect it. A time and code were agreed on. Begin made two requests, first, that they would not give any physical description of him, and, second, that they would not name the others there.

The atmosphere of the meeting had been truly cordial, as with men of sincere intentions. The Irgun had previously heard that Sandstrom, a former judge under the British in Egypt, was still subject to British influence but they found this not to be evident. Bunche had expressed his sympathy as a member of a persecuted minority in his own country. The only hint of political judgement came from Victor who asked a provocative question. Palestine, even on both sides of the Jordan, was a small country. A population problem would be created by the introduction of millions of people. What would happen in three hundred years? Begin turned the question back to him. What did Victor think would happen in three hundred years in China?

As they left Victor said fervently: "Au revoir in an independent Palestine."

It was close to midnight before the delegates returned to their hotel. Feeling in need of a drink, they went to the neighbouring Pilz Cafe. Unfortunately Garcia-Granados had seen the unmarked car at the side of the road with Sandstrom, Hoo and Bunche inside it. It did not take long for speculation to begin regarding the whereabouts of the men for over three hours. Victor had already become known as "something of a playboy" with a fondness for night life. It was assumed that he wanted to taste some of the more exciting aspects of life in Tel Aviv. It was understandable that Bunche would go along as his friend but not Sandstrom, the stiff, straight-laced and elderly Swede.

A Hebrew newspaper appeared on the streets with an extra edition announcing that the three men had been to a secret rendezvous with the murderous desperado leader of the Irgun. Sandstrom, Hoo and Bunche emphatically denied all rumours. George Symonides, UNSCOP's Press Officer, officially denied the story. The secret remained inviolate until the agreed moment when Carter Davidson was able to claim a scoop.

———————

Although they had been impressed by the cordiality of the secret meeting, Victor and his colleagues knew there was a great difference, as Bunche said in his report, between "getting a good impression and forming a correct opinion".

Nevertheless, the Committee's attitude was firming towards recommending partition and an end to British rule. Even the Soviet Union, having treated Zionism as a major heresy for thirty years, now advocated the establishment of a Jewish state.

From the earliest days of the Committee's investigations, it had been apparent that the Jewish nation was already in existence as what Bunche called "a dynamic reality". Palestine was a melting pot for Jews of the whole world. Within months of arriving, these Jews, with their different customs, became assimilated, bound in a fraternity fuelled by a single-minded determination which gave them a superhuman capacity to work and endure hardship.

———————

On 25th July 1947 the Committee withdrew to Geneva to write its report for the General Assembly. On departure, the plane failed to lift off and 2000 pounds of luggage had to be off-loaded. Halfway across the Mediterranean one of the motors started to belch smoke. As flames streamed out of the starboard engine, the plane pitched and bumped. They reached Athens without enough altitude left for circling and went straight in from the sea. With the luggage they would undoubtedly have crashed into it.

———————

The Committee began the gruelling task of producing their report by 1st September. The working group was not so much a committee of eleven men as eleven committees of one man each. There were only two vital elements on which there was unanimous agreement: first, that the Mandate had failed and must be ended; second, that

136

Palestine must be independent with neither an all-Jewish nor an all-Arab State.

The form of this independence was the subject of great dissension. The delegates had been selected from supposedly impartial nations. Even so, lifetime prejudices seethed to the surface. The deadlock was solid. A miracle was needed. Victor wrote in his diary that the Secretariat needed to show more initiative. At this rate he would never be back in New York by the end of August as planned.

Thanks largely to the efforts of Bunche who had worked day and night for a solution, the Committee completed its task five minutes before the deadline.

The recommendation by a majority of seven was for the partition of Palestine into an Arab State and a Jewish State, bound together in an economic union. The city of Jerusalem, as a Holy City for three faiths, would be administered separately as a UN Trusteeship.

The recommendation was adopted by the UN General Assembly on 29th November by thirty-three - thirteen with ten abstentions. The following day came news from Jerusalem that the three Irgun boys had been hanged.

The UN had created a new Arab State and a new Jewish Nation. It had happened in spite of the threats, the promises, the bribes; in spite of the power of various blocs which would have protected the Arab cause. Unquestionably, the most powerful bloc of all had been the six million Jews murdered in the holocaust. The Jews had proved, as Garcia-Granados said, that against all possible odds, faith in a cause and the spirit of sacrifice for an ideal would win through.

The UK had abstained, although it had raised no objection to the matter being placed before the Assembly as it was convinced that an agreement between Arabs and Jews was unattainable. In the event, the British refused to hand over anything or to co-operate on anything. Behind the scenes, there were intrigues to sabotage the partition plans. Finally, however, the British agreed to end the Palestine Mandate and permit the UN Commission and the peacekeeping force to enter Palestine.

The exhilaration was felt throughout the world, especially by the members of UNSCOP. However, this was the beginning of an even more difficult and fraught period in the history of Palestine.

Amid an explosive atmosphere, enraged Arab leaders threatened to rise up and annihilate the Jews, "filling the sea with their corpses."

The Grand Mufti organised a holy mission to attack Jewish settlements, blow up water pipelines, shops and synagogues, and murder civilians, all to intimidate the Jews against declaring a State. Despite the violence, the broken truces, British intransigence and American inconsistency, on 14th May 1948 the State of Israel came to birth.

In September of the same year, Count Folke Bernadotte, who had worked tirelessly as Mediator to secure a truce between the warring factions, was assassinated together with his chauffeur.

The shock and outrage that followed his death was inexpressible. The terrorism which had stained the cause of both sides had claimed its noblest victim. Ralph Bunche was appointed Mediator in his place, a role for which he subsequently received the Nobel Prize, and an Armistice was finally signed on 24th February 1949.

In the end the Jews were forced to set up their State by themselves with only the moral authority of the UN partition agreement behind them but with no assistance against armed aggression. The State was not a gift. They had to create it themselves at the price of an enormous and ongoing struggle.

The consequences of the UN decision to partition Palestine was to have repercussions on generations of Jews and Arabs. Hoo and Bunche were all too aware of the immense problems facing the area, not least for the displaced Palestinian population.

Within the UN, however, in the euphoria of what seemed an impossible solution, Victor was enjoying the most glorious moment of his career. From then on, his influence in the Jewish community was greatly enhanced. By the same token, the Arabs felt betrayed and their resentment did not diminish with the passage of time.

In consequence of his part in the negotiations, Victor was offered the post of governor of Jerusalem. But the Palestinian phase of his career was at an end. His restless spirit was already seeking new challenges. The creation of the Jewish Homeland had been an arduous task and he was thankful to relinquish it. In his diaries he remarked:

> It does not interest me to be buried there. I prefer travelling or a job serving my country directly. Religions and Holy Sites do not interest me.

Soon afterwards he was invited to set up the Commission to Korea, an undertaking which was to prove the most rewarding of his career.

CHAPTER NINE

Korea

The Realisation Of Syngman Rhee's Dream - A Proliferation Of Political Parties

Few nations had suffered so much from foreign rule as Korea. As a link between the mainland and the Japanese islands, the Korean Peninsula had been a constant bone of contention for 4,000 years. In fact, a truly independent Korea had only ever existed when neighbouring great powers were too weak to fight over it.

Since 1910 it had been ruled by Japan whose oppression in Korea increased as the War neared its end. In 1945, there were 300,000 Japanese soldiers in Korea. With their surrender in August of that year to the Americans and Russians North and South of the Thirty-eighth Parallel, the latter became the demarcation line for the occupying forces, with devastating consequences for Korea's future.

During the war, Victor, as Vice-Minister for Foreign Affairs in the Waichiaopu and Deputy to T V Soong, had been involved in the negotiations in Washington between the US State Department and the Korean Provisional Government in the person of Syngman Rhee. There was considerable rapprochement between the Chinese contingency and Rhee's delegation, though Rhee's efforts weren't always supported by American officials or even by the Korean Community in the US. Here were two countries who shared both a common desire to overthrow the Japanese occupation and a common recognition of their military and financial dependence on the US.

At the time Alger Hiss had been a high-ranking member of the American delegation headed by Secretary of State, Cordell Hull. Rhee made numerous appeals to Hull to see him personally and to be allowed to take an active part in the War. There was no response. Subsequently, when Hiss was tried for treason, it was suggested that his pro-Soviet attitude had prevailed on the State Department and that the primary aim of American policy was to accommodate the Kremlin at the expense of a small nation's claim for independence. It was also rumoured that there had been a secret agreement at Yalta to put Korea under Soviet control. Stalin had agreed to enter the War with the expectation of several rewards including Korea.

What is perfectly clear from the record is that long before the western world was aware of the rising danger of Soviet imperialism, Rhee saw that Russian ambitions were inclined towards Korea and that the American State Department was committed to a policy of partial, if reluctant, acquiescence in this aim.

Rhee had had to wait until November 1943, when at the Cairo Conference Roosevelt, Churchill and Chiang agreed to take formal cognisance of Korean claims for independence "in due course". The last phrase indicated both reluctance and ambiguity in view of the undefined position Russia was preparing to assume in Asia. Even so, the statement constituted a significant landmark.

In the summer of 1943, Rhee's Korean Commission Office in Washington had prepared a blueprint of the Korean Underground organisation and despatch it to Roosevelt. At a meeting of the Pacific War Council, Roosevelt asked Soong for his estimate of the worth of the Korean movement. Soong passed the question to Victor who asked Rhee and members of the Korean Communist Movement if they were prepared to form a coalition with Rilso Haan, a favourite of the State Department to unite their divergent forces. Rhee replied that Haan represented very few Koreans and that, in his judgement, to unite with Haan would have no other effect than to encourage the Korean Communists. At the subsequent meeting of the Pacific War Council, Soong reported to Roosevelt that the Koreans were too disunited to comprise any effective force.

At the San Francisco Conference in 1945, however, Rhee had done everything possible to secure a guarantee of Korean independence, calling together leaders of the dissident factions and pleading with them to stand together on a simple programme of independence for Korea. The question of leadership could be decided later.

At this time there were some sixty political parties made up largely of political prisoners out of Japanese camps and Provisional Government leaders out of exile, together with Socialists and Communists. In the name of the United Korean Committee, Rhee then requested the status of Observer, representing Korea. The request was refused.

At the point of his return to Korea in November 1945, Rhee was *persona non grata* with the US State Department because he had tried so hard during the War to have the Provisional Government recognised and was so adamantly opposed to co-operating with the North Koreans. He was not a zealot but he had been struggling for recognition of the Provisional Government by western Powers since 1919. He had a broad political understanding and his earnestness was tempered with humour and a personal magnetism. The Korean people regarded him as an almost legendary leader whose indomitable spirit had been an inspiration. To two generations the name of Syngman Rhee had symbolised reform, democracy and independence. All political leaders came forward to offer Rhee the Chairmanship of their party, including Pak Hun Yung, Chairman of the Communists! Rhee refused them all in order to lead personally all parties south of the Thirty-eighth Parallel under the Society for the Rapid Realisation of Independence.

The Americans were shocked by Rhee's rejection of the leadership offer, which they considered to be motivated by personal ambition. Furthermore, the State Department was eager to have some kind of agreement with the Soviet Union which would facilitate the withdrawal of American troops from Korea. Rhee had always refused to acquiesce to the Communists. Hence the uneasy and troubled relationship between Rhee and the Americans.

The elation felt by Korean patriots at their freedom from the Japanese yoke, took a severe knock at the Moscow Conference in December 1945, when the Allied Powers agreed that the solution for Korea would be a five-year Trusteeship supervised by the Soviet Union and the US, Great Britain and China. A transitional Korean administration would be formed by consultation between the occupying powers and the Korean people.

The Koreans were utterly shocked. Resistance to the scheme was virtually unanimous. Rhee and Kim Koo of the Korean Independence Party, who was Premier of the Provisional Government in Chungking, issued a strong denunciation of the plan. There were demonstrations in the streets of Seoul, shops closed in protest and the Korean press tried to exert its influence. Then, on 2nd January 1946, on Russian instructions, North Korea came out in favour of Trusteeship.

Rhee was asked to act in a consultative capacity to the US Military Government. He could see that the effect of the plan would be to extend Soviet influence directly over the whole of the Korean Peninsula and thus violate the Cairo promise of independence for Korea.

Rhee concluded that to admit the Soviet Union in any guise into South Korea would merely surrender the independence of the nation. His intransigence earned him the label of "extreme rightist". In January 1946, with scarcely any more influence to be wielded in the US, Mrs Rhee joined her husband in Korea. An Austrian by birth, she had always accompanied him dressed in Korean National costume and had given him high international credibility at social occasions, balancing his plain dress and agreeable, friendly manner with a more distinguished aspect. For the moment, however, it seemed that she could do no more.

The Soviet Union had no intention of unifying the two Koreas. If they couldn't get the whole country, they had no intention of surrendering the half they already held. The Thirty-eighth parallel seemed to be a permanent frontier.

The Trusteeship issue had the effect of creating a clear division between left and right. The American and Soviet sides were at a stalemate. The Korean economy was already in shambles as a result of Japanese exploitation and heavy industry in the North was controlled by the Communists. Two million refugees pouring South and a lack of technical and administrative skills exacerbated the situation in South Korea. The US authorities took control of the mines and instituted reforms but they lacked knowledge of local administration and often merely added to the confusion. General Hodge who was in South Korea operating under a Congressional enactment providing him with funds to "combat disease and unrest" in fact had a broader influence both militarily and politically. In December 1946 Rhee decided to fly to Washington and go above the head of General Hodge. By that time the situation in North Korea had become clear. Half a million troops appeared on the frontier ready to attack the South.

Yet Molotov had assured Marshall in Moscow that he agreed to a reunified and independent Korea. There was obviously a misunderstanding as to the meaning of "a reunified and independent Korea" just as there had been a misunderstanding of the term "status quo" with regard to Outer Mongolia. Russia had always looked greedily at Korea as a sphere of influence for strategic reasons. Her imperialistic designs had been cut short by Japan's victory in the Russo-Japanese War of 1905 and its annexation of Korea. As a result the Russian threat had been pushed into the background for a full generation. Now their day had dawned again. One of their conditions for entering the War had been the occupation of North Korea. The

US had assumed this was a temporary measure. The Russians saw it differently.

By September 1947 it was accepted that the Great Powers had failed to reach agreement on the Korean Question. On 23rd September 1947 it was put on the agenda of the General Assembly of the United Nations. In October the US proposed a withdrawal of all foreign troops in Korea. The resolution was adopted by the General Assembly and approved by the US Joint Chiefs of Staff and General MacArthur, although US troops did not in fact leave until late spring of 1949, six months after Russian troops left North Korea. On 14th November 1947 a resolution was adopted to hold free elections in Korea and establish an independent government under the observation of a UN Commission. At the same time, the UN Committee for the Unification and Rehabilitation of Korea (UNCURK) was organised to advise and consult with the new government.

Victor was appointed by Trygve Lie as his personal representative to get work started in Korea, together with a Dutchman Petrus Schmidt. After depressing years of deadlock, there appeared a glimmer of light. At the Soviet-American Conference in Seoul, there had been complete disagreement between Rhee and the US Government. Under virtual house confinement, he had experienced the blackest period of his career.

At the United Nations headquarters all the member nations agreed that elections should be held no later than 31st March, except the Soviet bloc who denounced the UN vote as illegal. They argued on the basis that Article 104 of the Charter excluded from the UN jurisdiction issues arising out of World War II. In those days, however, the US enjoyed overwhelming majority support in the General Assembly.

On 8th January 1948 the first group of UN Commission delegates, including members from India, the Philippines, Australia and Syria, arrived in Seoul. They were agreed by Rhee and some 200,000 Koreans. One of Victor's earliest despatches provides an indication of the atmosphere he found on his arrival and some of the potential dangers he encountered:

> All political parties, except the Communists, welcomed us
> most sincerely. Many Koreans say we are their last hope ...
> In Seoul, 100,000 - 250,000 people lined the streets for
> several hours in the cold, awaiting our arrival. Of course

143

they did not all come spontaneously: this demonstrates the influence of the Chief of Police and Rhee's Party who organised the whole show, although officially it was organised by a welcoming committee made up of all factions with no political tendencies …

The radio broadcasts from North Korea are hurling invectives at the Commission. They say its members are hirelings of American Imperialism which wants to colonise Korea, that even I and Schmidt are Americans and that the Commission will not be allowed into North Korea. There were even rumours of a Communist plot to assassinate me and I was offered a bodyguard by the American authorities. I refused because it would have created a bad impression. I imagine that, since we now have a Chairman, he might be assassinated in my stead.

The Chairman was the representative of India, K P S Menon. In a speech to the Korean nation, broadcast from Seoul on 28th January 1948, Ambassador Menon set the tone of serious purpose which characterised the Commission's attempt to ensure genuinely free elections. He reported:

The Commission has established three committees: one to study ways and means of securing a free atmosphere for the ensuing elections, another to study Korean opinion and another to study the electoral system.

At the first formal session of the Commission on 12th January, Victor made a speech as the personal representative of the Secretary-General of the UN. General Hodge expressed his full support. The Soviet Headquarters ignored the proceedings.

On 14th January Victor wrote:

The Commission members are all good and reasonable. The delegates keep coming to me for my opinion, perhaps because I know four of them from Chungking: Menon, Liu Yu-Wan, Patterson and Paul-Boncour. No other ASG would have had these advantages. Everything goes well except that the Soviets are not co-operating and I doubt very much that we will be able to go to North Korea.

144

I had an interview with General MacArthur in Tokyo which was very interesting. He expressed a view identical to Rhee's, that by forming a national government in South Korea, North Korea will sooner or later join it. Besides, the American view is to proceed with elections in South Korea whatever the Soviets do.

Victor suffered no false modesty when it came to his personal charisma. He felt he was the best man for the job, however unrewarding the outcome might be:

> ... I have a lot of prestige with the Koreans. They seem to trust me. This week, the Chief of Police, Dr Chugh, having drunk too much, told Liu and Patterson that no-one counted in the Commission except me. The other day I was with Menon and Marion Mao and as he asked my advice about something, she said to him: 'You don't dare do anything without Dr Hoo.' Because I think I can be useful to the Commission, I shall stay until the end. I could negotiate amongst the leaders of the South, although I think that if the meeting does take place, it won't bring about anything ... The question for the Koreans is whether they prefer a Communist Korea, but whole and without bloodshed, or a divided Korea with the South at least non-Communist and the probability of Civil War. In the first case, they should demand the retreat of foreign troops from both sides and negotiate with the North to save as much as possible. In the second case, the leaders in the South should agree amongst themselves, proceed to elections and constitute a government as quickly as possible in order to have the military and economic support of the US.

In spite of the problems of his present task, however, it seems Victor was already looking forward to the next one:

> Menon told me that there will be a UN Commission in Kashmir and expressed his hope that I would go to it. I would love to as it should be relatively easy and not as thankless as the two missions so far. Kashmir is the Switzerland of India. However, if I did go, when would I be

145

in New York, which I am now attached to, and where I have found new friends?

In fact I am a happy man: they respect me at the UN, I have interesting work to do and more travel than I want. I could even go to Tanganyika this summer. I can also save money, build a reputation and have a secure future, at least until the end of my contract with the UN. Here the newspapers were full of me because the Chairman wasn't here during the first few days and they took me for the Head of the Commission. Therefore, here, as in Palestine, I have become very popular. I hope it lasts!

In the ensuing days, the entries display some of the problems besetting the present task:

We are still waiting for a Soviet response which will probably be negative. The Chairman wrote to the two Commanders-in-Chief (American and Russian) saying he wanted to pay them a courtesy visit. The letter to the Russian Commander went from Seoul to Pyongyang by Russian courier. At the same time we cabled a letter to Lake Success asking Cordier to pass it to Gromyko. A few days later Gromyko replied, reiterating the negative attitude the Soviet Union has towards the Commission.

… The idea of referring to an Interim Committee is gaining ground. If the Commission decide to refer, Menon and I will go to New York. That's what Cordier said when I telephoned him. Although I am pleased that he suggested this, it will upset my plans to take my leave in China in order to join Margie and the children.

… We must now confirm Menon as Chairman and choose a Vice-Chairman. Neither Patterson nor Liu want the job. Paul-Boncour would like it but said he would not stay more than two months if the *per diem* is not increased. The other delegates would not make good vice-chairs and lack the ability to become Chairmen.

… The different political parties here are fighting to influence us to take a decision to benefit their own interests.

146

Kim Koo of the Korean Independence Party and Kim Kyo Sik for the middle right, seem to want to join to eliminate Rhee. They do not see that they are weakening themselves by this game. It is the old story of internal discords which can only benefit the real enemy. The two Kims are now suggesting a Conference with the leaders of the North. They are thus playing into the hands of the Communists who will impose their own conditions.

After meetings with Rhee's political competitors, Victor wrote:

We had a meeting with Kim Koo and Kim Kyo Sik and I got them to agree by asking the right question at the right moment. Kim Koo agreed to a meeting before the retreat of foreign troops, whereas he had previously insisted that such a meeting could only take place after their withdrawal.

... Speaking to Kim Kyo Sik alone, I told him that if the Koreans are willing and able to resist the North Korean Communists, they should hold their elections quickly and form a government. If they wait too long, the Americans might be forced by public opinion to quit Korea suddenly. If Korea had neither a government nor an army, this could be disastrous.

The Commission had by now accepted that if there was to be an election, it would be exclusively in the South, but in order to hold elections in the South only, it had to obtain a mandate from the Small Assembly. The latter however, had to be kept secret in order not to compromise the success of a North-South Conference. It was a question of timing. The longer the North-South Conference lasted the more it benefited the position of the North. It might then be too late for any elections at all.

... Through the efforts of Liu and myself, we succeeded in bringing together Rhee and the two Kims and persuaded them to accept a common programme of action. This is how it happened: after speaking to Kim Kyo Sik I called Rhee. I told him the Commission had noticed the discord between the political leaders of South Korea which made them hesitate to hold elections there. Rhee ardently wished for elections to take place and asked to have a meeting with Menon and myself, to assure us that disagreement between the South Korean parties was minimal. Rhee and the two Kims came to my room for the meeting and stayed for dinner. By asking precise questions and steering them to a convergence, the three finally agreed on the following:

1   That an attempt should be made to convene a conference of the Southern and Northern leaders. Rhee is no longer opposed to this and, if the Soviets agree, is even ready to favour it. If there is no conference or agreement before May, elections would go ahead in the South only in the first week of May.

2   The conference would aim to make a last attempt to unite the two parts of Korea and to blame the North if the conference was not successful.

This meeting of the Three made a big splash because they had not conferred together for two years and it increased the prestige of the Commission in the eyes of the Koreans.

On 14th February Victor and Menon flew back to New York to report to the Small Assembly. The journey took three days and two nights and Victor complained in his diary of jet-lag. In the plane Menon showed him the speech he intended to deliver to the Interim Committee on Korea. Victor suggested about thirty corrections, all of which Menon accepted.

In New York Victor faced the uncertainty of whether the US insistence on elections in South Korea would have enough support to influence the Small Assembly. He learned that France and the UK were unwilling to support the US on any question that separated the US from the Soviets. They did not in fact consider the Korean issue a high priority one. One member of the French delegation was heard to say that the US should not spread its efforts and money too thinly throughout the world. Of that Victor wrote:

It is a very cynical viewpoint which completely sacrifices Korea.

148

At Lake Success Victor had meetings with the Secretary General and Cordier. Both expected him to return to Seoul, although Lie left the decision to him. Cordier, however, strongly impressed upon Victor that he should return for the sake of UN prestige and also because Menon was leaving. Cordier suggested that Victor might be his replacement as Chairman. Victor replied that he would not be staying until the end of the Commission as he was due to take his home leave in Shanghai and would like to be in Paris for the Assembly.

Menon's speech on the Korean situation was well received and earned him considerable praise from the other delegates. He was described in an article as full of wit, understanding and firmness.

When it came to the vote, thirty-one delegations voted for elections, two against (Canada and Australia).

On 6th March Victor left New York for Korea again. Tensions and disagreements still existed at all levels. The most obvious were those between North and South but the South Koreans themselves remained fragmented in their political doctrines, most of which were based on personal rivalry and ambition. The US was now pressing for elections without delay, with or without the participation of the North.

As election time drew near, there was a growth of ill-feeling between Rhee, Kim Koo and Kim Kyo Sik. In an atmosphere of deep suspicion, charges and counter-charges flew in all directions.

Out of the blue, an invitation was issued by Kim Il Sung, the Premier of the People's Democratic Republic set up by the Soviets in North Korea. It invited all patriotic South Korean leaders to attend a meeting in Pyongyang to plan for a coalition government.

On 21st February Kim Koo announced his opposition to the UN election as effectively dividing the two Koreas forever. The main topic of disagreement amongst the various party leaders was whether they should wait until reunification of the whole country before holding elections. The two Kims went on a visit to North Korea and came back disillusioned. Yet they still officially opposed the elections scheduled for May in the South.

By the time the elections arrived, North Koreans had infiltrated the South with funds and secured control of large numbers of newspapers, media, movie theatres, giving the impression of being a large minority of the total population. The UN Commission on its arrival, added to the confusion and disorder by giving amnesty to several hundred Communists, agitators and terrorists who had put out a programme of sabotage, arson, murder and planned revolution. So the jails were now emptied of all the Communists who had been arrested for their lawless activities, allowing them to renew their propaganda against the UN Commission and threatening to attack any "traitors" who tried to vote in the "imperialist elections planned by the US through its puppet, the UN."

Nonetheless the first democratic elections in Korea's long 4,400 years of history took place as planned on 10th May 1948. 198 representatives were elected to the National Assembly, 100 seats being left vacant in case of possible future election in the North. A hundred people died on the day as a result of the Communist campaign of violence but the elections were fair. Rhee, who had been persuaded to stand for elections as a member of the Constituent Assembly which would draft a constitution and elect a President, got over ninety-five per cent of all registered votes in his district. The turn-out was ninety-two and a half per cent. The widely heralded boycott did not materialise.

The Koreans were enormously pleased that their new experiment in democracy had been launched so auspiciously. The UN Commission withdrew to Shanghai to draft the reports of Observers. These decided that there had been "a reasonable degree of free atmosphere wherein were exercised the democratic rights of freedom of speech, press and assembly," and that the election constituted "a valid expression of the free will of the electorate in those parts of Korea accessible to the Communists and in which the inhabitants constituted approximately two-thirds of the people of all Korea."

General Hodge officially expressed regret that free elections could not be held North of the Thirty-eighth Parallel at the same time. The US and the UN expressed their hope of eventually uniting North and South in one nation.

Looking back on his career, Victor felt that the most rewarding episode had been his Korean experience. He deeply believed that the ultimate aspiration of a nation was democracy and here he was able to be instrumental in such a process. The honour and respect he received from the Korean people in consequence was very gratifying to him. Perhaps they felt more able to relate to and trust in another Oriental. Certainly their history books gave him pride of place.

On 31st May the Assembly met to elect a Chairman. There were eighty-five Independents, forty-eight followers of Rhee, thirty members of the Democratic Party and thirty-seven splinter groups. Rhee was elected by 189 - 8 and over the next few weeks worked on the draft of a constitution.

On 19th July the Constitution was adopted. Rhee was elected first Teahan Minguk (President) of the Republic of Korea by a vote of 180 - 16 votes went to Kim Koo. On 3rd August Rhee's nominee for Prime Minister, Lee Bum Suk, was confirmed by 110 to 84.

The process of turning over authority to the new government from the American Military Government took several weeks but proceeded in orderly fashion. On 15th August the third anniversary of liberation, the newly formed Republic of Korea was proclaimed to the world. General MacArthur came for the ceremony. In his inaugural speech, Rhee, now aged seventy-three, emphasised the importance of democracy and the need to protect civil rights and individual liberties. He knew that he would now be expected to solve all problems and work miracles.

The Republic soon received diplomatic recognition from the US and fifty or so other countries. In December the UN proclaimed it the only legitimate Government of the Korean Peninsula.

There were a few more feeble gestures towards peaceful unification with the North, all ending in failure. Having founded the Korean Council of People's Commissars as a step towards establishing a permanent Communist regime, the Russians allowed negotiations to take place between representatives from North and South Korea at Pyongyang in April 1948. This turned out to be simply a brain-washing operation on the part of the North Koreans and nothing was achieved. Matters had gone too far for Korea to be unified through negotiations.

In the North, in defiance of the UN resolution, the People's Republic of Korea was established in September 1948, claiming to represent the whole country. Almost immediately it began harassing guerrilla raids on the South, together with a propaganda campaign and the fomenting of riots. By June 1949 both Soviet and American troops had been withdrawn. The big Powers had disposed of Korea for their own purposes and a microcosm of the Cold War was reproduced in Korea.

In the South, economic, social and political difficulties highlighted public disenchantment with the politicians. Shortage of essential goods, inflation and difficulties in maintaining public order led to Communist inspired riots and strikes. The South Korean armed forces were vastly inferior to the North's when, in June 1950, North Korean troops crossed the Thirty-eighth Parallel without warning. The invaders were not checked until they reached the Naktong River near Taegu.

Korea was at war and would remain so until 1953.

CHAPTER TEN

The Trusteeship Department - 1951

*Trouble in the Secretariat - Hope of a Cease-fire in Korea - MacArthur
v. Truman - Formosa waits for American Aid -
The Mission to East Africa*

The years following Victor's involvement with UNSCOP and Korea
were more fragmented and although there were highlights, such as
the Mission to East Africa in 1952, the rewards were marred by
disputes within the Secretariat over pay and contracts and conditions
generally.

In his diaries for 1951 Victor complained:

> Lie's indecision on the subject of ASG contracts is inhuman.
> He treats us worse than servants.

Finally, at an ASG meeting to celebrate his own new term of office,
Lie announced his decision to prolong the top ranking Directors'
contracts by five years and those of the ASG by three years.

Victor wrote in his diary:

> Lie told me he wanted to renew my contract but would like
> to appoint a Chinese Red if Mao is admitted to the UN.
> That is why he wants to give me a contract that can be
> terminated at any time. I replied that he should give me a
> contract of the same duration as the other four permanent
> members and, if it came to it, I would hand in my
> resignation. However, it seems I could well stay at the UN
> for another three years.

In February 1951 Victor and the other ASGs and Directors attended
a fiftieth anniversary dinner at the Waldorf for Lie and his family.

We presented him with a silver tray and there were several panegyric speeches which Bunche and I agreed were some of the most inept we had ever heard, with no ideas and no spontaneous humour. Lie made an impromptu speech expressing his confidence that there would not be a general war because the leaders were intelligent men and not crazy like Hitler or syphilitic like Mussolini. He also said that for the moment he would observe restraint in the international situation. It was the best speech of the evening.

However, as far as Victor's own security of tenure was concerned, Lie continued to procrastinate.

Yesterday, at an ASG meeting, he said he had still not decided finally about our contracts and that in the meantime we would be paid as usual.

By March they were still waiting. Victor complained in his diary:

He has not even signed the Directors' contracts. The highest official in the UN is thus in a less enviable situation than his subordinates. It is becoming more and more ridiculous.

The suspicion that they were not held in high regard within the Secretariat was fuelled by the penny-pinching attitude of other officials:

This week we had an ASG meeting where we examined two documents prepared by Price. It is curious how unaware he is of the mentality of others, especially foreigners, as well as of the work of other departments. He only sees the budgetary side and the rest doesn't count. It is because of him that we don't have new furniture in the new building and our furnishings are horrible compared to those of the League in Geneva.

Had it not been for the hunger for work and activity that had always been a mark of Victor's character, 1951 did not bode well. Bad feeling was exacerbated still further by the discovery that Lie had attempted to take away members' cars.

They say that in 1946 they wanted to buy a Cadillac for Lie and Buicks for the ASGs but Lie said *he* was the UN, so they only bought one car for him. He is always trying to minimise us.

In some ways, the almost daily entries in the diaries at this time provided Victor with a much needed release for his sense of grievance.

Internationally, Korea still dominated the UN's attention, together with speculation as to a possible invasion of the Chinese mainland by the Nationalists now confined to Formosa.

In January 1951, Chinese Communists again attacked the Americans trying to hold a line North of Seoul and the city was evacuated. At White Sulphur Springs, Victor met McAdams, Taft's advisor, and was told categorically that the American public was not yet ready to sacrifice everything for a Korean War.

The question of American military aid to Formosa in the event of a mainland invasion, was also the subject of considerable disagreement within the American State Department. In 1951 this led to one of the most public and controversial conflicts of the American administration, between Truman and General MacArthur.

The issue of Red China's admission to the UN was inevitably complicated by events in Korea. In January 1951 Victor wrote:

> I went to Washington for a few days with Mr and Mrs Tsien Tai, Liu Chieh and James Yu. The atmosphere was depressing. We spoke only of politics and especially of the last attempt by the Committee of Three to bring our Reds to negotiation.

There had also been attempts to bring together the Four Great Powers, including Red China, in a conference on the Far East "with specific reference to Formosa and China's representation in the UN."

> The fact that these principles were approved by the US shows that they would be prepared to recognise our Reds by sitting with them in the same conference. However, American public opinion thinks this ultimate attempt at negotiation would not be accepted by Mao, thus giving the UN justification for a resolution condemning Red China as aggressor. McAdams thinks the fate of the UN will be

decided soon and that, if Mao is admitted, the Americans will turn away from it.

In the past I would have liked to represent China at an international conference where she was branded aggressor, as this would prove a strong, united China. Today, 20th January, the US is going to present such a resolution but, alas, the circumstances are different from those I had hoped for. China isn't even playing the game of international Communism but simply of Soviet Russia. She sends her sons to be massacred for a cause that will not serve the real interests of the Chinese people and she rouses in the whole world respect for her strength, perhaps, but also feelings of hostility.

On 24th January the House of Representatives and the Senate unanimously adopted resolutions asking the UN to brand the Chinese Communists as aggressors. Victor wrote:

The Americans have thus at least shown the world their unity on the subject.

The resolution was adopted, although several countries suggested they were supporting the resolution against their will and insisted it did not exclude negotiations. The Soviets and Chou En Lai naturally seized this opportunity to denounce the resolution as having been imposed on the others by the US.

By March, however, the Americans were regaining their confidence in Korea and advancing. Victor wrote:

There are more of them in Korea than I thought, 250,000 excluding the airforce and navy. MacArthur published a speech today, separating the question of Formosa and China's representation in the UN from that of Korea, thereby contradicting Truman. Those who practise appeasement can now argue there is no reason not to settle Formosa before Korea.

The State Department later dissociated itself from this speech on the grounds that its threat to Chinese Communists jeopardised chances of a cease-fire and was a deliberate attempt to sabotage the possibility of negotiations. The gap between MacArthur's standpoint and that of the administration was widening alarmingly.

At the end of March a series of articles by Chennault in the *NY Herald Tribune* asked specifically for American aid to Formosa for a landing on the continent. Victor wrote in his diaries:

> He points out the lack of equipment and war material in Formosa. The soldiers have only one real cartridge a month for practice. We need six months' preparation before landing. In my opinion a landing would only be supported by the Americans if the Nationalists are beaten and find themselves in a desperate situation in Korea, or if there is a Third World War, or if the US feels strong enough to provoke a general war in order to combat Communism universally. Here in America, most people, except Chinese professors, hate Chiang Kai Shek. They would like to see the Communists defeated but not by supporting Chiang.

The introduction of television into politics was to bring about subtle but considerable differences and was to have drastic implications for the Truman administration, particularly in its handling of the controversy with MacArthur. Victor wrote:

> They say that Dewey lost the presidential elections in '48 because the public saw him on TV looking ridiculously like a bridegroom. The American public liked Gromyko because they did not see him but they hated Malik whom they saw and found him impenetrable compared to Austin whose feelings are apparent on his face. It will be disastrous for the Truman government which is now considered the most corrupt after Harding.

The fulsome entries in Victor's diaries during these months were helped by a gift from Margie in April of a Parker pen. He recorded enthusiastically:

> ... the latest model with a plastic reservoir. Let us see how long it lasts and how often I use it to write here.

He did not have to wait long before an excuse presented itself. A rumour through Wieschoff that he was trying to contact and get on good terms with the Chinese Communists infuriated him.

157

> This is idiotic. If it were true, why didn't I do it at a more favourable time. Either rumours are started to discredit me or else they ascribe intentions which these people themselves aspire to in my place. They think that everyone is a chameleon, as many petty people now are. Six months ago Lie would have been happy for me to be on good terms with the Reds but now it would be a reason to discredit me and this may account for it.

Personal rivalries and jealousies were rife within the Secretariat. Victor was to have more trouble with Wieschoff later in the year when the latter suggested that his reasons for going to Africa were merely to have the *per diem* and consolidate his position. Victor wrote bitterly:

> People like Wieschoff only think of politics and personal interests and don't realise others can do things through feelings of duty. He himself would probably like to go on the mission for the reasons he attributes to me.

In the US MacArthur had again provoked the fury of his government by suggesting that Formosa, now renamed Taiwan, should be helped to land on the Chinese Continent.

> MacArthur says it is he who is fighting for Europe by making war in Asia. It seems the Americans are again worried by the military situation in Korea. They think of our troops in Formosa whenever they fear being beaten and forget us as soon as things improve. This new outpouring from MacArthur could be the last straw. We'll soon see the reaction. The British can't stand him.

> Tomorrow Lie goes to the Near East for a month. He has an intuition that something will happen. I'm of the same opinion. I think that in Korea our Reds will retake the offensive. The question is whether the Russians will be part of it. I told Lie I'm entitled to home leave but will await his return …

The following day, 7th April, Lie left for Paris after a press conference in which he said he hoped for, but did not predict, a cease-fire in Korea. Victor wrote:

Lie urged us to put an end to the aggression in Korea with all the forces that the unified command could safely commit. He does not believe there will be a Third World War but says we must be prepared for the worse and hope for the best. Zinchenko is to be Acting Secretary General in his absence, no doubt to please the Russians.

The official White House response to MacArthur's letter announced that it had no intention of changing its policy of neutralisation of Formosa. On 11th April, however, Victor noted a *coup de tonnerre*:

> Tonight at one a.m. the White House announced that Truman has dismissed MacArthur and is replacing him with Ridgeway. The Chinese are dumbfounded. All the powers, especially Britain and India, are jubilant. Only Australia is sorry. This is going to provoke an almighty controversy in the US and everything will depend on the Reds. If they continue their plan of aggression, Truman is finished. Opinion in the US will be divided as in France over the Dreyfuss Affair. Truman refused to see Looke, the President of the American Legion, who has just done a world tour and declared his agreement with MacArthur's stance. It is really very petty.

By mid-April the MacArthur controversy had exploded over America. Victor wrote:

> The whole country is divided with a majority on the side of MacArthur, although all admit the President's right to dismiss a rebellious subordinate. Those who see clearly think, like Walter Winchell, that the greatest scandal is not the dismissal of MacArthur but the foreign policy which made it inevitable. Until now the press has never directly attacked Truman, for the Americans are usually respectful of the office of President, but this time they can't help it. The *Chicago Tribune* said the American nation had never been in greater danger, 'led by a fool who is surrounded by knaves.'

> Generally the division follows the alignment of the two political parties, the Republicans being for MacArthur and

the Democrats for Truman. However in the public arena it doesn't always follow. Today the radio announced that a husband who was for Truman was hit in the face by his sweet wife!

Worse was to follow. By August Truman's effigy was being hung in public demonstrations. *The Times* wrote:

"Seldom has a more unpopular man fired a more popular one. The public has an impression of a petulant, irascible President who stubbornly protected shoddy friends, a man who failed to give the nation clear leadership in these challenging times, whose Asia policy seemed to combine a kind of apologetic resistance with something between a hope and a prayer."

A speech by Truman in April had begun with the assertion that Communists in the Kremlin were engaged in a conspiracy to stamp out freedom all over the world. Victor observed that

... the speech was cleverer than usual but it contained a fundamental contradiction ...

Truman says the aim of the Reds is to unify Asia by annexation in order to crush the US. In this he seems to agree with MacArthur but he thinks that, by resisting aggression only in Korea, we could discourage the Reds from going too far and thus avoid a world war. Such a theory is of course very attractive as long as the Reds do stop. Truman concedes that it might well be that, in spite of their best efforts, the Reds spread the war but it would be tragically wrong, he says, for them to take the initiative in extending it.

Therefore, on the one hand he thinks the Reds want to take over the whole of Asia and on the other hand he thinks they might stop wanting to if there is enough resistance in Korea. He doesn't say that we would have to start all over again on another occasion, especially if the democratic states are in disarray which will surely be the case once peace is re-established. If, conversely, war continues indefinitely,

160

this would bring about such an economic crisis that the democracies would again be divided. In a sense MacArthur's dismissal could be a blessing in disguise for having roused public opinion and pointing out the fundamental problem of what American policy should be vis-à-vis Asia and the present situation.

The last sentiment was born out a few days later when Secretary of State Acheson, who had been against all aid to Formosa, announced that the US would, after all, give military assistance. Three days later, on 21st April, official US sources announced that a military mission of 100 persons would be sent to Formosa to help it defend itself. Victor commented:

> Surely this news will lift the spirit of all anti-Red Chinese. I think that from now on we are going uphill and that the lowest point for us in our international situation, reached just before Mao's intervention in Korea, will not return again. Our fate is again now officially linked to the fate of the US and thus logically, geopolitically, we are reunited with our ally *de toujours*.

Within the Secretariat there had been as much controversy and divided opinion over MacArthur as there was outside it. Victor wrote:

> In my department Bunche, Benson and Aleksander are all anti-MacArthur. At the ASG meeting Bunche opposed the suggestion that members of the Secretariat could go to the parade for MacArthur if they wished. He is really intolerant. I've never seen him so excited about something which does not concern him personally. He frankly hates MacArthur. It is interesting how passionate the arguments are surrounding the affair. These days it is the only topic of conversation. I wonder if there have been similar cases in Roman history of a disgraced general being hailed triumphantly by the crowd.

However, there were still many Americans who believed that Truman's more prudent policy would assure peace for longer. Victor recorded:

I lunched yesterday with George Sharp. He thinks the Korean War could last another twenty years, but that it is preferable to a world war. He thinks US strength should be conserved for Europe. In a word, he defends Truman's theory.

Last night at the dinner of French Ambassador Garreau, we spoke at length of the situation. De Kerillis energetically defended Truman's policy. He thinks the Americans are now short of armaments, planes and instructors (these being in Korea) and that materially the US cannot do what MacArthur would like. According to him, MacArthur has committed an act of high treason by forcing the US Government to admit her weakness. Like Sharp, de Kerillis thinks Europe is more important than China and we must think of defending Europe first. I replied that Russia was more likely to try and take Asia, the North East and Africa, without touching Europe at all.

He agreed that we could have had a war in better conditions in 1938 instead of giving in at Munich and that we might have kept Soviet co-operation instead of pushing them towards their present policy by betraying them then and throwing Hitler against the USSR.

In May Victor wrote:

MacArthur goes to Washington every day to testify in front of the two Senatorial Committees. Official communiqués are given to the press as soon as they happen. If nothing else, the frankness of MacArthur's criticism of the Government shows the strength of US democracy.

Victor continued to feel that his countrymen could only benefit from the MacArthur Affair and from the disclosures in the Senatorial Committee.

After these disclosures, the Republicans feel unified with Nationalist China and will be kind to us. The day will come, and I hope I see it, when China and the US will walk hand in hand with a common ideal of peace and freedom.

The future was not to be quite as uncomplicatedly ideal, however. Although the General Assembly voted on 19th May for economic sanctions against China and Red Korea, and American sympathy for Chiang Kai Shek increased with the Communist offensive in Korea, less than a week later the State Department announced a no-change policy towards China. Victor wrote:

It was like a cold shower. This kind of thing could only happen here. Lie believes the State Department dares not show itself conciliatory, for fear of appearing appeasing. On the subject of Formosa he thinks the UN could make it a trust territory, evict Chiang (as if it were so easy) and have a plebiscite after five years to see if it wants to be re-attached to China or Japan, or be independent. I told him he mustn't think Peking will adopt an attitude in China's interest, that it is the Russians who decide Chinese military operations in Korea and that only a solution acceptable to Russia would have any chance of success.

In June there was some progress towards a cease-fire. A speech by Soviet delegate Malik was followed by an editorial in a Communist Peking newspaper and articles in *Pravda* approving Truman's favourable attitude to a cease-fire. Conversations between the US Ambassador in Moscow and Gromyko agreed that negotiations could start between the belligerents without political conditions. An atmosphere of reserved optimism resulted. Victor wrote:

At the beginning Malik's declaration was considered too good to be true, like a legitimate wife often betrayed by her husband, who hears him all of a sudden say he will be faithful. The declaration and what followed awakened hopes everywhere except in Formosa and South Korea where they want a cease-fire as long as there is no loss of face and no compromise for the future. For the first time, Acheson declared that the Formosa question and the entry of Red China to the UN are not factors in the settlement of the Korean question.

Although from the start I said Malik's approach was something new, it was difficult to see if this meant a new attitude on Russia's part. At a dinner at Garreau's, Soldatov told me my heart was pointing in the wrong direction. I told him my father had not taken me to Japan because he felt Russia to be the country of the future. Soldatov replied that I did not seem to be in agreement with my father. I answered that I perhaps knew Russia better.

The Americans are now showing a rather childish enthusiasm to bring about the cease-fire. Lie is behaving like a *diable dans un bénitier*. He keeps making optimistic declarations about peace. In fact I suppose this is his role and can only be counted in his favour in the eyes of the world.

He [Lie] is very hostile to Syngman Rhee whom he considers reactionary and asked Cordier to get information in Korea to see if he could be replaced.

He [Lie] is probably of the same opinion with regard to Chiang Kai Shek. He told me at a fishing party that if I were in power he would support me. People like him have illusions on Far Eastern politics, as if all you needed to constitute a government was to be honest and liberal. He forgets that governments over there are not elected by popular vote and that it is the personality more than the programme which counts. It is the same in the US where Eisenhower could become President either as a Republican or as a Democrat.

The sincerity of the Communists in wanting a cease-fire remained in question, although Victor was inclined to take Malik's speech at face value:

Today I lunched with the Head of our Delegation, T F Tsiang who thinks as I do that the Reds want sincerely to 'behave' for a certain time. He said that the Red Chinese were economically exhausted in Korea and would have lost China by continuing the war. However, he thinks they will attack Burma. This would unite everyone against the Reds, which would be a great diplomatic error. The Reds would do better to attack Formosa once the Korean War is settled, because an attack would divide the democracies and would

164

not obtain the two-thirds majority needed at the UN for collective sanctions.

By March of the following year, optimism was fading regarding an armistice in Korea which seemed likely to depend on the choice of candidates for the two American parties.

> Lie thinks the Reds don't want Truman or Eisenhower but Taft. They will therefore only decide whether there will be an armistice or not after the official candidates are known.

It seemed there was nothing to do but sit back and wait.

In July Victor was able to enjoy a change of scene away from the squabbles and political and domestic frustrations of the Secretariat. In April Bunche had approached him to ask if he wanted to join the visiting mission to Africa. It was the UN's job to inspect all aspects of political, social and economic institutions in the trust territories to verify that the administrative powers were really preparing the population for full independence and self-government.

Victor was keen to go

> ... but not as a fifth wheel. Nor do I want them to say that I took advantage of my position to have a pleasure trip. I would only go in the interests of the UN and of the Department if I could play a useful role.

In May Lie had approved Victor's participation in the mission which excluded the malicious Wieschoff. Victor recorded:

> He must be furious, though from my experience of him I think I can do everything better. The present mission should be pleasant since my collaborators are all good and there are no troublemakers. Sayre has been replaced by Cargo who is pleasant and serious. Laking is also good. Marchena could be awkward but is easily manipulated if one uses tact.

The final membership comprised Marchena, President, Laking, Cargo, Kridakon, Dartigue, Rougier and Mademoiselle d'Anjou. They flew from Brussels to Usumbura on 22nd July 1951.

165

Despite some friction between d'Anjou and Rougier which Victor thought might best be solved if they slept together, the trip was largely a success.

At Usumbura they heard a speech by a colonial, Petillon on a ten-year plan for urbanising the town. Victor recorded:

> He has a wide view, rare amongst colonials, with much dynamism and faith in his work. He also has taste, evident in the colours and furniture of his office. He wants to plant palm trees along one road as it would look nice when the wind blows!

The trip from Usumbura to Kitega began to make inroads on the resources of the participants, however:

> Lots of dust and we were exhausted on arrival. Schmidt has no consideration for his passengers. We were rocked around like salad baskets and unable to sleep because Marchena can't sleep during the day and kept talking. On the way we passed a magnificent villa on Lake Tanganyika inhabited by a Belgian who was a priest but who dedicated his villa to a Phasam who had two of the priests massacred.

> It is along this lake that there is sleeping sickness. In a hospital I saw a male nurse give an intravenous injection to a ten-year old boy. The boy turned his head away and stoically winced and then went away with his arm folded against his biceps because there is no cotton wool! Preventative injections are given to everyone against sleeping sickness. Elsewhere I saw two vans taking X-rays of all the inhabitants on microfilms about two-thirds of a postcard. It costs fifty francs a photo. I don't believe it is done in other territories.

Because of the altitude, the climate bore comparison with Switzerland:

> The view is similarly beautiful but the mountains are deforested due to soil erosion.

On a practical level the mission found its task endlessly hindered by officials. On 1st August they received their first petitioner on general conditions there:

166

... a clerk in the administration who had enough courage to make the petition, although everyone here fears reprisals from the administration ...

Marchena's obtrusive personality continued to provide entertainment and irritation in equal measure. Victor wrote:

Marchena often clowns around and tells naughty stories, like the one about Mrs Roosevelt who scolded a South American during a trip for making cookies round on his stomach. He replied 'Come back tomorrow when I make doughnuts!'

Although Marchena shows pictures of his wife and children to everyone, on his bedside table there is a picture of a beautiful young blond whom he said he was with the night before his departure from New York. At dinner he told us his father had advised him never to be unfaithful in the afternoons. He says that's why his father has been happily married for thirty years.

When I told him that after a long period of abstinence the first coup can be a failure, he replied: 'It is with my wife that I will have the first try when I return.'

He told me the other day that male donkeys here fight by trying to catch each other's testicles and that is how one of them ends up being castrated. He is very single-minded!

On August 4th, they arrived at the Mission of the White Fathers at Kabbhayi. Victor recorded:

I have an austere room but clean and I slept well despite the hard mattress. This morning it is sixty-two degrees, so fresh. Yesterday a cable arrived saying everything was arranged for us to arrive in Tanganyika in two days. Last night I won a game of chess against the champion of Ruanda, an enormous native father who reminded me of a younger Paul Robeson. Finally there was a magnificent dinner: croquettes of lobster, *potage argenteuil*, turkey with dates, stewed fruit, coffee, white Alsace wine and liqueurs, the best meal since leaving Europe. After dinner a 'séance artistique' - native boys preparing for the noviciate in white robes sang religious and native songs in Latin and French. The whole thing was in perfect taste.

On the whole Victor remained impressed by conditions maintained by Belgium in Ruanda.

In Astrida we saw the best kept hospital for natives that I have ever seen, run by a Dr Panier. The beds had coloured bed covers that leant a happy note to the atmosphere. There were pillows for everyone with clean pillow cases and an anaesthetic machine in the delivery room.

We also visited the Institut St Jean for European pupils. It was even better than certain schools in Europe and America, with chairs, good quality desks, one room for pupils with sinks and running water, etc.

Yesterday, 2nd August, we visited the Queen Mother - the mother of the Muvami of Ruanda. She received us at the entrance of her castle in Shyogire. It resembles a miniature castle, with towers surrounded by a wall. She is about seventy, but must once have been very beautiful for her type. She had a large head-dress with long bristles which added to her stature and nobility. They say that in her youth she had one of her subject's eyes gouged out because she didn't like the way he looked at her.

After lunch, the President asked the Mwami, in front of his advisors and the Belgian officials, if he had anything to say. The Mwami said no and looked at the Resident Desseint! They are all afraid to speak up, understandably, as they don't wish to compromise their own position, especially when they are well treated by the administration.

At the National Park at Gabiro we spent the night in the bush and heard hyenas howl. The following day, crossing the park in an open van, we saw at less than 100 metres, buffaloes, wild boar, zebras and monkeys. It was the most enjoyable day yet as we did not have to visit hospitals or schools or see petitioners.

At the office in Biumba, Victor found more evidence of the administration's underhand dealings:

I finally found a poster advertising the mission but, curiously, the last paragraph - the most interesting for the population since it said the mission had come to see and hear them - was covered by another poster. It could have been accidental if the declaration had appeared everywhere, but it seems suspect when it was the only one we saw.

Since Kitega the members of the mission seem more tired and are trying to reduce the number of places to visit. Kisenyi, on the shores of Lake Kivu, is charming, apart from the constant dust. From the guest house we went to see the lava of the volcanoes at Sake in the Congo and photographed a delightful half-caste Arab girl with a jug on her head and a pretty naked bust uncovered at Marchena's request.

The friction between d'Anjou and the others by this time encompassed Victor. He wrote:

D'Anjou is a pain in the neck. I had not suspected her of being so bad at her work and difficult in character. Today we returned to Usumbura. She should have known she would have a lot of work, but nevertheless she left at 6.30 and did not come back after dinner. She started to cry when I made some remarks on her work.

On 31st August I received a letter of resignation from her in spite of the fact that the previous day I had returned her first letter of resignation in her own interest. The girl is impossible and I described her case to Bunche in a letter.

In Tanganyika, they found their hosts more forthcoming:

The British are doing everything to help us meet the Africans and are more liberal than the Belgians who only

169

showed us two tame Bamis. From Mwanga part of the mission went to Bukola where the Haga women are reputed to be the prostitutes of the territory. They are said to be beautiful and vain, with lazy husbands who make them work, so they leave Bukola to become prostitutes. We received a petition on this problem, probably from cuckolded husbands complaining that the British authorities would not restrict the movement of the wives and wanted to give them *cartes de circulation*. The mission should have heard the women as it had heard the men but no-one thought of it and I wasn't there.

In another place we attended a dance by the Wagogo in which they jumped lightly on the spot without moving in any direction. They are very proud and primitive, painted with an ochre-coloured glaze, their long hair with small artificial plaits smeared with amber-smelling grease and holes in their ears with bits of wood through them.

As always, Victor's sense of well-being was conditioned as much by the quality of food and drink available, as by the company at hand.

The coffee produced here in large quantities is so badly prepared that Marchena had a fit every time. Only in a British insane asylum did we have good coffee.

Complaints were not confined only to coffee. Victor confided in his journal:

Marchena is always telling incongruous stories to people he meets for the first time. It wasn't too bad in Ruanda Urundi but the British are shocked. One day, Marchena asked Berendsen a very precise question on the way to behave with a woman. Berendsen replied, 'Mr Chairman, I would be grateful if you would change the subject!' Kridakon and I nearly died laughing.

At Tobora, however, Marchena gave a piano concert to the African pupils at the Loleya School. He is very talented and it was a great success as most of them had never seen someone play the piano.

At Kisenyi, we met a very entertaining man called Rabaud of the League of the Protection of Human Rights. He was a revolutionary unionist, wild and full of *joie de vivre*. He told us that in order to discredit him in the eyes of the natives, the Belgians accused him of eating children. 'Me,' he cried, 'a vegetarian with no teeth!'

Some of the most interesting entries in the diary did not refer so much to the political or practical problems they encountered as to the novelty of the experiences on offer.

On another day they showed us an ingenious trap for catching native rats. It was an arch with an arrow. The arch was held with a string which at a certain point goes through a kind of bowl belonging to a wooden pipe in which there is a bait. When the rat breaks the string the arrow enters its neck for its head is held in the pipe bowl.

One of the problems the mission had heard about from Asiatics and Africans was racial discrimination in the toilets which were usually ranked according to three races. Victor had his own solution to the problem:

Between Iringa and Dodoma our car had to stop at a place where there were such toilets so I just pissed in the courtyard in front of everyone.

In an experimental station for tsetse that we saw in Tanganyika they have 200 blacks who do nothing except catch tsetse flies in the bush, to mark them and release them to see how far they can fly and what their lifespan is. They can mark 25,000 flies with different marks by making three points in a triangle on their backs with three different colours. In the same station they have scales to weigh a fly, to see if it has lost weight or not! The head of this station, Jackson, feeds the tsetse with his own blood!

On the 16th September the mission left Tanganyika in a special plane. Victor recorded:

The flight was quite bumpy. There were many air pockets and I vomited for the first time. This was also due to the piss-up the night before at Aruska where we had invited the Governor of Tanganyika, Sir Edward Twining and some of his colleagues to dinner. We went to bed at 1.30 a.m. after having started drinking gin. The next day the whole mission had a hangover.

At Tanga I noticed how good personal relations can influence general opinion. Before Tanga the mission wasn't generally sympathetic to the Indians or Pakistanis. But in Dar Es Salaam and at Tanga we were invited by the Krimajee family, who have been in Tanganyika for 150 years and are very rich and influential. The Indian Association in Tanga gave us the best possible impression by the calibre of its two Reps (Krimajee & Hussain) and the moderation and wisdom of their views greatly impressed us.

Most of the British officials, on the other hand, did not give a good impression and seem to be there only to receive their salaries. They told us that the 'ground nut scheme' was partly motivated by the desire to give work to demobilised British after the war who could not find work elsewhere.

At Moski we saw Kilimanjaro by moonlight. Its shape is very ordinary, a flat *monticule* with snow on the summit and easy to climb. What makes it majestic is its size and the fact that it is the only mountain in central Africa covered with snow all year.

At Moski, I met a Madame Cassel, of Russian origin, married to an Australian colonial. She gave a Russian dinner in my honour, placing me before Marchena, and we drank vodka. The Russian dishes were not very good, with some bad quality caviar, but the atmosphere was extremely pleasant. I knew Russia as well as she knew China. From the terrace of her house you could see Kilimanjaro by moonlight and we danced on the terrace. Looking at the mountain with my periscope, with a cigarette in my hand, I burned myself in the middle of my forehead so that for several days I looked like an Indian.

From Moski we went to see the Pare tribe in the mountains, one of the most advanced tribes here. They have succeeded in eliminating the Indian commercials and have a rare civic responsibility. For example, they are themselves building a road for motor cars in their mountains. Many of them are dressed in the European way. They have a Briton, Mason, who is very interested in spreading mass education. We saw groups of men and women sitting in the open, learning to read Kiswabili. Certificates are given to them at the end of the course.

At Aruska, a small town of prosperous European colonials, Mrs Ryden, wife of the President of the Tanganyika European Council, criticised by the government for her pro-native policy, invited us to her villa in the outskirts. From there we had a splendid view of the lake and mountains. We also saw the Governor General of Tanganyika, who looks like Charles Laughton and is much more pleasant and liberal than I expected. He told us we could see ostriches near Aruska who bury their heads in the sand but do not lay any eggs. He meant the colonials.

It was in Tanganyika that we saw a black woman with enormous breasts, each the size of a cow's udder. Marchena started to laugh and shriek with pleasure.

In Nairobi we were greeted with great friendliness by the Governor General, Sir Philip Mitchell, and his colleagues of the East African High Commission. We were told that our mission was much nicer than the previous one, that our approach was different and more objective, with no hostile preconceptions. Our hotel reminded one of Europe or America from the point of view of service and comfort but they don't admit Asians and we had to intervene with the manager to accept Pant, the Indian Commissioner.

In Nairobi, they visited the new building, EAAFRO - the scientific research organisation of East Africa.

I saw things I had never seen before, like a spectrograph to determine soil fertility which takes less time than a chemical analysis, a research laboratory on termites, with a mother termite as long as a finger in alcohol, maps taken by

173

cameras from aeroplanes and a kind of magnifying glass for the two eyes which makes the map look three-dimensional. Soil fertility and the type of culture suited to it can be judged by the colour and configuration of the ground.

We left Nairobi again with a hangover. Marchena, who had found an American woman, had only slept two hours, but I and the others went to bed early by ourselves.

In Mogadishu I was struck by the artistic taste of the Italians, compared to the British and Belgians. Here the architectural style is Arabic and there are no buildings, even modern ones, that do not blend into the general style of the city. The Somalis are a very fine race. Nowhere in the world have I seen so many handsome men and beautiful women. The most frequent diseases here are venereal. Syphilis is even congenital. The women are vain and all wear jewellery, amber or hollow gold, even the little girls. The European women, by contract, all looked pale and tired. The climate is not very agreeable and I did not feel well there myself.

The country is filled with political parties growing like mushrooms. The best organised is the Somali Youth League which criticises everything the administration does. It had the discipline and organisation of the Communist Party and it is suspected that it has contacts with it in Addis Ababa. The SYL says that everything worked better under the British. One wonders about their motive: desire to see the British return or to play a dominant role when Somalia becomes independent. In two schools children complained to the mission about the administration. Some members wondered if they hadn't been prepared by the SYL.

On 17th October 1951 the mission returned to New York just three months after its departure.

Everyone is happy that the mission is over. We were starting to get fed up with each other. The visit to Somalia was the most useful because we learned things we could not have

174

found out otherwise, like the relations between the members of the Consultative Council who hate each other, one being 100 per cent pro-Italian and the other 100 per cent pro-SYL. We also gained an insight into the unreasonable attitude and arrogance of the SYL which increased our indulgence towards the Italians who have a thankless task: the country is poor, economically barren without the miracle of petrol. Italy only stopped administering a year ago, after ten years' absence, and had to give independence in nine years. The mission thinks Italy will want to leave before the ten year period is up. In Rome we were told that Italy is only administering Somalia to have a voice in African affairs.

Though thankful to be out of Africa, the return to Europe was not entirely felicitous.

In London I went to have lunch alone at Simpsons. What a disappointment. Nobody asked for roast beef, and as I insisted, they gave me three small slices, very thin and of doubtful aspect. The oysters I ordered weren't fresh either. I feel British standards have been lowered a lot. They are nicer to foreigners whereas before they were very condescending.

In Rome and Brussels the Ministers of the Colonies invited the mission to lunch or dinner. In London they offered us a cup of coffee with biscuits!

On 15th November Victor left for the General Assembly in Paris, although arguments and difficulties within the administration had made it impossible for him to finish his report. Laking and Cargo set the tone for all the reports, dragging out the sessions indefinitely and Marchena, every anxious to please, failed to assert his authority as Chairman.

Laking and Cargo are objective and say what they think is right but all this takes an infinite time. However, I am sure the reports will be good.

On 20th November he was still on the *Ile de France.*

F T Liu came back from leave in China before my departure. He says the Communist regime is well installed in China and could not be toppled by the Nationalists without a general war. The student youth supports the Reds. The Chinese population in general only reproach the regime on three counts: for the suppression of freedom, for waging war in Korea, and for sending food to Russia when there is not enough for them to eat themselves. For the rest, they think the Reds are better than the Nationalists: there are no more beggars in Shanghai, the trains work better, there is no corruption, etc.

On the ship I met a man who had been in New Guinea for twenty-one years. I gave him the report of the Trusteeship Council on New Guinea to read. He likes the natives but says they are still in the Stone Age and will need a couple of centuries before they can govern themselves. They have hundreds of different languages but none for abstract concepts. For example, they have no word for forest or tree. To say 'I love you' they say, 'I lead with your death or my entrails run after you.'

In certain primitive tribes a woman giving birth for the first time hides in a cave with other women and a sow. During the birth the women beat her. Afterwards they no longer touch her and she cuts the cord herself. She takes the child and throws it against a stone and then the sow eats it.

Some of the most fascinating and informative encounters came to Victor coincidentally. On 21st November he wrote

Today we arrived at Le Havre. Yesterday the captain of *the Ile de France* gave a select lunch in his cabin, inviting two priests, and including Dupeyrat and me. For the first time in my life I tasted *Blanquette de Lenous*, a bubbly wine of the Pyrenees which was delicious. I'll order some in Paris and impress Lie.

Boutet told of a meal he had had with Pétain in February 1943 where Pétain could not remember what Boutet had told him a few moments previously. Boutet thinks Pétain

176

only had his mind awake in the morning but would sign anything in the afternoon. He said Mme Pétain told him the Jews weren't persecuted enough!

Father Dupeyrat spoke of his experiences in New Guinea and of two inexplicable examples of witchcraft: in the first, a native, Xaverion, had become Catholic but the Vatican considered his first marriage, contracted at the age of six, as still valid. The native, disappointed, then became a witch and one evening came sixteen miles to see Father Dupeyrat in the bush. Before his arrival Dupeyrat heard the steps of a typical big bird, the casoar as well as immediately after the native left. Given the distance covered, Dupeyrat believes the native had transformed himself into a casoar.

He says that sorcerers who wish to kill someone put certain things, as well as an object belonging to the victim, in a bamboo tube. On the appointed day they break the bamboo tube, the victim dies but if he is Christian it doesn't work unless the sorcerer obtains some sperm to put in the tube. Dupeyrat connects this to the Catholic belief that, by committing an impure act, you lose divine protection.

He also told us how sorcerers put poisonous snakes in a bamboo tube with a piece of the victim's clothing. They make the snake suffer by heating the tube and hitting it, then put the tube at the place where the victim has to pass and at the given time open the tube and the snake jumps on the victim.

Dupeyrat has noted down for me his views on the Trusteeship Council Report on New Guinea. He thinks we have to go very slowly in the development of the Papuans and that by teaching them trades it only benefits the Europeans who employ them. On the other hand he is in favour of compulsory work in the fields to teach them how to cultivate.

He is very nice and full of the fires of enthusiasm. He admitted that he did not himself understand the dogma of the Trinity and explained it to the Papuans as a person

177

with one arm and three legs. We became great friends. He drinks and smokes as much as he can.

By the beginning of December Victor was settled in Paris, in the luxurious apartment of a Madame Jallu:

...where I have a bathroom, bedroom and study and can use the other rooms to invite my friends. I thought of staying until the end of the General Assembly in January but Lie, Cordier and Price are pressuring me to finish the work of my Fourth Committee (Trusteeship) before Christmas. Anyway, Paris is no longer as much fun as before. Strangely, I am the only one asked by Lie to finish my Committee so early. Aleksander and I think Bunche is behind it as he wants to return to New York for Christmas and is trying everything to shorten the discussions even at the expense of good work.

As he saw that I was not very enthusiastic and predicted that the delegates would rebel if they had to sit twice a day, he wants to force me by telling Lie and Cordier that it is I who is delaying the work. It is the first time I have known Bunche to be so selfish towards his colleagues.

As Victor had predicted, the Fourth Committee was far from finished by Christmas, although Bunche was not required to come back afterwards. Even though the rift was ostensibly smoothed over, the incident had thrown new light on Bunche's character and the already troubled relations between the two men were never quite as close again.

CHAPTER ELEVEN

Trusteeship 1952

A Return To Taiwan - The McCarthy Witch Hunt -Eisenhower Replaces Truman - Lie Resigns

In March 1952 Victor decided to take home leave in Taiwan, prompted largely by the enthusiastic response within the Secretariat to an exposé he had written on the subject. All Secretariat members of a certain rank and their spouses were entitled to "home leave" every other year. Headquarters being in New York it was felt that a holiday in one's own country was a right rather than a privilege. Staff members from mainland China who couldn't or wouldn't return to their native town were entitled to a paid trip to Taiwan or Hong Kong.

He recorded events surrounding the visit with his usual candour:

> Awaiting my plane for Taipei I went to see a Japanese striptease - two Japanese women dancing, wearing a cache sex and stars made of shiny paper on their nipples. This kind of scene didn't exist before the end of the war. The hall had one subject, sex, and showed the savagery of Japanese soldiers on an island. Such a subject would not have been possible during the military times here. It is the American influence - striptease, sex and down with the military. Some of these performances would probably be prohibited even in Chicago. One girl with only small underpants on, and a piece of cardboard piping in her hand. She came through the spectators and allowed them to look under her chemise with the piping. Another one made all the movements of copulation with her back to the audience, her bottom covered with a few threads of silk. The most exciting was a Japanese girl in traditional

costume who undressed completely at the end. It shows that European clothing accustoms us to seeing flesh and exudes excitement. The girls were all young, tall and sporty - a new type of Japanese woman emerging from contact with western civilisation. Afterwards I went to the Ally of Kokusai Gekijo where there was a performance of 'Tokyo Odori' - 300 artistes, all young girls, even in the role of men.

Before landing in Taipei, they had to draw the curtains to prevent passengers from taking photographs. To Victor's surprise, a crowd of photographers and reporters, as well as others from the Waichiaopu, had assembled to meet him.

These days the press is full of news about the probable truce in Korea and as they knew I dealt in Trusteeship, some thought I was coming to arrange Taiwan as a Trust Territory. My declaration that I was there on home leave dissipated any doubts.

The Pu had organised a secretary, a car and a hotel for Victor - an old Japanese temple on a hill at the edge of the city. (There were many signs of the fifty-year Japanese colonisation of Taiwan.) He quickly became irritated by what he saw as an excess of zeal on the part of the secretary, who had a room next to his and:

... barely left me for a minute, so that I wondered if it was a surveillance. Nobody could see me without passing through him. On the other hand I was given every facility and my least desires were granted. Eventually I realised he had never been abroad and simply didn't realise he was in the way!

Victor was gratified by the fact that everyone seemed pleased with the visit:

... perhaps because I am one of the first to come without having to and without looking for favours. Perhaps I am also for them a sign of better things to come. They have found a little petrol in Taiwan and searches are continuing with the Americans. If we could find petrol in large quantities, our economic problems would be solved.

180

Although it was understood that Victor could not pass public comment on political questions due to his international status, various opportunities were arranged for reporters to meet him. At one such meeting, Victor asked how many of the journalists were from Taipei and discovered there was only one out of fifty:

> I then said that the people of Taiwan should participate more in China's activities so they could feel that China's problems were theirs. When I asked if there was censorship of the press, they answered no, but each newspaper is careful not to publish certain things. I kept trying to ask questions on the relations between the Taiwanese and the continent. These are obviously important for the future and I still don't have a precise idea of what they are. In general the Taiwanese are happier, especially since the agrarian reforms of Cheng Chen which have benefited Taiwanese farmers. Nevertheless they are contemptuous of continentals whom they consider less efficient and organised than the Japanese.
>
> Concerning the recruitment of Taiwanese, Sun Li Jen confirmed that they are good soldiers, but that they need to raise the standard of living of soldiers in general. They say they can recruit ten per cent of the population which would made 800,000. Unfortunately, I didn't really have a chance to speak to the Taiwanese. Those I did meet, like Huang Chuan Ching, are considered collaborators.

On 23rd April Victor was invited to a dinner for foreign diplomatic representatives at K C Wu's. He was not impressed:

> I could feel that these were not diplomats who had chosen Taiwan. They were not of a high class and not the type of worldly diplomats that one meets in large capitals.

Two days later he dined with Chiang Kai Shek and his wife at a dinner for American Congressmen, where there was an incident over protocol which for once concerned the Americans rather than the Chinese. A Republican representative, Wilson, complained that he had been placed after the Democrats who had less seniority. Victor noted:

Apparently he makes the same complaint at every dinner. Chiang remarked that they are like children. Yet in New York the Americans would not understand Lie's insistence on the question of placing at table.

It was some time since Victor had last met Chiang Kai Shek.

He hasn't changed physically although his back is a little more bent. One can now smoke as much as one wants in his presence - his wife was smoking like a chimney. He has learned to tap on the shoulders of the Americans when they make him laugh. One told an amusing story about the Americans alerting Chiang at 6.30 a.m., whilst he was praying, to tell him an unknown submarine had been picked up by radar. Chiang said it was impossible in that area and in fact it turned out to be dolphins.

Madame Chiang has put on weight and her face is puffed up. She explained at the lunch I had alone with her that it was due to certain injections against an allergy suffered by the whole Soong family, especially TV and TL, and that she is filled with fluid. She has grown older and looks increasingly like her elder sister, Madame Kung. After the dinner, the Congressmen surrounded her and took her hand, complimenting her on her beauty 'like a flower'. For the last year she has been taking lessons in Chinese painting and is very enthusiastic about it. She says she paints with the speed and strength of a man.

A few days later, I was summoned by Chiang to his office. He was alone at the end of a long table, with two secretaries behind him who took notes of the conversation. He asked me several short questions and it was I who spoke all the time. The interview lasted fifteen minutes, which is long for Chiang. He asked what the international situation was, if I had anything to tell him or any suggestions to make, and if the UN was better disposed towards us.

I told him that foreign opinion on China is changing because they realise that our Reds are not agrarian reformers and Mao will not be like Tito. Abroad they believe that the Russians will not start a war but the Americans, therefore the whole free world, expects military, financial or economic aid, as they cannot continue indefinitely without going bankrupt and it is then that a change could occur. My feeling is that we are not appreciated for ourselves but for the strategic and military contribution we might give if necessary. The moment of our usefulness to the others will come when there is a change in the international situation. The Americans are looking for friends everywhere, even those they used to boycott, like Franco and Tito. As far as the UN goes, they are more favourably disposed towards us, not because of our merit but because our Reds have been so intractable. It was the Korean War which opened everyone's eyes.

My suggestions to Chiang were to prepare for the landing but also to prepare politically the necessary measures to follow, which are as important as a military victory. Thirdly, we must be united.

He asked how Lie was. Chiang reckons he doesn't like us. I explained that Lie wanted to please the Americans, and isn't working for the entry of the Chinese Reds into the UN. When I left, Chiang was very friendly and pleasant and gave the impression that he thought our diplomats at the UN were doing good work.

When Madame Chiang invited me to lunch, I suspected that she wanted me to take something to TV (Soong, her brother) or HH (Kung, her brother-in-law) and indeed she gave me three large parcels and a letter for HH. She asked me about the American presidential elections and the chances of the different candidates.

The lunch was European but she had her own diet, with salad from her garden. She swallowed a large steak with the same rapidity as TV while I did not have time to finish mine. After lunch I took out my panscope to look at the garden. She was very curious and asked if it was a new gadget. I invited her to keep it as a souvenir. She was delighted and said it was exactly what she needed for her excursions. Thus I gave one to Prince Douala in Cameroon in 1949 and one to Madame Chiang in 1952.

Hollington (Tong) came to see me in the morning and I chatted with him over breakfast. Indications are that the Americans want to retake the initiative in the Far East. He says the ideal solution would be to avoid a general war but to have the chance to land and hold China south of the Yangtse. He said our Reds were expecting us to land after the start of the Korean War and were ready to evacuate the coast and retreat to Lanchow.

There is a feeling that Mao derived two advantages from the Korean War, getting arms from Russian for free and using the former Kuomingtang troops in the war. The Vice-Minister of War in Taiwan says if there is a truce, Mao will not attack Taiwan but Indochina. In 1950, apparently, the Russians agreed that he should attack Taiwan but Mao was not ready.

Despite its limitations - "cleanliness and order left a lot to be desired, the running water never works and water runs when the taps are turned off," - Taiwan impressed Victor on some levels:

The day of my departure I visited the experimental station for sugar. They showed me that from a by-product of sugar they can produce paper, plastic, rum which we tasted and which wasn't very good, streptomycin and cannon powder.

He was also deeply impressed by his treatment:

Everyone was so kind to me that I was profoundly touched and at a buffet dinner given by Foreign Minister, George Yeh, in my honour with all the high officials of the Pu, I was so moved that after three sentences I had tears in my eyes and my voice was strangled by sobs. I don't know what the others thought. In Taipei I even had whisky, cognac and Lucky Strikes in my hotel room on arrival.

On 24th May Victor returned to New York. In his subsequent exposé of the situation he had found in Taiwan, he noted an improvement in the economic situation as well as an increase in military strength. This was due largely to a reduction of waste in government expenditure and increasing confidence as a result of American aid.

Within the Secretariat the same frictions continued to irritate:

Aleksander told me that Lie is going to propose a reorganisation plan for the Secretariat with only three ASGs: French, British and Russian, the departments headed by Directors under one of them. Certainly the manner in which Lie uses his deputies does not justify their existence. He could very well do without any of them.

When he asked my opinion, I said I preferred to replace the quantity of ASG with quality, by paying a higher salary to a smaller number of deputies, although salary is not a measure of competence or prestige. Lie replied that if you pay someone a lot it increases his prestige. But I said we would be criticised for having such high salaries.

Regarding the plan itself, the Russians will want to keep a 'deputy' at the head of the Security Department but the administrative powers will never want a Russian in charge of Trusteeship. Similarly, they would not consider putting the non-self-governing territories in the Political Department. We could put them in the EcoSoc Department but we cannot separate this Division from Trusteeship. Furthermore, the Information Department has never been political and it would be bad to put in under the Political Deputy. We cannot integrate the departments more and it would bring about criticism if we said we could. It would be better to have one 'deputy' and directors without putting all the departments under one or other of the three deputies.

Lie warned us that he would 'give us hell' if we agitated against the plan but that we could express our opinion if the Consultative Council or the Fifth Committee asked our advice.

Aleksander told me there is only contempt for the boss in

185

the Secretariat but added that Bunche was personally very attached to me and would do everything to help me. Today, 26th September, is Kerno's (Ivan Kerno, Head of Legal Department) sixtieth birthday and the day his employment at the UN ends. What a nice birthday present! Lie is applying the age limit to him whilst making an exception of Price and Pelt.

Dissatisfaction with Lie's directorship extended to his political pronouncements:

At the ASG meeting this morning, he said the Reds are seeking domination of the world by any means and do not keep their promises. I almost remarked in front of everyone that this is what the Chinese have been saying since 1946. When I said it to him afterwards at the cocktail party for Kerno, he didn't seem to like the remark.

This morning the *New York Post* suggested Lie would cease being Secretary General on 1st February 1954 to become Norway's Prime Minister. At lunch he told us he hadn't said that and could stay another two years because he knows how to get votes but that he would have gone if there was a better SG than him, etc. I have never seen such an egotist.

At least his own life, for the moment, was seen to be above reproach:

Aleksander was right when he said the other day that I did not have petty complexes because I have had luck in my life and success in my career.

The extent to which the limitations of his luck in marriage had contributed to the success of his career was not an issue Victor agonised over.

A scandal in the US involving Nixon drew ironic comment from him:

Nixon has been accused by the Democrats of having received $18,000 from an American group. Everyone thought it would be detrimental to Eisenhower to keep him as Vice President as Eisenhower's campaign is supposed to be a crusade against corruption. However, Nixon broadcast an explanation on television lasting half an hour which had an unbelievable effect on the American masses. The speech had no legal logic, he avoided the main issues, but cleverly played on the average American's emotions. He talked of his wife and two kids, of his dog, of the fact that his wife had no mink coat, of Alger Hiss, of the corruption in Washington, etc. and it would appear that in consequence he is more popular and better known than before!

At a cocktail party on 2nd October Victor's vanity received some unexpected flattery when:

The French delegate Pignon suddenly suggested I should have the Légion d'Honneur and that he would see what he could do. I told him that, as an international official, I cannot accept decorations and I told him my Légion d'Honneur story after the negotiations with Martel. In that instance, my refusal of the Cravate of Commandeur led to my successor becoming Grand Officier!

At a Charity Fund Raising Dinner of the China Institute at the Waldorf, Victor commented on the brilliance of two speeches made by Dewey and a Mrs Maurice Moore:

It was a little depressing and comforting at the same time - depressing because of the atmosphere and from the tone itself of the speeches where we could not help feeling that what remains of China now is Formosa and the Chinese abroad; comforting to hear that the Americans still have faith in us. Mrs Moore concluded well in asking the Americans not to give us charity or to feel sorry for us but simply to open the door and hold out a hand to the Chinese intellectuals sheltering here.

One occasion that stands out in my memory was a reception for the Chiefs of tribes from the African Trust Territories. They had come to UN Headquarters to attend a session of the Trusteeship Council and a reception had been organised in their honour. These Chiefs were decked out in their most colourful costumes and were clearly thrilled to be at this gathering. Some of them were officially divine in their own tribes and as such were not allowed to converse with mortals except via their intermediaries. My brother and I mingled freely and managed to make the "divine ones" forget their status and they soon cut out their intermediaries to chat directly to us.

By late 1952 the McCarthy Witch Hunt was affecting the UN as much as other institutions of American life and increasing numbers of UN officials were being called to give evidence of their political affiliations. That year Father took my brother and me to have Thanksgiving dinner with Ralph Bunche and his family. They lived not far from us and we were friendly with his two daughters and son. Ralph expressed his fear of the Witch Hunt. Although he had never been a Communist, the prevailing hysteria could possibly implicate a person who might have flirted with socialism in his student days between the two World Wars. Victor recorded:

> Jack Harris was summoned to the McCarran Committee[1] and provoked the furry of O'Connor because he refused to answer the question asking if he was a Communist. O'Connor then said he was sure he was and that the UN was honeycombed with Communists. We have more than twenty officials waiting to be heard by the Committee and it will give a bad impression of the UN to Americans who always like to exaggerate and generalise.

Due to public opinion, Lie decided to give special leave to those officials who refused to answer the Committee on the grounds of their constitutional right not to incriminate themselves. Later in October Lie announced that he was terminating the temporary contracts of three of the ten people to whom he had given forced leave, justifying the decision by saying that he had received confidential reports on the three. Victor recorded:

> Keenleyside gave Lie a memo advising him to take the question to the Assembly. Lie returned it with the remark that Keenleyside was a good man but had never been in practical politics. He said: 'If I had followed your advice, I know where I would be now.'

---

[1] set up to prevent Americans of questionable loyalty to the US Government from working in the United Nations.

Later, Georges-Picot [ASG in charge of Social Affairs] explained Lie's turn-about as a result of Price threatening to resign publicly if Lie didn't act. Price had added that he would then like to see how the Senate would vote for funds to the UN! Price subsequently asked me if I knew whether there were any Communists amongst the Chinese for whom the Committee had recommended permanent contracts. I promised to get information on this. These days there is a wave of unjustified criticism of the UN.

The result of the American elections brought some satisfaction:

I had predicted that, if Eisenhower was elected, it would be by a landslide but that, if Stevenson was elected, it would be by a small majority. The vote for Eisenhower shows that the American people are fed up with the Truman administration and foreign policy humiliations in Korea and China and want change even at the risk of compromising their present prosperity. Even the farmers and workers voted for change. It was a good example of democracy in practice. I also predicted that everyone would rally behind the elected President, whoever he was, and that's what happened. I also think the Americans will rally more easily behind Eisenhower who has already united his party and will have the support of the southern Democrats, unlike Stevenson. Everyone agrees Stevenson is intellectually superior but the former is better known and closer to the man in the street. The women voted for Eisenhower because they have more intuition. Eisenhower is for a crusade whereas Stevenson is for containment 'Acheson-style' and that doesn't appeal to American dynamism. Naturally the Chinese are delighted.

On 16th November 1952 there was another *coup de tonnerre* when Lie announced his resignation:

What emotions these days at the UN! When Lie read out his letter to us, he was so moved he shed tears. Georges-Picot reckons he's a good actor. When he'd finished, I was the first to speak. I suggested that it was such a surprise that, not knowing the background, it was difficult to express

189

an opinion. Lie said he wasn't asking our opinion since his decision is final.

At first I thought his resignation was a ploy to have himself reconfirmed because a successor could not be found. However, I then heard he had already signed a contract with an American company for a well-paid honorific post. Lie was disgusted with Russia's attitude towards him, with the lack of support from other powers, with the McCarran Committee, the Fifth Committee and the Consultative Commission, with American pressure to dismiss certain American officials, and with the difficulties of settling these problems. As he has new employment, it doesn't matter to him if he leaves the UN at this crisis point and he has the hero's vote because he gives as the reason for his resignation the desire to facilitate the settlement of the Korean Question, as if this could have some bearing on the Soviet attitude. If the Five cannot get together on a successor, he could still agree to stay and his prestige would be enhanced. Those at the UN who know the candidates, prefer Entezam [Iranian Foreign Minister, and a friend of Victor's since university days]. China will certainly vote against any Indian candidate.

The suicide of one of those indicted by the McCarthy Committee and dismissed by Lie threw the Secretariat into confusion:

Bunche was completely bewildered and looked terrible. He had helped Lie draft the announcement of the suicide in which there is a clear attack against the smear by the McCarran Committee. This declaration obviously did not please the Committee and three of the Senators subsequently said it was irresponsible. I do not think it is the fault of the Committee that the American Government pressured Lie to dismiss the Americans, nor is it Lie's fault for deciding to dismiss them. The McCarran Committee wanted to deal with Weintraub, Feller and Bunche but did not want to proceed until they were 100 per cent sure. Perhaps Feller heard about it and preferred to commit suicide so as not to jeopardise the UN, except that the suicide itself suggests an admittance of guilt to the man in the street.

190

We will probably never know the truth. Today there is a memorial ceremony for Feller and Weizmann but I do not want to go on my birthday. Furthermore, Feller was always in favour of admitting the Chinese Reds to the UN and rejoiced like a child when it was decided to hear a delegation of our Reds in the first committee and the Security Council. However, I am told that he was also in favour of UN intervention in Korean which suggests he was not a Communist himself.

At the end of November Lie announced that he had decided to bring in Bunche to work on the drafting of his speeches and declarations. Victor recorded:

He asked me my opinion and I said I thought he would be very good, although his aggressive tone is less suited to the SG than to American electoral fights. The declaration on Feller's suicide is a perfect example. Bunche was depressed after Feller's death, thinking probably that the Republicans would be against him but Eisenhower's recent compliment - 'How the hell can the Government afford to let you go?' - has restored his confidence. He's probably decided now that he'll control everything in the UN!

The upheavals within the Secretariat had left Victor also wondering about his future. On 27th November he wrote:

Yesterday, after the dinner I gave at my place for Foreign Minister George Yeh, Liu Chieh said he'd told George that I was ready to serve my country and return to Formosa if I was needed. George replied that I should take his place. Liu then told him I had no desire to be Foreign Minister but that I would be good as Ambassador to France. I think Liu would like to take my place as ASG but he is not the type to intrigue against me. At most, his solution would be attractive to all the interested parties and for the country too. When I told him of the difficulties I've had with Bunche, he did not look pleased! What a difference there is between a Black American and a Chinese of the old tradition. I am curious to know how things will develop.

Victor's future in the UN depended, it seemed to him, on whether Lie stayed or went:

> If he stays, I would not mind leaving. If Entezam is elected, I would prefer to stay.

Sometimes his own speculations overcame the more practical side of his nature. He confided in his diaries:

> I think I would do well in Paris if I had enough money for expenses. I could become the most popular Chinese Ambassador in France since Tchen Kitong. And in France personal relations can help a great deal in official work, not like in Moscow. It was in France that I started my career and it will perhaps be there that I end it!

Once again, however, he was a victim of Lie's procrastination:

> One day he told us he would stay if they could not decide on a successor. Another day, when the papers announced that the Russians were going to nominate the Polish Foreign Minister as their candidate, he said he would prefer to leave! As the Assembly will only adjourn in February, that is when his successor will be decided. This means I will not be able to go to the Pacific with the visiting mission as I have to be there if there is a new Secretary General.

In America, the McCarran Committee was making life in the UN increasingly uncomfortable:

> There is now such anti-UN feeling in the US because of the Committee's revelations, that the only golf club that allowed UN players has written to say we can no longer go!

It was at this moment that the possibility of a return to Taiwan appeared to be gaining ground. He wrote in December:

> I dined with George Yeh at the Barberry and he asked me to be his successor. Chiang Kai Shek was impressed by my visit to Taiwan and told him after my departure that if I was no longer in the Secretariat, I should return there. George

doesn't want to stay any more for financial reasons. I replied that I was ready to serve my country anywhere and have no objection to returning to Taiwan as long as another ASG is appointed before I leave. I added that I had no desire to be his successor but would be happy with another post where I had to deal with foreigners, like a mixed commission, and that, for a temporary post, I could get leave from the UN. But George made me no other offer than to become his successor. I told him he would not want to stay if there was a change of cabinet. He seemed to think that I would remain at the UN until the end of my contract.

In the event Victor kept to his decision not to go to the Pacific with the visiting mission, partly because he still felt that any change in the Secretariat necessitated his being there but, more importantly, because it was no longer pleasant to work in the visiting missions under administrative countries ...

> ... who want to control everything. Members who go on the missions now are more and more the instruments of the administering powers, or at least goody-goodies who say what they are told.

Life in the Secretariat might not be comfortable but at least he would be on the spot as events unfolded in 1953.

CHAPTER TWELVE

Trusteeship 1953

Death Of Stalin - Dag Hammarskjold Becomes Secretary General - A Truce In Korea

Throughout 1953 the McCarran Committee continued its investigations. Some of the Americans dismissed after invoking the Fifth Amendment wanted to call the administrative tribunal and to organise a collection within the Secretariat to pay for the legal fees involved.

Asked for his opinion, Victor remained non-committal. A circular suggesting donations could remain anonymous failed to convince him:

> I gave nothing for the following reasons. In Harris' case there is some evidence that he is a Communist and it would be ironic if I were to help one. Secondly, I was present at the meeting where the decision was made to dismiss those who would not answer certain questions and I can hardly therefore contribute now to an appeal against this decision. In any case, if I contribute to Harris, I'll have to contribute to the others in my department and who knows how many there could be. He is richer than I am anyway. Price reckons the whole thing is a Communist ploy.

Victor justified his decision and submerged any misgivings by arguing that those who had contributed did so for questionable reasons, either they were Jews showing solidarity for Harris, whose name had been changed from Harkowitz in 1938, or they were afraid and anxious to use Harris as a test case. Failing that, they had been pressured by Aleksander and others to contribute.

As if he still needed convincing, Victor made a point over the next few weeks of recording any instances of "American instability" that he came across:

> Countess de Leusse told me that her son Lon, who has an income of $100,000 a year, has to walk with a stick following polio but is completely normal sexually. He has had to divorce his wife, a beautiful, tall young woman of good family, because she drank, beat him and disappeared for a week with a black musician. Apparently Mrs Eisenhower is also an alcoholic and gets drunk. In Tokyo there was a case where the wife of an American officer stabbed her husband to death and the radio recently reported that a son wanted to kill his mother with a beer bottle because she refused to give him six dollars for the rent of a room!

In February there was "great excitement at the Secretariat" over a sinister development. Americans were suddenly being asked to fill in long questionnaires on their past and to submit fingerprints. Victor was concerned that other governments might follow suit, resulting in only those approved by their governments being appointed.

> Experience has shown me that people like Aleksander don't follow the instructions of their superiors in the Secretariat and do as they please on the pretext that it is in UN interest. According to Price, all opposition in the Secretariat is controlled by outside Communist forces. The battle between Reds and non-Reds is everywhere, even in our daily lives here. At the last ASG meeting, where the report was discussed, Lie opposed an amendment suggesting that loyalty to one's country could not be in conflict with loyalty towards the UN. Such a conflict might not exist for Americans but could well exist for a citizen of a Communist country.

Early in February there was welcome news when the press announced an end to the neutralisation of Formosa. Victor wrote:

> This doesn't mean they would let the Reds take over, simply that we would no longer be prevented from attacking the Continent. MacArthur is pleased with the news, though

Eisenhower's decision and the change in attitude is causing considerable controversy.

Within the Secretariat, Victor felt the news had enhanced his own government's prestige. He wrote

> The members of the Secretariat seem more respectful towards me and Lie is becoming excessively kind to me. After denigrating us for years, the American papers are now looking up to us. Stevenson went to Formosa and expressed admiration for the progress we had made, saying it was the most significant fact of our time. It's all rather different from the speeches he made during the election campaign, when he advocated forgetting China in favour of India. The progress made by Chiang's government in Formosa could be the most important historical accomplishment for centuries in the Far East and Formosa is an essential part of the Pacific defence of the free world.

> In February 1953 Stalin died, though official Russian declarations suggested that his policies would be followed to the letter by his successors. The world waited to see whether Stalin's death would allow greater independence for Mao and whether he would end the war in Korea and aid to Vietnam in return for a chance for Red China to enter the UN.

Victor's feeling, as far as the UN was concerned, was that the Soviet Union would not relinquish its stand on anything and was likely to be "more ticklish internationally" than before, so as not to imply weakness.

By April, however, it was clear that the Russians were at a crossroads in their history. Victor declared he had never seen a country change course so radically in its foreign and internal policy, although he foresaw more aggression in the future "since the Communists always have world domination as their goal."

For the moment, however, it seemed that the new Russian leader, Malenkov, was going out of his way to please the Russian people and the rest of the world. Regret was expressed for the death of British pilots shot down by Soviets and amendments were being proposed on the question of disarmament. Within Russia, the price of food and other goods had been reduced, certain prisoners had been granted an amnesty, nine Jewish doctors had been released and their trial denounced, Malenkov resigned as Secretary of the Communist Party and appointed another to the post, and Beria had been arrested. As Victor noted, the meeting of Russian generals to approve the arrest indicated the increasing role played by the Red Army and the power struggle going on in the Kremlin. "It is the first time in my memory," he added, "that such a meeting has taken place in Russia. Stalin would never have tolerated it."

There were further altercations with Bunche during 1953 when his name was mooted in connection with a committee to study Apartheid in South Africa. Victor was asked belatedly whether Bunche's absence would affect the work of his department. Victor complained in his diaries:

> This is typical of Lie and Bunche. When they need me they remember my existence and my rights! They know very well that the person I could do without in my department is Bunche. Since he returned in triumph from Palestine and earned the Nobel Peace Prize, he is no longer interested in the department. He spends all his time seeing important people, preparing lectures and answering letters. It is almost impossible for his subordinates to see him on urgent matters concerning the department. All he does is build himself up for heaven knows what role in the future since he will not work for his own government nor for the cause of black people. No doubt he is preparing for another role as international mediator. Someone suggested the other day that the service he is doing to the black cause is simply to exist. Lie told us one day that the only two Americans in the Secretariat who gave Alger Hiss as reference where Bunche and Foote!

Victor was not alone in his criticism of Bunche. In May he wrote:

> Aleksander, who is unhappy about Bunche's behaviour, came to cry on my shoulder. He thinks Bunche is sabotaging the department. He hasn't read any documents for five years but is jealous if anything is done that doesn't please him. He goes off on lecture tours and Aleksander cannot speak to him for weeks on end. He wants to minimise Aleksander's

work to give himself more importance and to appear indispensable to the department whereas in fact his presence is actually an obstacle to good work. Aleksander is ulcerated.

Inside the Secretariat Dag Hammarskjold had finally been appointed Secretary General. Lie described him as very formal and aristocratic, a brilliant man but one who was not close to the people and was more interested in economics than politics. Those in his immediate staff attested to his spiritual excellence, his intellectual greatness and remoteness. He seemed to suffer from melancholy and loneliness. Victor wrote:

> The rumour is that he is also homosexual because the Americans can't understand that he could be a bachelor at forty-eight. Lie is staying on at the UN for the moment to break him in. He suggested Hammarskjold should appoint as his Chef de Cabinet, Lindt, whom he brought with him, in place of Cordier. It is typical of Lie to do such a thing to Cordier who has served him so faithfully.

In August he reported:

> We are in the middle of a honeymoon period. The Secretariat is like a man divorced from the wife he hated in order to marry another younger and prettier, with all the good qualities the former lacked. Perhaps Dag is simply trying to make a good impression. Unlike Lie, he eats and queues in the cafeteria and goes in the lift with everyone else. He spoke to everyone individually, in order, as he put it, to get to know our problems and personal philosophy and to establish an *esprit de corps*, pointing out that we are already united by the common ideal of the UN, and he says he will maintain the autonomy of the Secretariat in the matter of staff. For the poor members of the Secretariat who have never been treated like human beings, it is too good to be true.

> Yesterday he called for me and we spoke for half an hour. He finished the interview by saying that I would be welcome in his office whenever I want. He asked me to be frank with

him and I promised to tell him the truth, even if it was to criticise him. I told him just to be natural, and if he has certain idiosyncrasies we will have to adapt to them as we are more numerous, rather than him having to adapt to all of us. He says he will not be able to make a real decision on Lie's reorganisation of the Secretariat for at least a year. He also said the Swedes like the Chinese who have an ancient culture and must have time to reflect before they act. Better to proceed slowly but surely.

I told him of the understanding between Lie and myself, that I would not stay if the Chinese Reds were admitted to the UN and that this understanding would continue to be valid between him and me. He said that Lie had spoken to him about it.

In the press there were rumours that Eisenhower's conditions for settlement in the Far East were the division of Korea at a line eighty miles North of the present one, a cease-fire in Indochina and UN Trusteeship for Formosa. Victor wrote:

For us it would be adding insult to injury. As usual the Americans, when they see our usefulness diminishing, start denigrating us. In Washington they are saying our troops have no chance of reconquering China and Chiang's government is no good. The General Assembly has voted to condemn us for our action in Burma under General Li Mi. We were completely isolated with only China abstaining.

On top of this, there has been a Red offensive by the Vietnamese, helped by Chinese Reds against Laos in the direction of Thailand. Some reports suggest it is synchronised with the Reds' peace offensive in Korea.

Domestically, at least, things continued to improve:

What a change in the atmosphere here. The new Secretary General is so different from Lie. He insists that we can discuss anything useful in the ASG meetings and asks us to take on questions of common interest. In two years Lie did

199

not do this. Everyone in the Secretariat feels encouraged to work well. I foresee that personal loyalty will link us to Dag and will further reinforce the loyalty that we have to the principles of the UN. He has said two things that affect me personally, that he will only make staff changes after mature thought and that those reaching sixty could stay if they are useful and cannot be replaced. Therefore, unless the Chinese Reds enter the UN, it seems my position is stronger than it was under Lie.

In June he recorded a lunch with Max Beer and Georges-Picot, who had just returned from Geneva with Hammarskjold.

Both were full of praise for him. Georges-Picot said that Dag writes and improvises his speeches and was very well received in Geneva. The Swiss hated Lie, who was arrogant and had dissuaded the meeting of the General Assembly in Geneva on the grounds that Geneva was too small, the street too narrow, etc. Beer said journalists hated him too for his arrogance and that it was Lie himself who had spread the rumour that Dag is homosexual. He suggested that was good for Dag because coming from Lie nobody would believe it. Georges-Picot's feeling is that Dag simply has no sexual needs. Beer agreed with me that he is the best SG available because he is absolutely neutral, knowing no-one in the Secretariat which was not the case with the other candidates.

In July Hammarskjold's record for brilliant manoeuvring was marred by his declaration that he had been asked during a recent European press conference whether he would accept Lie's memo on the necessity to admit Red China to the UN. In June the American Senate had voted unanimously to oppose its admission. Hammarskjold had answered that he would accept Lie's recommendation but that there was the question of the practicality of the psychological atmosphere to take into consideration ...

The Secretary General had also made a declaration condemning the release of prisoners by Syngman Rhee, saying that he could not always be silent. Victor wrote:

200

Personally I think the subject was ill-chosen to make the first declaration because all he did was to take the side of official UN opinion to hit on the weakest. From the viewpoint of moral courage it wasn't brilliant. By his courage and unshakeable attitude, Rhee has become a world figure. He now has admirers, even amongst his enemies, who call him 'the seventy-eight year-old President.' K C Wu told me yesterday that Eisenhower himself had told his close entourage that he understood Rhee's attitude. This is a relief to all those who defend a cause deemed lost by the majority and is an attitude often compared with that of Czechoslovakia at Munich in 1948. I wonder if Chiang had adopted the same attitude to the Marshall Mission, whether we would not be in a better position now.

As always with Victor, the small irritations often ranked side by side with the larger issues. In the same entry he complains of having to pay customs duty for the first time in his life: thirty-eight dollars for the importation of a Swiss gun ...

... and it doesn't even work! If I had made a trip to Europe, I would have avoided paying duty by putting it in my baggage.

In the little spare time he had Victor was learning Spanish. The Chairman of the Fourth Commission, a Venezuelan, could only speak Spanish and Victor foresaw complications if the debate became heated. Although with his facility for acquiring languages he found no problem with reading and understanding, for the first time, his age and everything else he had to think about, made progress difficult.

It is the first language I have had to learn indirectly, instead of absorbing it in the air of the country that spoke it, as I did in childhood.

In August 1953 a truce was signed in Korea and the Assembly met to arrange the political conference. Victor wrote:

Never before have the allies signed a truce with so little agreement between themselves on the way to solve certain

201

problems and with so little confidence in the good faith of the enemy. The US and South Korea signed an agreement of mutual defence yesterday and a common declaration by Dulles and Rhee said they would withdraw from the Conference in ninety days if the Reds were found wanting in good faith. Personally, I think the Communists will reject the resolution on the composition of the conference, which excludes India, and we'll be back to where we started.

Dulles' record for indiscretion and public errors doesn't help the US. Because of the importance of America, the slightest utterance affects other countries. There have been four things recently: his indiscretion at a press dinner on the possibility of putting Formosa under Trusteeship, support for Adenauer before the German elections, the possibility of a change in policy on Trieste, which irritated the Italians, and his exhortation to the Japanese to make an effort at rearmament, which irritated them.

However, faced with Soviet opposition to the composition of the political conference in Korea, Dulles remained "firm but moderate".

His speech put forward a programme to reduce international tension that was certainly more constructive than any by Acheson.

Despite the evidence in Vishinsky's speech at the Assembly that Soviet policy hadn't changed, Victor noted that the American public itself seemed less hostile to him and was prepared to laugh at his attempts at humour. It could well be that one day the American public will change its opinion of the Soviets and hostility could turn to appeasement, but less quickly and radically than the European public. Certainly he is full of kindness towards me. When someone asked if we knew each other, he said: 'Of course, we are old friends.'

In November Victor attended a lecture by a Professor Calogeropoulos on "Evolution of UN Law" and had an opportunity to point out a basic misconception of the purpose of the UN.

I spoke up afterwards and was the only one warmly applauded by the audience. The lecturer limited himself to the settlement of international differences and aggression. I remarked that the Charter is wider than that, that it tries to prevent conflicts from starting by settling the economic problems of dependent people. If the Charter were to be applied completely, these conflicts would not exist.

Two international visitors to the UN that autumn also failed to impress Victor:

> The Japanese heir apparent, Akihito, came to see Dag and the ASGs were introduced to him over champagne. He looks overbred and has no personality. When I told him my father had twice been Minister in Japan, he barely responded.

> Later, when Chiang Ching Kuo (son of Chiang Kai Shek) arrived, Dag asked me to show him the building but didn't invite me to join their interview on the pretext that he wanted to give the ASGs an international character. I suspect that what he actually wants is to show his independence and ability to deal with all situations and to minimise, like Lie, the importance of the ASGs.

It seemed as if the honeymoon with the new Secretary General was faltering. Inside the Secretariat, rumours had reached Victor's ears that he was being considered as a successor to Pelt in Geneva, as Director representing the SG at the UN office. Victor recorded:

> If this is true, it means Dag does intend to reorganise the Secretariat and reduce the number of ASGs. He may also be humouring me for political reasons of course, not wanting to break off with the Nationalists for the moment and keeping open the possibility of putting a Chinese Red in my place in Geneva so as not to give him control of the Trusteeship Department.

> Dag won't express an opinion on the subject. He is too clever. He'll wait until the last moment before taking a decision that will affect the whole organisation. When I saw Pelt I told him I had nothing to do with the rumours and no-one in a responsible position had spoken to me about it. He looked grateful and relieved.

A larger picture was beginning to emerge of Dag's complex character. When Victor prepared a speech for him on the opening of the last session of the Trusteeship Council, Dag had omitted Victor's allusion to the well-being of the people in trust territories. Victor observed in his diaries:

> ... This tends to back up Lall's opinion that Dag is not colonial-minded...

Another speech by Dag at a dinner in his honour was dismissed by Victor as badly pronounced and too deep to be understood. The gap between himself and the Secretary General was widening.

> He likes to show off his knowledge, or rather his culture, by quoting various authors, and then he misreads them. He loves to make plans, to such an extent that when he was elected Secretary General they apparently heaved a sigh of relief in Sweden that they wouldn't have to spend all their time studying new proposals!

The plans for the reorganisation of the Secretariat were about to assume such complex proportions that Victor was driven to observe that Dag seemed to have made a mountain out of a molehill:

> It seems that eight ASGs might be abolished in favour of a deputy Secretary General. Suddenly the poor ASGs are wondering, as they did in the time of Lie, what will become of them. Today Bunche is to be installed as Chairman of the Foreign Policy Association. I question whether it's compatible with his functions at the Secretariat. It will certainly take up time, of which he doesn't have much anyway.

Finally, at an ASG meeting on 7th November, Hammarskjold revealed his plans for streamlining the Secretariat which had been inspired, as far as the abolition of the ASGs were concerned, by his predecessor's plan. Victor recorded:

> Having said it, he added with a smile that it was not a debate but a dictate. Only Cordier wasn't taken by surprise, but then he stands to be the main beneficiary in the reorganisation, as long as he stays in his present post.

A few days later, Hammarskjold lived up to his reputation for making plans, by offering a revised one which kept some of the ASGs as Under Secretaries.

My feeling is that he wants to appease the ASGs. On 17th November he spoke to me alone for an hour. He started by saying that he had never before been faced with such an impossible situation concerning the staff. As far as my own position goes, he reiterated that he could keep me beyond my age limit and that in 1954 there would be no change either of title or function. I reminded him that in his recent memo he had promised to save a million dollars but he said this could easily be saved by reducing the world programme of certain UN organisms and not filling vacant posts.

Regarding the entry of the Chinese Reds to the UN, he doesn't think the question will arise before autumn 1955, because of the political conference on Korea. However, he thinks they might enter thereafter. I told him if they did, I would leave. Dag said the administering powers would not want a Communist heading Trusteeship and he would therefore give the Chinese Reds the Conference Department. He asked me if India would do well for Trusteeship but I said they had proved too anti-colonial.

He plans to appoint Bunche and Chernychev [ASG in charge of Political & Security Affairs] to represent the two great powers as Under Secretaries without portfolio. Personally, I doubt the Republicans will want Bunche as Principal American in the Secretariat. His task would be to liaise between Americans and Arabs. Yesterday Bunche, who'd heard of the plan and learned that Dag was talking of a South American for Trusteeship, expressed his displeasure at having to leave Trusteeship. He says he's dealt with colonial matters all his life and thinks it's the administering powers who have provoked our transfer from Trusteeship in favour of a South American who would be their lackey. I said nothing to him about Dag's suggestion of putting Bokhari in charge of Trusteeship but, if Dag is really considering Bokhari, Bunche may be right about the administering powers. It is interesting that as soon as there was talk of Bunche's transfer, the latter started taking active interest again in departmental matters, for the first time since Palestine and the Nobel Prize.

Both Bunche and Aleksander think Dag will want to keep me until the Reds enter, which could take a long time. Garreau reckons I'll have a long beard and stay in the Secretariat until the end of my days. I told him it was no fun as I could be missing other opportunities. Since my fate depends on the good luck of Taiwan, I would prefer to be Ambassador abroad to remaining in the Secretariat where I am doing no useful work for my country except to maintain China's prestige and protect the interests of the Chinese officials.

I'm told by Chiping Kiang [Chinese delegate on the Trusteeship Council] that not only the Arab Bloc but also their friends hold me in high esteem as head of my department and that they cannot see anyone doing better. A South American would have to be trusted because the South American countries can change their attitudes and if it were an Asian country, there would be jealousy amongst other Asian countries. The Chinese Delegation feels that if the Soviet ASG for the Security Department is not moved and it is only me who is moved to ease the eventual appointment of a Chinese Red, it would oppose it.

Although Dag says he will change nothing next year and that subsequently I'll remain head of one of the departments, I doubt that everything will go as he thinks. Aleksander is sure Dag will be obliged to resign sooner or later because he is creating difficulties for himself with his plans, which are more theoretical than practical. Many people say Dag is still a bit young! We have the feeling he's put himself in a hornet's nest with his plan and is prepared to make concessions as long as a plan of some kind is approved by the Assembly. He used the expression 'so I don't lose face' which suggests he knows he could lose face.

On 19th December Hammarskjold's reorganisation plan was passed by the Assembly with only the Soviet Bloc voting against. A reunion shortly before with Lie had done nothing to soften Victor's antipathy. Hammarskjold might have had faults but they paled beside those of his predecessor:

> Lie, whom I have seen again and with whom I went to a shoot, is naturally happy about the difficulties encountered by Dag and even said, full of confidence: 'You will see, one day I will come back.' He really has some illusions! I have never seen a man as vulgar and arrogant as Lie. Playing bridge, he lost his temper when I asked him how he would play after he claimed the remaining tricks and exposed his cards, and when I showed him the adding mistakes he'd made in writing down the penalties. It is only my composure that prevented a ridiculous argument. Bunche told me confidentially that whilst Lie was still Secretary General he wormed out of him the promise to nominate him as candidate for the Nobel Peace Prize. This time Lie invited him to lunch alone with him to remind him of his promise! Really!

CHAPTER THIRTEEN

Trusteeship 1954

The Treachery of K C Wu - A Return to Taiwan - The Geneva Conference - Red China's Admission to the UN Under Fire - The End of an Era

Hammarskjold's plans for the reorganisation of the Secretariat continued in 1954 amidst such manic activity that Bunche was heard to wish that the Secretary General might marry and give some respite to his colleagues. Hammarskjold was known by all to work evenings, nights, weekends, at times borrowing other people's secretaries for dictation when his own were exhausted.

Politically, the Russians were manoeuvring to have a Conference of the Five including Red China and hinted that such a conference could bring peace in Indochina. Victor commented in his diaries:

> I am sure that Red China's admittance to the conference will bring nothing tangible. The only happy thing was the return of the anti-Red prisoners. The first Chinese prisoners were greeted in Formosa as heroes.

In February he noted that since the death of Stalin the Russians had at least become more pleasant socially.

> At the Trusteeship Council last summer, for example, the Soviet delegate, Zoroff, come to my cocktail party, whereas Soldatov never came. Vishinsky has also become more agreeable. The other evening at a dinner given by Dag for Bayar, the President of the Turkish Republic, Vishinsky happened to be walking next to me as we left the table to go to the salon. We talked along the whole length of the hall. I spoke to him of Russian literature and was amazed

at his memory for fables and proverbs. He then said that T
F Tsiang (head of the Chinese Delegation at the UN) was a
wise man, although of course he did not agree politically
with him. I related this subsequently to TF who was at the
same dinner. A few days later, Vishinsky was also present at
a dinner given by the Philippino Delegation in honour of
Romulo, although at the Paris Assembly he had called
Romulo an empty barrel. At the dinner for Bayar, Vishinsky
told me I looked forty-five and asked if he looked sixty. I
suggested sixty-three and he replied that he was seventy.

In February at a cocktail party given by Bokhari Victor again spoke
to Vishinsky and his wife.

Gladwyn Jebb was there and told Vishinsky I was a 'white
guard'. I almost replied that it takes an Englishman to betray
us. Vishinsky surely knows what I stand for.

The impasse in Korea and Indochina depressed Victor but when
there was movement it seemed to him that it could only be
detrimental to their cause.

The only agreement obtained at the Conference of the Four
in Berlin is to meet with the Chinese Reds in April to discuss
Korea and Indochina. Naturally this conference will come
to nothing if the western Powers do not make new
concessions and even then they will be cheated but this
decision will make the French even more ready to appease
the Reds and delay the ratification of the European Treaty
of Defence. Apparently it was French public opinion that
forced Dulles to accept this decision. The French will try
anything to get out of the Indochina stalemate. The lessons
we have learnt with the Reds do not seem to benefit others.

On 1st March, at a buffet dinner given by the Indian Delegation
at India House, he met Tsarapkin, the Soviet delegate, who prompted
him to be more forthright than usual:

Tsarapkin came over to shake my hand and praise my
Russian, raising his whisky glass to the Chinese people. I
did the same and drank to the Russian people. Thereupon

he said: 'If you are for the Chinese people, you must be for the new Chinese government.' I replied that I could not be for a government that killed ten million people. He said that was propaganda by foreign papers, to which I replied that it had been confirmed in their own papers. Tsarapkin protested that all revolutions had their victims and that the new government had given land to the peasants. 'Not enough,' I said. 'More will be given,' he replied. I told him there would not be enough land and the conversation ended there. It is the first time I have revealed my opposition to the Mao government so openly to a Soviet. Yet they must have known, unless they were stupid enough to think they could have me on their side. At least this way there can be no possible misunderstanding.

This was not the case when Hammarskjold, who was leaving for ten days in Europe, asked Victor to stand in for him. Initially Victor was flattered:

It is the first time he has asked an ASG to do it but it is a sensible measure in case an urgent matter arises or he is involved in an accident.

However, no more was said about Victor's substitution, even at the press conference on the day of Hammarskjold's departure. Victor, confused as to his role, called Cordier to ask whether he should attend the press conference and was told that he should. The following day the "daily report" mentioned Hammarskjold's departure again but said nothing about Victor replacing him.

Next day Kerno wanted the Acting Secretary General to open the session of his new review board. He telephoned Dag who said I was Acting. Thereupon I called Cordier to ask where I stood. He replied, half-annoyed and half-mocking, that he would send a circular to the ASGs and Directors telling them I was Acting.

The following day the Security Council was to meet and in order not to offend Chernychev I telephoned to ask if I should sit in for the Secretary General. He said it was up to me and I therefore decided not to go since the place is often empty. Cordier subsequently told me I should have gone because Dag had followed the Palestine debates very closely and that Chernychev had discouraged me from going so as not to be diminished himself! What a mess.

Internationally the news continued to be worrying.

At the Berlin Conference, according to the papers, Molotov told Dulles that the Soviet Union had given a stockpile of atom bombs to Red China. I foresaw a year ago that the Red Chinese could well drop an atom bomb on Taiwan. The effect on American opinion would be less than if a bomb was dropped on them and would make the western Powers even more prepared to accept a disadvantageous compromise.

Even in the American press there are now calls to admit our Reds to the UN. A correspondent in the *New York Times* in Paris suggested that in France many people would be willing to admit them in exchange for peace in Indochina as if they didn't know that a Red promise is worth nothing!

On 20th March Hammarskjold returned from London:

He looked fresh and very pleased. He must be very satisfied with his post as Secretary General which gives him a sense of power and affords him the frenetic activity which he craves. As Secretary General he can be the greatest dictator in the world and can appoint and dismiss people more easily than a prime minister in a democratic country. Whilst he was away I sensed how jealous Cordier was of his own position as Executive Assistant to the SG which allows him to control everything in the Secretariat. He thoroughly enjoys functioning as Secretary General when the latter is busy or absent.

In London Dag made a speech with Gladwyn Jebb at the Pilgrims where both of them supported the admission of the Chinese Reds to the UN. Yesterday the *New York Times* published an editorial criticising Dag. He replied that, if we want to have a universal organisation, all the strong centres should be represented but that he had already said their admission should be subject to conditions. This suggests he is sensitive to criticism and prepared to retreat if necessary.

A quarrel between the Chinese government and K C Wu was also making headlines in America. Wu, accused in the Chinese press of having been an accomplice of Wang Shih Chieh, had been dismissed by Chiang. In his counter-attack he had described the government as dictatorial and undemocratic. Victor recorded:

> In Formosa they are shocked. Wu has been excluded from the Kuomingtang and labelled a traitor, as one who profited by his visit to the US to attack Chiang whom he had served for twenty years, etc. It has created a lot of commotion. Knowing KC well, I am sure his declarations were made intentionally. When I spoke to him in October about his impressions since arriving in the US, he told me that the Americans are sympathetic to Formosa but that in present circumstances they would not help us to attack the continent.

> His present announcements suggest either that he wants to capitalise on these observations or else he doesn't want to return to China and hopes his declarations will give him the excuse of being a political refugee. Alternatively, he hopes to gain sympathy from the Americans and return as a patriot and democrat in the event of a government reorganisation. He won't succeed since the Chinese are unlikely to forget the dirty trick he is playing on the very people to whom he owes everything. If he really does succeed in returning in this role, it would prove that China is very sick, weakened and impotent, and no more than a puppet in American hands.

The machinations going on both in the Chinese government and in the Secretariat were causing Victor a lot of heart-searching:

> I am told the Chinese section at the Secretariat are saying that I am deliberately going on home leave to Formosa at the time of the cabinet reorganisation. Whether they think

212

I have political ambitions, or that the government will want to keep me, I don't know. Yu Tsoming [V's Personal Assistant on Chinese affairs] has political ambitions for me and advised me to accept the foreign affairs portfolio if it is offered to me. It is only one step from that, to saying that I am seeking it myself, and it is possible that Yu himself is campaigning for me simply to make it possible for him to enter the Foreign Office if the Chinese Reds are admitted to the UN. This time he has arranged to stay in Taiwan all the time I am there whereas last time he only stayed in Taiwan for the first days of my visit. Actually it is not a proposal I would be seriously tempted by. It would not be fun to be Foreign Minister now and I would have more internal and external matters to worry me.

On 28th March Victor's entry in the diary underscores his previous fears of French motives at the Geneva Conference:

The American press has frankly revealed its concern that the Reds might make attractive proposals to the French in exchange for recognition and admission to the UN, since the French would not have to effect it. The US would then be isolated with her allies blaming her for the failure of the Conference.

Although the French subsequently sent a note to the Chinese government assuring them that they would minimise the importance of Red China at Geneva, Victor remained sceptical

They can say it but, as soon as the Chinese Reds offer them something tangible in Geneva, they will be the first to bow to them.

In March Dulles made a speech to the Overseas Press Club, defining the US attitude to Red China and the Geneva Conference. Victor commented:

This speech has certainly comforted the anti-Reds, especially in Asia, and Reston wrote yesterday in the *New York Times* that Chiang Kai Shek's stock has gone up. His main arguments, which I agree with, are that recognition

213

would have a disastrous effect on the twelve million overseas Chinese who, having no other Chinese government to go to, would become a Fifth Column for the Reds.

Of greater impact in the American and Russian papers was the horrific destruction of the hydrogen bombs. Victor wrote:

Each article is more scary than the next. Nehru is terrorised, the British also, and propose that the testing of these bombs be banned, as they have already caused victims amongst Japanese who were beyond the danger zone.

On 8th April 1954, Victor left New York on home leave. He recorded:

I arranged to visit Manila and Bangkok. Berkeley Gage is there as Ambassador and Kridakon has written to me several times from Bangkok expressing the hope that I would visit him.

There was now open speculation amongst the Chinese diplomats as to whether Victor was to become Foreign Minister. Victor wrote sceptically:

No doubt this explains their extreme kindness. In Manila C P Cheng gave a dinner in my honour. Apparently he made a fortune on the Burma Road during the war because he controlled transport. This explains his luxurious lifestyle. It seems he has recently divorced his wife for the nanny of his three children.

Our Ambassador told me that the richest Chinese abroad are those who emigrated to the Philippines and have high-ranking jobs as bankers or manufacturers. At the golf club he pointed out four Chinese at the first tee who were worth $100 million altogether!

I must say it is very pleasant here amongst the diplomatic corps, except for a few months when it is horribly hot. They see each other often and play bridge or tennis together. Unfortunately I was in Manila on Good Friday and Thursday when, being good Catholics, they close all the shops, bars and cinemas. Most of the people were at Baggio. Our Ambassador himself only came back because of my arrival.

Easter Sunday was spent at the house of Kridakon's brother-in-law. Victor recorded:

> ... a perfect day by the sea two hours from Bangkok. It was so hot that we stood in the pool drinking whisky and smoking. Berkeley Gage, the new UK Ambassador to Thailand was also there and I was able to liaise between him and Kridakon, who is the European Director at the Foreign Ministry. Gage invited me to stay at the Embassy, which would have been pleasant and economical, but I could not accept for political reasons. One evening after dinner I went with the Kridakons to visit Gage, who was in pyjamas, and we drank a quantity of whisky. This brought Gage and Kridakon even closer.

Finding that the Foreign Ministry had put a motor boat at his disposal to see the river, Victor invited Berkeley Gage to come along and he in turn invited two ladies, a Mrs Holmes and Lady Aniruth Debna. Victor's susceptibility to female charm was fuelled by the presence of the latter. He recorded:

> ... a Cantonese woman brought over to Siam at the age of twelve by one of the King's favourites. They say she came from a tea house, then married the favourite by whom she had two or three children. Later he became increasingly homosexual and they led separate lives, though still together. Eventually he died, leaving his widow a large fortune, to take lovers as she pleased. One of these fell in love with her daughter and was promptly assassinated! Ani, as she is called, is very worldly and well-dressed, with beautiful jewellery. She is quite good looking, though about fifty. Unfortunately her English is difficult to understand. On my departure she sent me a silver lighter with the royal emblem which shows her good taste and knowledge of the world. Moreover, it is the latest model which can be used in high winds. Her current lover is in the police and Berkeley and I teased her in the boat that the two police boats escorting us, were here to protect her from us.

In all ways Bangkok suited Victor's appetite for the good life:

> There are two race courses, several golf clubs and bungalows used as *maisons de passe*. In other words, life is nonchalant and nobody is on time.

The only shadow to fall across an otherwise perfect stay concerned the arrival of the *New York Times* with an article on changes in the Secretariat.

> It revealed what we had been saying before my departure, namely that Bunche would be Under Secretary without portfolio, Bokhari Head of Dept of Public Information and Cohen Head of Trusteeship but there was one addition that I hadn't heard of - that I would reach my age limit on 16th November 1954 and 'was expected to leave'. This wouldn't have mattered quite so much except that a summary of the article had already been published on the day of my arrival, so that everyone I met in Bangkok knew my age!

On 12th May, the eve of Victor's departure for Tokyo, he had an interview with Chiang Kai Shek in Taipei.

> He invited me to sit facing him but did not shake hands. I said it was an honour to be able to congratulate him in person on his re-election. He asked if I could participate in the inauguration but I explained that I must return for the Trusteeship Council Session.

It was Chiang who then repaired the blow to Victor's self-esteem by asking how old he was and saying he looked young for his age.

> When he asked for news of the UN I told him the Americans were more aware of the Red threat now than they were two years ago and realised it would be suicide to yield any more. I also told him that all the non-Red and non-Kuomingtang hoped the government would appeal to their service and that if we returned to China we should have the political support of the largest possible number of Chinese.

He said he was aware of this and that there were already many non-Kuomingtang in the government, T F Tsiang, for example. He said he hoped I would continue in the UN.

In Hong Kong criticism of Chiang's government had been more forthright:

In Hong Kong I heard that Hu Shih has agreed to become Vice President if Chiang Kai Shek does not oppose it. It is regrettable that the President and Vice President are both military men and Kuomingtang. As I suggested to Chiang, the government would have more authority if it was less exclusively Kuomingtang. In Hong Kong they felt that government policy was often so stupid that it failed to attract the sympathy and enthusiasm of the Chinese in general. They asked me to transmit these views to Chiang Kai Shek, which I did, though without saying where I obtained them. One person suggested there should be more political parties in order to gain the support of the people. I replied that the Chinese hate political parties and are only interested in what the government does. My impression is that they find the government far too dictatorial. They still think our only salvation is to support Chiang, but they are hoping for a more liberal policy.

In Hong Kong I was struck by the gulf between the very rich who have everything, like Harold Lee and Li Shu Fan, and the great mass of the poor, especially those who came in as refugees. Many young women refugees become dancing girls in the night-clubs. In some clubs there is no fee for entry but you pay eight dollars an hour for a dancing girl. The successful ones only stay with a client ten to twenty minutes, so a girl who is popular can easily make ten to fifteen times eight dollars, of which a portion goes to the establishment. One of the young girls, almost a virgin, was prepared for anything because she had to send money to her sister in Peking. She was of good family and told me she had been to university.

On arrival at Taipei Victor and the other passengers were no longer required to draw the curtains as they had been two years earlier. Victor reported:

A crowd of friends came to meet me, including George Yeh. This time I was not invited by the Foreign Ministry to stay at an hotel and no member of the Foreign Office came to be my secretary. They welcomed me as a friend who had come from afar, without giving any particular importance to the event as they had in 1952, so I will be freer in my movements.

In Hong Kong a Mrs Y C Wang had invited Victor to live in her house in Taipei. It turned out to be one of the best furnished houses in the city and Victor was led to speculate that poor Wang in future was likely to be bombarded with requests to lend his house to friends.

In his diary he wrote of Wang Chao Chin's pride in having been re-elected to the Provincial Assembly, after an eighty per cent turn-out in Taiwan's first democratic elections.

Wang told me he did not have an electoral platform but went round to all the villages. His name sounds like 'all in youth'. According to him that is what impressed the imagination of his electors. Actually I thought it was a little like a circus!

The new mayor of Taipei has also been elected and the Kuomingtang candidate was beaten, perhaps due more to the fact that he was a bad candidate than that he was Kuomingtang. Some die-hard Kuomingtang want the election annulled but Chiang showed his political wisdom by opposing this, perhaps in consequence of the good effects of K C Wu's letters.

Victor was saddened to observe that some of his friends and colleagues, including Wang Chung Kui, had aged visibly since his visit two years earlier.

Wang rarely goes out, no longer has the same energy and has to be carried in a chair when he goes up to his office. He rarely reads now and smokes less. On the other hand Yoshizawa hasn't changed much. He still has all his teeth, plays golf and remarried before coming to Formosa. He remembers me as well as my father very well.

218

When I met Cheng Chen at Chiang's reception for the Americans on 1st May, he told me to go and see Wang Shih Chieh who he said had behaved like a gentleman when was dismissed by Chiang, did not complain and made no declarations. They appreciate such behaviour, especially since the tirades of K C Wu.

When I told Wang everyone in Formosa looked more relaxed and calm than in '52, he said it was a false sense of security. He thinks that in a year we will be involved in war. He reckons Chiang Ching Kuo is honest but less liberal than his father. Our military men in Taipei tell me that the Vietminh could take Dienbienphu when they want but are not doing so in order to have a bargaining card at the Geneva Conference.

Cheng Chen gave a dinner at which only he, his wife, George Yeh, the Secretary General of the Yuan Executive, and myself were present. We spoke frankly and I told him we should have a political plan to gain the support of all Chinese in China the day we land. Secondly, we must rally around us all the non-Reds and not just appoint Kuomingtang members to high positions. We need more money for propaganda and we must ally ourselves to the Taiwanese because if things turn out badly the UN will insist on a plebiscite in Taiwan.

Wherever he went, Victor seemed to hear the same complaints against Chiang's leadership.

One of the most honest and interesting conversations I had this time, as in 1952, was with Sun Li Jen. He has always been very critical of the old man. This time he came to see me one evening with George Yeh and we chatted over Scotch. He said there had been 500 suicides in the army and their morale generally is less good than in '52. He accuses the old man of appointing yes-men and of wanting to control everything. When I asked him, he said that sexual problems don't exist in the army because when one is badly fed and tired one doesn't think of sex.

Generally, economic conditions in Taiwan have improved. Chinese ladies think it is better than in Chungking during the war because the currency is stable and one can budget. There is one doctor for 2,000 people and 7-800 dentists in Taiwan.

Chiang is less strict on prostitution here than he was in Chungking. After years of Japanese culture the mores are rather free. In the suburbs of Chungking there are sulphur baths and one can get masseuses for seventy dollars but they cannot do a massage. They are simply prostitutes and have to have medical cards. One such establishment was right next to a cathedral.

Victor's endemic resentment at having to pay excess baggage was not provoked on this occasion and put the finishing touch to the pleasant impression he had of his visit to Taiwan:

When I left, I had fifty pounds of excess baggage and was allowed to take more than the regulation $200. My baggage wasn't opened either. In China there are always ways to get round things when the authorities want to co-operate. I remember during the war in Chungking, in order to go abroad it was actually possible to find someone else to take one's place for the anti-epidemic injections.

In Taipei the two questions always asked of me were whether the USSR had made progress in manufacturing the hydrogen bomb and when and how the Chinese Reds would be admitted to the UN.

On the ship home, the *President Wilson,* Victor had his usual success with the American ladies on board ...

... who liked my replies at a lecture on the UN given by an old American. When I was asked how Mrs Roosevelt and Mrs Pandit could be compared, I replied that Mrs Pandit was certainly prettier. They laughed. Then they insisted that I also give a lecture. I gave one on Trusteeship and non-self governing territories, with no notes, which greatly impressed the audience and I had more people than the

220

previous lecturer. After this I became very popular but it was not the same as with a Latin public. There was always a certain reserve due to the difference in race.

In New York, Victor's arrival coincided with that of Haile Selassie, Emperor of Ethiopia. He wrote:

> The Americans received him as one they wished to honour: ticker tape parades along Broadway, receptions at City Hall, lunch with the Mayor, and honorary degree at Columbia University, etc. This is an encouragement for us, remembering how he was vilified at the time of the Italian invasion. He was accused of being a slave driver and robber of public funds (as Connelly had accused Chiang). And now his just cause has triumphed. We would like to see Chiang feted in the same way, the day he triumphs over the Reds.

The situation in Indochina, however, was going from bad to worse. Victor wrote despairingly:

> Eisenhower seems to have forgotten what he said about the danger of losing Indochina. The Americans now say they would not intervene alone and that the loss of Indochina is not the loss of Asia. The Geneva Conference is making no progress, the British seem to be prepared to rally to the Americans for the defence pact of Asia, but the French, instead of doing the same, have another ministerial crisis. In short, the democracies are making the same mistakes again. It all reminds me of the worst time of the Japanese aggression in Manchuria, Italian aggression in Ethiopia and of Hitler in Czechoslovakia. Naturally the Americans are more dynamic than the British and French before 1939 but they may decide to turn back into their shells in disgust.

> Khoman told me that at the Geneva Conference the Chinese Reds and the Russians rose when Chou or Molotov entered but wouldn't rise for anyone else, even the Chairman. He thinks Red Chinese prestige has increased due to the Conference and that many Europeans, even the

West Germans, have taken advantage of contact with the Chinese Reds to exploit the possibility of developing trade.

The Conference has shown that there is no agreement between the anti-Communist powers, whereas the Reds show a united front. France has had a change of cabinet and the Council President has promised to obtain an honourable peace, which is interpreted by everyone as peace at any price, or to resign on 20th July.

Indications are that the Americans are also ready to abandon Indochina. Khoman is dismayed. He agrees with me that if we lose Indochina, even if the Americans are prepared to help militarily, the war would be waged in his country, Thailand, instead of Indochina. Many people think that, militarily, Thailand would not have a great combative strength. The Americans must feel unhappy and isolated but the American public does not want war in Indochina unless it is led energetically by the government.

Overtures by the Russians led Victor to wonder what they might have in mind for him. He recorded:

Tsarapkin has been very kind to me. He invited me to a reception for Russian chess players and asked how things were in Formosa. He warned me to be careful, that Formosa would be detached from China. I replied that in Formosa we were thinking of rejoining China to Formosa. He laughed and suggested that would be to put the coat on the button. He also told me not to forget the Russian language as it would be useful to me! So the Reds are making overtures to me. I'm told that, as in Hong Kong, the Chinese Reds have a very good opinion of me and of Liu Chieh, finding that I am loyal!

In America, K C Wu's anti-government propaganda was doing nothing to help the Nationalist cause.

Khoman told me that that the articles by Wu are detrimental to the Philippines and to Thailand because they discredit Formosa, which is anti-Red. He even wonders if Wu is not deliberately playing the Red game. I told him I did not think Wu was pro-Communist but wants to make out he is a liberal in order to return to Formosa with American support.

More and more, they are talking of the early entry of the Chinese Reds to the UN, though Dulles says the US could prevent this and thus avoid having to leave the UN. In any case the Democrats and the Republicans are vying with each other in their protests against Mao's entry. It therefore appears that they will not be admitted this year at least. Churchill's trip to Washington roused fears in the Americans that Britain would want Red China in but American reaction was so strong and spontaneous that Churchill felt obliged to announce that his government would oppose admission in present circumstances. This suggests that when the Americans are really angry the British will yield.

On 21st July Victor recorded the signing of the truce in Geneva ...

... under the best conditions possible in the circumstances. The tragedy is that the present circumstances could have been avoided. Tsien Tai agrees with me that our Reds will not undertake a military coup at the moment because there will be elections in Vietnam in two years and the Reds will do everything to win them. To this effect they are going to infiltrate South Vietnam on the partition line and behave as decently as they can in the North. When the elections have given them what they want, it will be easy for them to gain the rest of the peninsula because everybody there will be demoralised.

In August he wrote:

I have finally found an explanation for the change in American policy towards Indochina. According to the Alsop brothers in their editorial, all the American military were in favour of an intervention, but Humphrey, the Secretary of the Treasury, and Milton Eisenhower, prevailed in advising prudence. I wonder what Truman would have done in Eisenhower's place, or what Eisenhower would have done in Truman's place in 1950 when South Korea was invaded. The official explanation for the change was that the French government had not asked the American government to intervene militarily.

When the President of South Korea, Syngman Rhee came to visit Hammarskjold, Victor was interested to note the difference in his treatment compared with other Chiefs of State. For them, Hammarskjold had given official dinners with champagne. There was no such thing for Rhee. Hammarskjold, being a rabid neutralist, probably has no sympathy for him. When I saw Rhee at a reception at the Korean Consulate, he did not seem to recognise me but his wife called me by name and spoke to me in a kind way, asking for news of Margie and the children, whom she often saw in Washington in 1942.

On 14th April newspapers published the suggestion by Chou En Lai and the Red government that Taiwan should be liberated. Chou said it was an internal matter and that the foreign powers should abstain from intervening or suffer the consequences. Victor commented:

In my opinion it is a manoeuvre, firstly, to divide the US and other countries because most of them would not want to defend Taiwan, especially now that the Reds have publicly announced their intention of taking it over; secondly, to rally China in favour of action against the US under the pretext of patriotic and nationalistic action.

In August he was proved right:

As I thought, the British have announced that they would not defend Formosa or include her in the territories that the SEATO Conference is guaranteeing. One the other hand, Australia announced that an attack against Formosa would have serious consequences. For Australia, as well as New Zealand of course, Formosa in Red hands would be a threat to their own security. However, the British, whilst not guaranteeing Formosa against Red attack, have never suggested that it should be given away. They would rather have Trusteeship for Formosa but they have not specified who would be the administering power. Churchill said over a year ago that we should not allow the invasion and massacre of Chiang and those who followed him to Formosa.

Within the Secretariat there was talk of Victor's transfer to the Conference Department the following year. Victor wrote:

I agreed with Dag that my case would be reconsidered if there was a change in the political situation in the Far East. Dag thinks three possibilities could present themselves: that the Reds replace us, that there are two Chinese representations or that there is none. What if the Reds did not enter for another ten years, I asked?

He predicts that pressure will become stronger in favour of entry, however, and that in the US opinion could change suddenly, as it did for American policy towards Germany and Japan. I thought the case was different because the US won over Japan and Germany and thus had reason to change their policy whereas a policy change towards Red China would mean surrender by the US.

In September the Chinese Communists started bombing the offshore islands of Formosa with artillery. Victor wrote:

We have retaliated with air, sea and land bombings. The Americans have not said whether they will help to defend the islands, in order to keep the enemy guessing. The Red bombing lessened in intensity thanks to our countermeasures and there is no concentration of ships for an attempted landing, so we don't know why they started it. Probably it is simply part of a war of nerves.

Although Chou himself had declared his intention of liberating Taiwan, in October the Americans, fearful of an escalation in the war, asked Taiwan to stop its attacks against Red China, so as not to aggravate the situation. Victor protested in his journal:

Thus it is the Reds who are protected! Even in the US they are starting to appease them.

225

By the end of October the word was that Taiwan was ready to land on the continent the following year, even without American help, feeling that it would be better to take the initiative if the Communists were going to invade Taiwan.

In November Victor reported a conversation in which George Yeh claimed the Americans were in favour of a Nationalist occupation of Hainan but that it might have cost 100,000 men whom Chiang Kai Shek wanted to keep for an invasion of China.

> George thinks that if we had occupied Hainan the Red Chinese would not have been able to help the Red Indochinese because we could have bombed their communication lines. George doesn't think the Chinese Reds will try to invade Formosa.

In November Victor's sometime friend and enemy, Vishinsky died in New York. He wrote:

> The day of Vishinsky's death I was lunching with de Kerillis. As I had a chauffeur-driven car, we went to the Soviet delegation to sign the register. A crowd of photographers took our picture at the entrance which horrified Kerillis because he is always afraid of the FBI. I hope that my Chinese friends will understand that an international official having to deal with the Soviet delegation and attend their receptions is not at fault for doing what a Chinese delegate cannot do.

The same month, Peking radio announced that thirteen Americans, including eleven prisoners of the Korean War, had been condemned by the Red Chinese to long prison sentences. Victor observed cynically:

> It is the best thing that has happened to us since the Red Chinese attack against South Korea. The Americans are furious. Even the British called it an outrage. This will certainly diminish the chances of Red China entering the UN. The British are to stop pressing the US to settle the Formosa question by negotiation. It's a pity there are no American women amongst the condemned. That would really have fanned American anger!

Above Victor with Hammarskjold (center) and Chief of Protocol, Count Jehan de Noüe (right)

Right Victor, representing the Secretary General at the Security Council, sitting next to Andrei Gromyko (Iacov Malik behind Gromyko)

With Krishna Menon
ndia and Fernand van
ngenhoven of Belgium
Opposite below Victor
lcoming Pope Paul VI
o the United Nations

Above Victor welcoming Lyndon and
Lady Bird Johnson to the United
Nations
Left United Nations Headquarters,
New York City

*Left A rare
evening out
together, for
Victor's 60th
birthday
Below Mona and
Mrs Patricia
Tsien, daughter
Dr V K Wellington
Koo, New York
1995*

On 5th December he wrote:

> George Yeh has signed a treaty of mutual defence with the
> US for an undetermined time, with provision for the two
> parties to denounce it with a year's notice. However, even
> in the US the press is starting to talk of the possibility of
> having two Chinas at the UN.

In mid-December, after the General Assembly voted to ask the
Secretary General to try and obtain the freedom of the condemned
prisoners, Hammarskjold telegraphed a message to Chou En Lai
suggesting he should see him in Peking and take Victor. For once
Victor was not anxious to step into the limelight:

> I told him if I went I would never be able to come back
> again. I am sure Dag understands I would be the least
> qualified person to go to Peking with him. My presence
> would only irritate the Reds unnecessarily and for me it
> would be fatal. My friends would never forgive me and I would
> not even be able to see my friends and relatives in Peking.

In a conversation with Pelt in November the two men had agreed
that notwithstanding his limitations, Hammarskjold was a greater
intellectual than Lie and had the virtue of considering himself as
being as expendable as anyone else. Victor recorded:

> Lie by contrast was always too egotistical to sacrifice himself
> and only resigned in the expectation of staying.

A week later, however, Hammarskjold created mayhem amongst
the members of the Secretariat by writing to all the high officials
with details of their salaries and indemnities.

> It transpires that everyone has a raise of $1-4,000 except
> me, Chernychev and Cohen, who have a decrease of $2,000!
> Naturally, we are furious. Chernychev was the first to speak
> to Dag, to no effect. Cohen did not have his interview and
> I haven't yet asked to see him. If Dag does not receive us, it
> would prove that not only is he irresponsible and without
> administrative experience, but a coward without heart or
> manners.

I have the feeling, but it is perhaps wishful thinking, that there will eventually be an enormous scandal, either by the revelation that he is homosexual or as a result of his attitude or some decision that leaves no doubt about his mental state. I realise now why in some countries they are not allowed into the administration, not because of the act itself but because of their mental disequilibrium.

Whenever I attended a UN function, Father always warned me not to stay close to Hammarskjold after the initial salutation. It had become a known fact that he was allergic to women.

Victor's disenchantment with the Secretary General had evidently reached an all-time low at having to take a relative drop in salary.

As I am disgusted at the offhand and unfair manner in which we have been treated, I thought of resigning in order to better serve my country in another job. I spoke first to Yu Tsoming, then to George Yeh and T F Tsiang. The latter two, especially George, want me to stay for the country's sake because they wonder if another Chinese would be appointed if I leave. Hu Shih, whom I saw the next day, is of the same opinion. George says I am the best qualified Chinese to deal with my job at the Secretariat. Thus I am useful to my country by virtue of my presence there, irrespective of the work I do. It doesn't do much for one's enthusiasm.

At the close of session in December Victor took leave of the department "with regret but without apprehension." He declared in his farewell speech:

First of all, I had the privilege of having the two Bs, Bunche and Benson, appointed and then came the others. We organised the department and now it runs smoothly. I would like to pay tribute to their devotion to their duties and their assistance to me. The reservoir of goodwill which I have built up among delegates will be useful to me in my new functions when you complain about translations, interpretations, records, etc. I say to you all au revoir and not adieu.

228

Thereupon, as I had covered Pignon with praise, he proposed a motion of thanks to me and Bunche, supported by Itani of the Lebanon who will come to the Conference Department for Arabic, and by Rivas, the Venezuelan Vice President.

Chou En Lai has replied to the Secretary General agreeing to receive him in Peking. If he succeeds in his negotiations, he will be very popular in the US and in the whole world. Moreover, this could change American opinion of our Reds and prepare the ground to admit them to the UN. The Reds could well be cleverer than Hitler, Tojo or Mussolini! Perhaps it is the end of an era for us all.

CHAPTER FOURTEEN

The Conference Department

Learning The Fifth Official Language - The Suez Crisis - Visit Of Queen Elizabeth II - Khruschev At The United Nations - Chiang Kai Shek Is Intransigent

On 4th January 1955 Victor took up his new post as Under Secretary for Conference Services. Hammarskjold, who had been to Peking to see Chou En Lai in an attempt to secure the freedom of the eleven prisoners held by the Communists, returned a week later. He had evidently been impressed by what he saw, particularly the encouragement given to art by the Communists. Victor retorted:

> I told him it was the same with all dictatorships. I doubt if the trip actually achieved anything but at least they didn't close the door in his face. Eisenhower wants the people to believe everything is going well for electoral reasons and the UN wants it in order to stop American criticism.

Any optimism was short-lived. On 29th January Chinese Communists occupied Yu-Kiang and the Americans were driven to make a move which, though threatening, was seen by Victor as more of a diplomatic manoeuvre than a real sign of aggression. At the same time as declaring their willingness to accept a cease-fire in the China waters, American battleships were moving towards Formosa and Congress was authorising Eisenhower to declare war if necessary to defend the island.

> It sounds good, but it could be no more than a ploy to persuade American public opinion to accept a Red Chinese regime as a *fait accompli*. The Americans need to pound

their fists on the table before feeling morally justified in making concessions.

T F Tsiang told me there is an agreement between us and the Americans to evacuate the Tachen Isles, to hold Quemoy and Matsu, and for us not to invoke the veto against negotiations at the UN for a cease-fire with the Reds. If negotiations progress, it is possible that under pressure the British and other allies may create two Chinas, with the Reds occupying the islands of the continent. Today, for the first time, the papers announced a plan by Eden to this effect.

Yesterday New Zealand invoked the Security Council on the question of a cease-fire in the coastal islands. One wonders if the Reds will come to the Council. Our fate depends on their skill. If they are as clever in their negotiations with us, they will have a chance of success in the long run.

Before the Red coup against Yu-Kiang, *Paris-Match* published a horoscope predicting events in France, prophesying that the Queen of England would die in 1955 and that in the same year the atom bomb would be used in a war between the US and the Reds over Formosa. The situation is certainly volatile.

On 31st January the Security Council's invitation to the Chinese Communists to come and discuss the cease-fire was met by Chou with an absolute refusal. Victor confided in his diaries:

One has a definite impression from the papers that the Americans would be prepared to give up the coastal islands if the Reds would agree to a cease-fire. Tsien Tai reckons Quemoy will be abandoned to the Reds in a year.

Upon taking charge of the Conference Service Department, Victor became head of the largest department with the biggest budget although with the least political charge. It covered the responsibility for scheduling all meetings from the General Assembly downwards - wherever in the world they might be held. This included arranging

231

for the translators, interpreters, recruitment of staff, document control, library, printing.

Within the department Victor was carrying out the usual tasks falling to a new head of staff and dealing with a few problems he hadn't anticipated. In March he wrote:

> I intended inviting all my colleagues (more than 1,000) in batches of seventy to a cocktail party in my room. Vaughan [Director, Office of General Services] said this would spoil my new rug and furniture and that I could give my cocktails in the Press Bar. He promised it wouldn't cost me any more. We'll see if he's right. I am told that the members of my department greatly appreciate my invitations. Vaughan thinks I am only doing it to show that I am spending my expenses allowance. I told him it had nothing to do with that and I used to do it even in the Trusteeship Department where the question was irrelevant.

In April he had to deal with his first serious domestic incident when Michell, Head of Conference Division in the department, disappeared for three days and was finally discovered drinking in a bar. Victor recorded:

> I am told that he is in the habit of getting drunk like that for whole days at a time, without his wife knowing. This time his disappearance was noticed because he had with him certain documents that we needed. As he had always been a good worker, I managed to get him off with a reprimand in front of Robertson, Chief of Personnel. Michell promised to give up drinking completely, at least for a time, and Dag agreed to forget about the incident if Szeming Sze, the Head of our Medical Service, would give him a certificate suggesting that it was an isolated case. This was granted after a medical examination, only Robertson insists that the certificate be put in Michell's personal file. I suggested, as a compromise, that the certificate be withdrawn from the file if by the end of the year Michell still does not drink and behaves OK. Robertson agreed.

In July Victor took three weeks leave in Mexico and, finding his Spanish still lacked fluency, forged an introduction to a Mexican lady who was also a Spanish teacher. He wrote:

> She gave me lessons in a classroom at the university which made me feel quite young again. When we first met, she'd worn an ugly coat. This time she was wearing a light grey suit, her hair was well done, she had a pink slip which showed below her skirt and was very elegant and gracious in her movements. Much more interesting, in other words!

Whilst in Mexico, he elected to stay in a family apartment belonging to a widow with two daughters who had studied in America. By normal standards, his timetable was relaxed. On 18th July he wrote:

> The days have gone very quickly, a little monotonous but very restful - up between 8 and 8.30, breakfast 9 - 9.30, study Spanish for a couple of hours, partly in the park opposite the house on one of the benches. Sometimes I go to town before lunch for some shopping. Lunch (two sandwiches) between one and two p.m.. Then an hour's siesta. From 3.30 - 5 p.m., a Spanish lesson at the university. Then a walk in the gardens in the town centre, buying *El Universal* and reading it in a cafe, usually the Voladez which is the most popular. Then dinner at the house, followed by reading in my room, or a visit to the movies, or conversation or poker with the girls and their student friends. I am making rapid progress, but I still don't know enough to express myself on complicated matters and make continual mistakes. If I stayed in a Spanish country for six months and worked as I am doing now, I would be able to speak fluently.

On leaving, he was peeved to discover that he had been charged for an additional sandwich each day

> ... even though the two they gave me at lunch were not enough. That means, presumably, that I was only supposed to eat one!

233

Returning to New York via Mexico City, he at least had the satisfaction of being congratulated on his Spanish at an Embassy dinner. He wrote smugly:

> They said it was incredible, a *tour de force* and other flattering terms, so the trip achieved something.

Once back in the office, he was immediately assailed with problems. In late July a meeting was announced between Mao's ambassadors and the US in Geneva to settle the question of the repatriation of American prisoners and Chinese students. Certain papers speculated that they might also discuss the problem of a cease-fire in the Taiwan Straits and Red China's admittance to the UN.

Chou's sudden decision to liberate the eleven American pilots fuelled expectations of progress, though this was soon marred by the pilots reports of the torture they had suffered and the Chinese Reds' demand to have the right through a third power to control all Chinese in the US. Victor wrote:

> Despite Chou's cable to Dag, wishing him a happy fiftieth birthday and hoping for good relations, it would seem after all that China is not likely to be admitted to the UN this year.

Eisenhower's heart attack in September, despite its implications for the presidential candidacy the following year, was seen by Victor as perhaps a blessing in disguise as far as Formosa was concerned. Victor reflected:

> Eisenhower was becoming more and more an appeaser. If Nixon stays, it will be better for us but he is too young to be a serious candidate. If before the elections he has the chance to govern and show himself an able statesman, it would be to our advantage as he has travelled in the Far East and has even laid down precise conditions to the Reds for their admission to the UN.

Inside the United Nations, he noted the "large scale bargaining" which was going on in November 1955:

> Krishna Menon [Head of the Indian delegation] succeeded in persuading the General Assembly not to raise the

Algerian question in the present session which means that France will return. The Arabs are not opposing it so that France can vote at the Security Council in favour of the package deal for the admission of eighteen new members, including Outer Mongolia, which will admit a few new Arab States to the UN. With Eisenhower's recovery, the US is giving in again. They now accept Mongolia and are forcing us not to use our veto whilst in Taiwan the papers are clamouring for us to use it.

With the admission of new members, pressure will be greater for the admission of our Reds. Thus we are at a new turning point in history. By their intransigence the Russians always obtain concessions. The Americans don't know what to do in order not to lose votes in the election. Everything is going adrift. Russian propaganda is succeeding. On top of everything else they've just exploded their strongest hydrogen bomb. They certainly know how to synchronise their effects! What a *coup de théâtre*!

Up to the last minute they hoped China would abstain. T F Tsiang's veto against Mongolia was the third veto of the session and provoked all the following Russian vetoes. Most of the delegations were furious and there was talk of expelling us in 1955, when suddenly the USSR requested an extraordinary session of the Security Council and proposed to eliminate Mongolia and Japan. Thus the crisis is solved for the moment and the veto against Japan is transferred to Russia. Our position in any case is strengthened until the Autumn Assembly. For once, events have turned in our favour, although they are still blaming us. The US are the most bothered because they are keen on helping Japan.

Yesterday Khoman suggested we should abstain on Mongolia in order to allow the admission of Japan. He says that would obtain the favour of all but I think it would be making a concession for nothing and it would be better to wait. Japan was furious with us but then the USSR used the veto three times against Japan at a Council meeting in which the US proposed her admission, so Japanese opinion turned against her.

In April 1955 Hammarskjold went to Palestine under the authority of the UN in an attempt to prevent hostilities breaking out between Jews and Arabs. Victor acknowledged that ...

> ... most people, especially in the US, think that if anyone could succeed in such a mission it is Dag. He is a very good negotiator, knowing what he wants and saying things without offending the others. The Soviets, who have previously favoured the Arabs, have also recently declared their support for UN action in the Middle East to secure peace. This further reinforces Dag's position.

On his arrival, hostilities had increased but Hammarskjold obtained a promise from Egypt and Israel to abstain from hostile actions which calmed the situation. Victor wrote:

> It is a great personal success for Dag and increases his prestige and that of the UN. There is now talk of entrusting him with the mission to find a settlement to the Palestinian problem.

Hammarskjold's subsequent acceptance of the mission left Victor in charge as his 'representative' at UN headquarters. This brought its own diplomatic problems when the Bulgarian delegate refused to deal with him. Hammarskjold's problems and those of the Middle East could be equally petty. Victor recorded:

> An example of useless complications in the relations between Jews and Arabs arose when a few goats crossed the frontier from Arab to Jewish territory. The Jews kept the goats and demanded fifty shillings per goat per day to allow them to graze there. The bill come to £251 which is more than it costs per day for every Arab refugee.

In October Victor went to Taipei where inevitably talk still centred on whether the Chinese Communists intended to attack the coastal islands and what the Americans would do if they did. Victor wrote:

If the Reds bomb our islands we will bomb the mainland and they will then bomb our air bases in Taipei and this will force the Americans to enter the game. If we manage to hold our isles, it would already be a victory. That is why we are ready for war at any moment. When I was in Taiwan in '52, I reproached my friends there for not building hotels to attract tourists. They replied that they wouldn't be there long. Yesterday our information bulletins announced that we have taken on a whole programme of hotel building and initiated a commission for the development of tourism. This indicates a change of spirit in Formosa. They now realise they will have to stay for an indeterminate time.

His return to New York on 3rd November 1956 coincided with the Anglo-French coup against Egypt of the Suez Canal. Victor wrote:

Not knowing it, I did not go to my office and this was the very day the UN sat until five a.m.

His judgement on the crisis was merciless:

The coup is without precedent in history: two great powers undertaking a military mission against a small country, without sufficient preparation, under a ridiculous pretext and without finishing the task. They stopped suddenly, for fear of Russian 'volunteers' and what they got was exactly the opposite of what they wanted, i.e. the fall of Nasser and freedom of navigation on the Suez Canal. The result was to strengthen Nasser's position, make him more intransigent than ever and the Canal will be blocked for months. The Suez conflict is unique in history; it is the concentration of all the conflicts in the world - east and west, Communism and capitalism, nationalism and colonialism. In the past there have only been conflicts of local interest but in Suez all interests are involved.

In June there was an incident in Taipei which forced Americans to re-appraise their position there. The acquittal of an American sergeant who had shot a Chinese peeping Tom looking at his wife in the shower set off a wave of riots. Victor wrote:

237

The violence was spontaneous. 10-30,000 civilians looted the Embassy buildings, tore down the American flag, etc. The Chinese authorities confirmed that the riots weren't organised, although the Americans believe the rioters were Red agitators. Until now this was the only country where there had never been a demonstration against the US. It shook the Americans who took for granted that all Taiwan was on their side. The incident will reinforce the position of those in America and elsewhere who advocate a re-evaluation of American policy towards us. It could be fatal. They may well say that, since they cannot count on the Taiwanese population and since Chiang Kai Shek is not immortal, it is better to act realistically and find another policy. We are doing everything to avoid this. Chiang said on the radio yesterday that he takes full responsibility for the incidents and asks everyone to behave themselves.

On 24th November 1957 Victor recorded a speech made by Britain's Queen Elizabeth in the General Assembly:

She is very simple and pleasant, like an ordinary young English woman rather than a sovereign. I complimented her on her French which I had heard when she read a speech at the Ottawa Parliament. She was visibly pleased and said modestly, 'But I am not bilingual like many Canadians.' I told her I spoke with authority as Head of Conference Services and asked her if she spoke Spanish. She said no. To Prince Philip I said that I had met his brother Mountbatten and his wife during the war in Chungking. He corrected me, saying they were his aunt and uncle.

At a cocktail party in December 1957, Hammarskjold approached Victor on the subject of continuing their "gentlemen's agreement" to keep him in the Secretariat.

He asked if I would make difficulties about staying and I said no. He added that since I had been head of my department morale had completely changed for the better. I said that I'd been lucky and couldn't take all the credit. In fact we've had everything in my department except a

238

murder: forged cheques, pregnancies, illegitimate births, an official in an insane asylum, debts, muggings in the street and suicides!

The next day in his office he said that, due to my age, he couldn't give me another five-year contract. He could give me a two-year one, but he knew this would not give me satisfaction. He is going to think about a formula and we will speak about it again in January. He said he would understand if I did not want to stay and would probably appoint a Japanese in my place but since I've done good work he would like to keep me.

May 1958 was not a good month for the American government. Victor wrote:

For the moment everything is going badly for the Democrats: the three Russian sputniks are superior from all viewpoints to the American satellites, the reception of the Nixons in Caracas could turn out very badly for them, and then there is the situation in Lebanon and in France and Algeria.

International reactions backed up his feelings:

The effect of the sputniks on US prestige and the confidence of their allies have been disastrous. I predicted at the start that the effect would be worse than the Little Rock events. The decision to send paratroops to the Caribbean after the demonstrations in Caracas against Nixon is unbelievably stupid. It could not have prevented anything and has wounded the feelings of all South Americans.

Later in the year, it was his health that preoccupied Victor. In July, on board the *President Hoover* between Yokohama and Manila, he discovered he had gall stones.

It started with cramps in my stomach, ten days after dining with Marthe Brusset at the Forum. We had been recommended marrow on toast and the following day

Marthe and I had bad indigestion. With her it lasted two days. I had it less severely but the malaise in my stomach lasted several days. The cramps came at a lunch in honour of Wang Shao Ku. It was so painful I had to leave the table and was swimming in cold sweat. Dr Irwin of the UN advised me to have X-rays. They showed I had no ulcers but ten days after the first fit I had another one at five a.m. which lasted five hours. After each one I had a fever for two days.

Luckily, I met Madame Farrin at a cocktail party at Marthe's and she advised me to see Dr Snapper whom I'd consulted in 1946 before the ulcer operation on my stomach. She told me she had also had gall stones but that it could be cured without an operation. After four days of X-rays, Snapper found two or three large stones, the size of twenty-five cent pieces. It is better to have small ones because they cannot obstruct the billial canal. Snapper recommends a diet and some pills. He said I must have had the stones for years and that I might have no more fits for the rest of my life. We will see.

On 3rd August 1958 Victor arrived in Hong Kong.

A delegation was sent to welcome me and two little girls presented flowers. It is because of the UN's resolution providing aid to Chinese refugees from Hong Kong that I am greeted with so much eagerness. They think I can do something to speed or increase this aid. At a tea in my honour I explained that I was simply a member of the Secretariat and that it was the delegations and countries concerned who made the decisions. Having promised to visit the refugee camps, I complimented the people responsible for aid and added that, if I hadn't known I was in a refugee camp, I would not have guessed it as the morale and physical conditions seemed so good. Posters on the walls referred to me as the saviour of the refugees. I wonder if they will greet me with as much warmth in a few years' time!

Rare in the diaries, he also mentioned Margie at this time, if only in passing:

Margie is staying on in Hong Kong for the winter. She is following a treatment of acupuncture and taking Chinese medicine which I hope will benefit her.

In March the following year Dulles was diagnosed as having cancer. Victor wrote:

Now even his opponents find him indispensable. Alsop said his prestige increased when they saw that his firm policy on Matsu and Quemoy worked, whereas Acheson, Stevenson and the others all preached the abandoning of these islands. He is the only one who knows what he wants and is steadfast in front of the Reds. Only Dag is still against him and his policies. When we had lunch, he started to speak about the situation in China and said that during his recent trip to India, Thailand, Vietnam, Laos and Afghanistan, the people he met were all against Chiang Kai Shek, without saying precisely why. He believes the majority of the Chinese people accept the Red regime and that Chinese refugees only represent ten per cent of the population which leaves 500 million in favour.

He doesn't believe Cheng Pao Hua's assertion that the Red regime is economically and politically bankrupt and says the Chinese colony in Cambodia is for the Chinese Reds. I replied that this colony is pro-Red because the Cambodian government has recognised Red China and that it would be the same in other Asian countries if the Red regime is recognised. This is why the Americans will not admit Peking to the UN. I told him there were far more than ten per cent of the Chinese people who are anti-Red and that he should go himself to Formosa to learn the situation.

He thinks that a source of possible conflict will be Cambodia's invasion of Vietnam. In his view the Chinese Reds have succeeded in their agrarian reforms and Red China has made greater economic progress than India. He is therefore against Dulles and Dewey and gives the impression, like the Burmese Prime Minister, that he will sleep more easily when Red China is a member of the UN.

241

A conversation with Wang Shih Chieh in October '59 cast an interesting if sad hindsight on the war against Chinese Communists and the opportunities for American aid that had been missed. Victor wrote afterwards:

> It seems that at a given time in 1948 the American government, seeing the situation deteriorating, asked Wang, through the intermediary of General Marshall, if we would accept MacArthur as Commander-in-Chief in China. Wang cabled Chiang but the latter was afraid that MacArthur would be difficult to control and gave an evasive reply when every minute counted. Wang had also suggested Henry Luce as US Ambassador to China, but, because the Republicans had lost the Presidential elections, Luce wasn't sent. Wang believes that the combination of MacArthur and Luce would have saved the situation because they would have obtained more aid from the US.

> Moreover, before Pearl Harbour, the British had suggested a ten-year alliance with us. Chiang refused because he was for Indian independence and it's because of that that the British have always put spokes in our wheels and favoured our Reds.

In September 1959, Hammarskjold organised a dinner in honour of Khruschev. In July Victor had attended a fashion show which the Soviets were giving for the first time abroad at The Coliseum. He wrote:

> Naturally, it was an imitation of the same kind of show in Paris and elsewhere but not as good. The models were all young women, well proportioned but with no refinement in their features. I could not help commenting to Kochtkov the following day that the Soviets are re-introducing the Class system, since not everyone can buy the dresses and mink coats we saw. He replied that there were no classes in Russia, simply some very rich people who could buy these things. He had not understood my meaning. Was it worth making a revolution that killed millions of people only to re-introduce economic and political inequality between the citizens? I am told that in Russia they now want to inherit from their parents.

242

When T F Tsiang told the newspapers he had declined the invitation to attend the dinner for Khruschev, a journalist had asked if Victor Hoo was invited. He replied that, as an international civil servant, he went to all the receptions given by the Soviet and satellite delegations, and that his absence would have spoiled relations, not only with the Soviet delegations but with his Soviet subordinates in the department with whom he had to keep on good terms. It was not the first or last time that Victor had to walk this particular diplomatic tightrope.

A meeting of Khruschev and Eisenhower at Camp David, although it dealt only superficially with the problem of Red China, had ended with Khruschev saying: "We will remain friends, even though you support Chiang and we support Mao." Victor wrote:

> The problem is that Ike has now gone to visit eleven countries to talk of peace and democracy. If he mentions the spirit of Camp David, which is so emphasised by Soviet propaganda, the result of the trip will be to spread that propaganda in places where it would have had little chance of success, and all with American tax payers' money!

His scepticism was justified a few months later when the Russians used the U2 incident as an excuse to cancel the Summit Conference. Victor noted:

> This will become a classic case for international law manuals in the future because it is the first time that a government and Head of State has openly admitted spying. Khruschev said that Ike was no longer welcome in the USSR where he was due to go on an official visit. Soon after that Ike's visit to Japan was cancelled due to uncontrollable student demonstrations. To fill his time, Ike finally visited Taiwan and the Philippines which would not have happened if he had gone to Russia. He must be very disappointed, having believed he would be the artisan of an East-West agreement. It is precisely him that Khruschev refuses to negotiate with. How ironic. This shows what it means to appease the Reds. Khruschev said in a press conference that at Camp David Ike told him to call him 'my friend'. Khruschev said he almost vomited.

Dag's prestige, on the other hand, has increased enormously since the Congo invoked the Security Council against the presence of Belgian troops. As usual, faced with the ineptitude of governments and their statesmen, he alone comes up with ideas and plans actions, be they good or bad. In the present case he took seriously the threat of Soviet military intervention in the Congo in favour of Lumumba, and his plan of action, which had been accepted by the Security Council, derives from this fear which, according to him, is real and could start a world war.

The situation in the Congo is certainly complicated and Dag will need all his skills to meet it: on one side Lumumba is supported by the Russians, on the other Tchombe has the Belgians' sympathy. The Congolese themselves are divided. We will have to see what comes of it. In any case, a UN success would enormously enhance its prestige, though Dag could also come a cropper. The Russian press calls him an instrument of colonialists and imperialists.

By the end of September 1960 the Cold War seemed to be escalating. Victor observed:

In spite of his peaceful declarations, having aborted the Summit, Khruschev wants to ransack the UN. Having failed to impose Lumumba in the Congo, the Russians are now attacking Dag. Khruschev even wants to link disarmament to him. He says the latter is not possible because it would imply the use of UN armed forces which under Dag would be on the side of the western Powers. Thus we have first to accept Khruschev's proposal to have three men in place of a single Secretary General in order to settle the disarmament problem.

Never before has the General Assembly started with such violent disputes. Khruschev openly attacked the US, the Secretary General, the colonial powers and the UN seat in New York. This provoked a reply from Wadsworth [the US delegate] which was not conciliatory.

244

I feel increasingly that a neutral block is forming which could have a decisive impact on all questions. The two opposing blocks will be more and more isolated and it will be the neutrals at the UN who will have their say. This Assembly is characterised by the first recognition of Red China by a Latin American power, Cuba.

As October wore on, the world situation continued to worsen. Victor confided:

I feel like I did in 1932-38 in Geneva in the midst of an impotent League of Nations where everything was going wrong - except that at the League things were bad because the powers controlling it could not or would not take the necessary decisions. At the UN the US grip is weakening because of the neutral group which is gradually increasing and which sometimes joins the Soviet Block. This is especially noticeable since the admission of the new members in 1960.

Khruschev has behaved like a clown but, even though the new African countries condemned his attitude as unworthy of the UN, they were impressed by what could be interpreted as an attitude of power and defiance towards the free world.

I have never seen such a spectacle at an international meeting: banging his fist on the desk to express disapproval of the speaker, interrupting MacMillan's speech, taking off his shoe to bang on the desk. The Soviet attack against Dag personally and against the structure of the Secretariat also had an effect. Even though only the satellite states supported his proposal to have three Secretaries General, each with the right of veto, the effect of the attack has been that Lumumba seems to have regained power because the African countries are no longer unanimous in supporting Dag's action. Dag is holding on and replied very well to Khruschev's criticism but this does not prevent him from giving in where he can without dropping his principles.

His despair over the deteriorating state of East-West relations did not prevent Victor from relishing the occasional compliment. At a dinner given by Hammarskjold for the King and Queen of Denmark, the King had asked which China Dr Hoo belonged to and on hearing that it was the China of Chiang Kai Shek, asked to be introduced to him. Victor recalled:

> I was the only one invited to sit with him. He told me he was in China in 1930 for three or four months. I remembered that on that occasion they had pulled down the slums of Nanking and Madame Sun Yat Sen had protested. I also told him that I had visited Greenland. He put on his glasses to look at my decorations. I was tempted to point out that I did not have a Danish decoration! What a pity Tsiang did not accept the invitation, otherwise it would have been him the King had spoken to in front of everyone. I was chosen because I was the only Chinese at the dinner.

On 25th December 1960 Victor was spending his first Christmas on a plane and enjoying his first flight in a jet. It was the initial lap of a world trip, starting at Lisbon. His diaries record a number of interesting and occasionally amorous encounters. He wrote:

> In Lisbon the flamenco dancers open and close their mouths without singing. They tell me that they cry *sa-sa-sa* to the rhythm of the dance, to mark the effort they make. I replied that they could do the same thing whilst making love!

> In Geneva, at Sacha de Mauficerli as usual I met some interesting women: Mme de Vilmorin, Comtesse de la Barre, Mme van der See. The latter wanted to exchange my Japanese cigarette case for hers in gold and it ended up with my case staying with her for nothing in return. Mme de la Barre tried to arouse me. She is lovely and has Chinese blood. In Paris, thanks to Vergeot, I enquired at the Palais de la Légion d'Honneur and discovered that I have been registered as Commandeur de la Légion d'Honneur since 1944. How about that!

> In Rome I attended a charming buffet supper at Ambassador James Yu's where Chinese students sang *Madame Butterfly*. Two others played Chopin and Ravel while

yet another played a divorce scene of a Chinese couple with sentences made out of the names of Chinese movies. Another sang an American and Italian love song saying: 'How many lips have kissed you, I really don't want to know.' The other guests were Chinese from Taiwan rushing to the Belgian Congo at UNESCO's request to be teachers there.

In February he was en route from New Delhi to Bangkok and Hong Kong. He wrote:

Of all the countries I have visited during this trip, I find the Indians the least pleasant. The servants in the hotels seem only to be waiting for a tip. I feel their antagonism. There are hoards of servants that one never sees but who come up one after the other to say they will not be there tomorrow. The people have no sense of responsibility and do everything without enthusiasm. Lall and his wife were very kind and looked after me with great solicitude. And yet, the day before my departure, he asked me to buy him 500 shooting cartridges which he will reimburse with Indian products for which I have no need.

On 12th March he returned to New York. Although his diaries had been largely given over to casual impressions, there were a few political and philosophical asides:

Once, when I complained about the Communist threat, noting that in world history there is always some danger that comes to spoil things, my interlocutor replied that a constant threat is necessary for survival. In the case of migrating tropical fish, for example, only a percentage of the fish arrive alive. Experiments have shown that the percentage increases amazingly when they introduce a catfish which eats some of them!

In Taipei Victor had seen Chiang twice, once in his villa where he was invited to take tea with Chiang and a Guatemalan Minister. On this occasion Victor gave his opinion privately to Chiang that it might become necessary to accept the representation of the two Chinas at the UN or be forced out. Chiang replied by quoting a Chinese proverb: "It is better to be a broken piece of jade than to be an entire slate tile." It was clear that this intransigent position would never be modified in Chiang's lifetime.

> When they had gone, he asked me what I had to say on the Taiwan situation. I told him that the issue of our representation at the UN will depend on whether Britain's vote is the same as that of the US. He told me it would be. When I said that I would come to Taiwan if I was no longer at the Secretariat, said there were many things he could use me for. He added that our work at the UN is very important and that we have to persevere. He thinks that if things continue as they are the Reds will fail in China as soon as we land there. He did not elaborate as to how we would be able to land, however.

> I had tea alone with Madame Chiang for an hour and she asked me about Margie and her health. She said Margie should pray, and that she herself meets every week with about thirty women to pray. We did not speak of politics. She gave me three of her books, including a collection of her paintings.

May 1961 saw the launch of the Space Race between the Russians and the US. Victor followed its progress and the difference in approach, with interest.

> What a difference there is between the Americans and the Russians as far as propaganda goes. The Russians only announced their first man in space after the event and we don't know for sure that Yuri Gagarin went around the earth. The Russians had warned newspaper men of the imminent departure of one or two men but then nothing more was said. Rumour says that the first, who must have been the son of Ilouchine, went mad when he returned to earth. The Americans, on the other hand, announced the departure in advance, together with all the delays. Fortunately, the flight was a success.

Despite the popular support that had greeted Kennedy's nomination as President, Victor noted that things generally were not going well for the new administration:

Kennedy is losing his prestige. The failure of the Cuban invasion and events in Laos are partly responsible. He promises a lot but there is little follow-up. The American government did everything to help the invasion but then stopped in mid-tracks after advice from Stevenson and the State Department. American support was too feeble and did not persevere, in contrast to the Russians. Subsequently it was announced that Kennedy was seeing Nixon, Eisenhower, Hoover, etc. probably to gain their support for help to the Cuban rebels. Thereupon Zorin gave a press conference declaring that Russia would intervene if there was foreign aid to the anti-Castro Cubans; since then nothing from the American side. The whole coup fell through. What Kennedy finally delivered was hot air.

On 3rd June Kennedy met Khruschev for the first time. Victor observed:

What a change from the international situation of the time of Dulles. Then, such a meeting would have provoked a violent reaction by the Western Powers. In Britain they say that Kennedy personifies two Englishmen: Churchill when he speaks and Chamberlain when he acts!

The American press says the meeting was useful because it gave the two a chance to size each other up. However, as Khruschev is more experienced in the handling of people it is surely he who has benefited from the sizing up. After the meeting Kennedy referred to it as sombre, whereas Khruschev had apparently never been in such a good mood and was rolling about on the floor and clowning as usual.

On 20th June Hammarskjold summoned Victor to his office.

I thought it would be about my contract and I was right. He says he is under terrible pressure and cannot prolong my contract beyond the end of this year. I told him I did not mind but that he had to talk to T F Tsiang. He said he would but that he wanted to warn me first. He also told me he would not appoint a Red Chinese.

I wonder if Dag is hoping to be accepted by the Russians, or at least supported by a majority of the members for a third term, by appearing so eager to reorganise the secretariat. Why can't he prolong certain contracts, like mine and Cordier's, until the expiration of his own contract? It is what Lie would have done.

Secretly, Victor suspected that Hammarskjold did in fact want the option of appointing a Red Chinese in his place. This was confirmed by T F Tsiang:

It appears that, whilst implying to Vaughan and myself that he would not appoint a Chinese, Dag asked TF to recommend one. What game is he playing? This won't please the neutrals or the Afro-Asians. I told TF to ensure that my successor signs his contract before my departure. TF told me that the Americans will no longer vote for Outer Mongolia's admission to the UN and will not be in favour of two Chinas.

On Monday 18th September, on the eve of the sixteenth session of the General Assembly, Victor woke and turning on his radio, heard the news that the plane taking Hammarskjold to Rhodesia for a meeting with Tchombe was feared to have disappeared.

Later in the day the debris of an aeroplane was seen in the forest by a search plane.

Finally, at 12.15, we received news from the teletype that Dag's body had been identified next to the plane's debris. There were fifteen people with him, including Wieschoff, Fabry, Bill Ronallo and Miss Lande, a Canadian secretary. There was only one survivor, an American guard who said that at the last moment, when the plane was about to land, Dag decided not to. Thereupon there were several explosions in the plane and it crashed.

They think that perhaps the explosions could have been caused by bullets hitting the petrol tanks. This would indicate an assassination. As yet they do not know the cause of the accident. Vinnichenko told me yesterday that someone returning from the Congo said that, at the last airport where Dag's plane landed, Indian soldiers accompanying him had played a funeral march in error. His death occurred on the same date as Bernadotte's in Palestine: 17th September.

Never has a death provoked so much emotion in the whole world, even those of Stalin and Roosevelt. Dag died in the course of duty, in mysterious circumstances and his disappearance creates problems which could have unforeseen consequences: his succession, considering the Soviets' insistence on Triska, will be very difficult; the situation in Katanga and the Congo could become dangerous given the absence of a UN organism able to agree precise instructions on what to do; and the situation at the Secretariat, where Dag alone decided a multitude of current and urgent matters, can only be confused.

Bunche's subsequent communiqué, issued in the name of the Secretariat, but without consulting its members, added to the problems rather than solved them. As Special Representative of the SG in the Congo, Bunche felt he could speak for all the staff of the Secretariat and he chose not to consult the ASGs. Victor wrote:

The following day I spoke to Bunche. I told him I was his friend and wanted to help him but that several of our colleagues are unhappy and it would be better to consult them first. Two days later he rang me at 11.30 p.m. to inform me that there will be a concert on 28th September at the UN in memory of Dag. The Philadelphia Philharmonic Orchestra will play Beethoven's Ninth, his favourite. I told him then that we must consider who will be sent to Dag's funeral in Sweden.

On 18th September a press conference was summoned to announce officially the death of the Secretary General. The next day the Assembly opened and closed again after a minute of silence.

Investigations had discovered that Hammarskjold's plane had made a considerable detour from Leopoldville to Nadal to avoid a Katangan fighter aircraft. A few days later a truce was nonetheless concluded between the UN and the Katangan authorities. Victor commented:

251

This proves that it could succeed even in Dag's absence. He wanted to do everything himself and that is why the void will be difficult to fill. We are unlikely to find someone as active, intelligent and devoted, and with as many ideas as him.

On the 30th September the bodies of Wieschoff, Ronallo and Julian (the only survivor, who died a few days later) arrived by plane at Idlewild where the Secretariat staff assisted at a simple ceremony. The coffins, covered with flags, were placed on rollers and the families of the deceased stood behind them. Victor noted:

> Before leaving for the Congo the last time, Wieschoff took out a very large insurance policy on his life and asked to be buried at his small country house five hours from New York. At the same time, Dag wrote a letter to Peer Lund, asking him 'in case of need' to file his papers, keeping the private papers and leaving the others to the UN. In his last book, *Markings*, Dag mentions death seventy-three times. It is as if the two had a presentiment of death.

It was particularly distressing to learn subsequently that Hammarskjold probably did not die immediately in the crash. His body was found at some distance from the wreck and his fingernails were torn and dirty, suggesting that he had pulled himself away from the fuselage. The cause of the crash was never fully explained although there were many versions, some with eerie inferences.

———————

Within the UN Victor's disenchantment was growing:

> Never before has the UN been so low. Even the League, though it was impotent to do anything, never disavowed the principles of the Pact. The UN is also impotent but is sacrificing its principles. It has already made a package deal to admit new members and has done it again with Outer Mongolia and Mauritania whilst declaring it opposes their admission. In effect the Soviets have obtained what they wanted, except that they would have preferred China to use her veto on Mongolia so that they could use the veto on Mauritania. As China did not participate in the vote,

Russia abstained on Mauritania. The new members only agree in order to denounce imperialism and colonialism. On other matters they have no ideas and often abstain. That is what allowed the Communist members to delay the vote of the resolution asking Russia not to explode her fifty megaton bomb.

On 5th November 1961, the General Assembly finally and unanimously elected U Thant acting Secretary General. Victor wrote:

It is a great success. Who would have thought at the time of the League that one day an Asian would be Secretary General! It shows how the world has changed. U Thant is more social than Dag and goes to all the cocktail parties given by the delegations. Women like to speak to him and he listens with a lot of patience.

He has not yet told me if I'm staying and this worries me because, if he says nothing, I have to go after 31st December and I need time to pack. On the other hand I can't start to pack if I am staying. Cordier is in the same situation and told me he would need time to settle those things of which he is in charge. At the moment they are discussing the question of our representation in the General Assembly. Naturally, most of the speeches are unfavourable to us but they are not attacking us. It is the US who is criticised, especially by the Communist countries. If it were not for US opposition, the Red Chinese would be admitted to the UN without hesitation but there would not be a majority to expel us.

On 12th December Victor received confirmation from U Thant that his contract would not be renewed:

He said he would speak to T F Tsiang and asked what I would do. I told him I would return to Formosa.

Once the news was out that Victor was going, he was touched by the regret expressed by members of the department, especially the White Russians.

What moved me most was a blind typist who came to my office to express her regret. Altogether, I had only spoken to her two or three times! The farewell reception is on 3rd January. Peissel asked me what I would like as a gift and I told him a portable radio and a typewriter.

On 28th December, however, just before a farewell lunch in his honour, Victor was contacted by U Thant after T F Tsiang had requested an audience.

U Thant presumes he wants to discuss the post of Chinese Under Secretary and wonders why he has left it so late. He had concluded that the Chinese government wasn't interested after all in having a Chinese Under Secretary after my departure.

I tried to excuse TF, saying he was very busy because of the question of Chinese representation and had also been ill, but that the Chinese government considers the question of having a Chinese Under Secretary as being linked with the matter of Chinese representation. U Thant then said, if that was so, he would prefer to keep me in place of Heuttematter, Commissioner for Technical Assistance. I replied that I had not followed Technical Assistance matters and would prefer to leave the UN early and obtain a post as ambassador abroad. He pointed out that a new Chinese Under Secretary would not be as well liked or accepted and that another new person would not know about Technical Assistance either. I then asked what we should do about the farewell lunch. He said that, since the silver tray with the inscription was already there, the lunch should go ahead and he could appoint me after the farewell reception on 3rd January. I suggested he should see TF before making a final decision.

Thereupon the farewell lunch took place. In his speech, U Thant said that Victor combined the eastern and western virtues and that he had become an institution at the Secretariat. Victor recorded:

I replied that I had never stayed so long (fifteen years) in one place, that I am a hunter, not a climber and like to

254

spread myself horizontally, not vertically, that I have applied Confucian precepts: to be sincere and truthful in word, and honourable and prudent in action, and thus to get along even with barbarians. I said the principle of not doing to others what you didn't wish them to do to you, was more realistic than the Christian idea of doing to others what you would like them to do to you because then, if you had a diamond, you would have to give it away, whereas, according to Confucius, you just need not steal one. I added that if I could no longer serve the UN I would always serve its principles by serving my country and my people since their ideals are the same: keeping the peace and the dignity and value of the individual, developing social progress and a better standard of life.

Bunche then made a speech praising Victor's character and contribution to Trusteeship. He also told a few stories, including the fact that in Victor's address book he has the names of friends all over the world, especially ladies of a certain age with Bentleys and Rolls Royces! Hamilton (Director of Personnel) said only that he would do homage to Victor as a perfect gentleman.

After the excitement and sadness of the farewell lunch, Victor mused:

> Now I will let fate decide my future. I would like to travel and I am sure to do well with the people in Technical Assistance but if I leave the UN now my future might be brighter. Therefore, if U Thant asks me to stay, I can do so with a clear conscience because it will be he who wants me to stay. Morally my position will be beyond reproach and I would find in it an immense personal satisfaction.

> In this case, two predictions that Margie obtained will be realised: one, by Buddhist sticks, that I will not change because I am like a pearl of such value that they cannot do without me; the other, from Hong Kong, that I have to be quiet for two weeks in November and from 15th November my position will be better than ever.

The optimism of his personal predictions was small compensation, however, for the global predictions Victor had received for 1962.

They say five planets will be in the same axis. Three planets were in the same axis when Christ and Buddha were born. Today the radio said Hindu astrologers predict a terrible catastrophe for 2nd February 1962 when seven planets are aligned. They say it will be war, or the end of the UN, or the world will explode like a ripe melon. In which case, the question whether I remain at the UN or not, will be merely academic!

CHAPTER FIFTEEN

Technical Assistance

Reprieved From Retirement - Continuous Travel - Worries About The Future

U Thant's appointment as Secretary General in October 1961, heralded, or seemed to herald, a more relaxed atmosphere at the UN. Whereas Hammarskjold had been cold and aloof, U Thant was approachable, women enjoyed talking to him and he listened with a gentle and compassionate expression.

His attitudes were summed up in his memoirs:

> We have a common stake in human progress and prosperity. Prosperity, like peace, is indivisible. Most important is the survival of humanity itself.

These were precisely the goals of Technical Assistance. Just as the main purpose of the UN was to end wars between nations by promoting social progress, better living standards and a reduction in the gap between rich and poor, so Technical Assistance was seen as the best hope for achieving this.

The idea had been initiated by Truman in the 1947 Marshall Plan for the economic rehabilitation of Europe, an imaginative concept aimed at restoring and strengthening the non-Communist world. In 1948 his Point Four Program invited other countries to pool their technical resources through the UN and the Specialised Agencies. The American initiative quickly influenced other members of the UN who were already thinking along the same lines. This was the first major international aid programme aiming at the transfer of skills from the developed to the under-developed countries.

When Victor took over as Commissioner for Technical Assistance in 1962, his commitment to its fundamental objective - the creation

257

of economically self-sustaining nations independent of domination by any external power - was as absolute as his commitment to the vision of democracy in the world had been a generation earlier.

His move to Technical Assistance coincided, aptly, with a call by the UN General Assembly to the conscience of mankind. Even until the late 1950s it had been taken for granted that some nations maintained a high standard of living whilst others endured conditions of backwardness and poverty. Similarly, within each country it was assumed that under-privilege, malnutrition, ill-health and lack of education were the inevitable lot of the less fortunate members of society.

The idea that these societies also had a right to share in the benefits of progress had deep-rooted implications for the UN Charter of 1945 which had been drafted almost entirely by major countries, not small countries wishing to assert themselves.

The decade 1960-70 was to be labelled a UN Decade of Development in the fight against hunger, poverty, ignorance and disease. The goal was a five per cent increase each year in the aggregate income of the developing countries, an ambitious target given the expected increase in population.

Victor found the UN Programme of particular interest because of its international character. By 1966 120 countries were contributing to its funds and facilities and pledges had reached $146 million.

Whereas in Trusteeship, his struggles had been against those powers reluctant to see the dismantling of their colonial system, here he faced a world waiting to be improved. He had something to build on. The aims of Technical Assistance underscored his own beliefs in man's innate dignity and his right to determine his own political and social destiny. His task now was to persuade others to accept these ideals. His message was the same as Emerson's and was often quoted by him in these years:

Nothing great was ever achieved without enthusiasm.

In the early '60s anything seemed possible. Science and technology were taking vast strides. A man would soon travel to the moon, disease was being eradicated, unlimited cheap fuel was no longer an idle dream, the frontiers of knowledge seemed suddenly to have no limits. The future was bright with promise.

For Victor himself, however, there was less to hope for. By 1961 he had already passed the official UN retirement age by six years.

He was aware, as was everyone else, that his continued employment was a matter of political convenience for both the Chinese Government and the UN Secretariat. This was frowned upon especially by those who were in line for Victor's job. There were articles criticising the Secretariat and describing Victor's situation in harsh tones, though without mentioning names.

However much his own ideals fell in with those of Technical Assistance, he was also uncomfortably aware that he had nonetheless been demoted. This was highlighted by a reduction in his expense allowance of $2,000 a year. His subordination to Philippe de Seynes, who had been an equal as an ASG, was also an irritant and Hammarskjold's formula for such situations "co-ordinated but not subordinated", provided small comfort to his ego.

He was worried, too, about his lack of technical and scientific background. Although he had been at the UN sixteen years, he was unfamiliar with Technical Assistance matters and since industry, trade and transport - anything that did not fall to the Specialised Agencies - fell to him, effectively co-ordinating the resources of the Economic and Social Department presented something of a challenge. At Headquarters, however, he soon discovered that the real work was done by the Director of the Bureau of Operations, Henry Block and, as far as foreign visits were concerned, he was promised a full brief on his arrival at the country in question.

He wanted to continue working and this was a job that not only satisfied his wanderlust and his desire to service his country but left him with sufficient time to pursue his social life as well as pay attention to his increasing concern over his health. With advancing age and with his ulcer problem, he was aware that his health and stamina were not unlimited. He started to watch his diet and made sure he had a nap after lunch every day, no matter what the circumstances. After taking up an invitation to lunch at someone's house, he would startle the hostess by asking if he could lie down on her bed. There would sometimes be a scramble to clear away underwear from the bedroom! The rest of the company would have to make somewhat stilted conversation for half an hour until he re-emerged, fully refreshed.

———————

Victor's first trip as Commissioner was scheduled almost immediately on joining the Department. On 25th February he flew to London, then to Rome and Athens. The entry on 24th March 1962 reads:

My first trip as Commissioner was a greater success than I had hoped. First, I took the trip well without getting too tired. I went to bed before eleven p.m. whenever I could. I had no dysentery, no vomiting and no pain, unlike some of the others with me.

In London he managed to contact friends he hadn't seen since 1946 and found time to record in his diary his pleasure at the English accent and the fact that porters accepted his tips politely without looking at them first.

He was less impressed with the higher echelons of English diplomatic life:

They really are stingy - the English won't even offer you a cigarette if they can avoid it.

He had looked forward to meeting Barbara Castle in London - not so much in her capacity as Minister for Overseas Affairs but as a woman on whom he could practise his considerable charms. He noted ruefully following the meeting:

Mona warned me she seemed especially 'dedicated'. After an hour I gave up trying to extricate her from her subject. She certainly is a true professional.

The stop-over in Athens was memorable, according to the diaries, merely for the paucity of hospitality:

... almost as bad as the British. At our Embassy, I was offered a bowl of noodles with a small fish, cucumbers and Chinese carrots - the cheapest meal I've ever had in an Embassy. The Ambassador would have taken me to a restaurant but his wife asked if I wouldn't prefer to rest and stay at the Embassy.

In Rome the treatment was more befitting:

Ortona gave a lunch at the Restaurant Palazzi in my honour and in Paris I visited Dechaume and Foncet who gave a lunch for me at the Doyen. Foncet said we belong to the Technical Assistance Internationale. The French seem keen to collaborate with the UN in Technical Assistance. This must be the only area in which they have been anxious to collaborate.

At the time of my father's appointment to Technical Assistance, I was working as Personal Assistant to Barbara Hutton, the Woolworth heiress and her apartment in Paris' 16th Arondissement was my work base. The apartment had many things to recommend it, including a collection of Chinese porcelain second only to that owned by Chiang Kai Shek. When my father came through Paris in 1962, Barbara was away in the Far East with a new escort and I had her permission to use the apartment and her domestic staff for parties. It was the perfect setting for diplomatic socialising and Victor recorded in his diaries:

> I invited my Paris friends to a cocktail party at Barbara Hutton's in Mona's name. It was a great success and those who did not come must have regretted it the next day when they learned whose house it had been in.

> Whilst in Paris, I went with Mona to the Théâtre de Dix Heures. What struck me was that virtually all the songs were about de Gaulle, which highlights the lack of variety in the Parisian imagination and there was not a single song about the bombs which go off every day in Paris. This demonstrates the extent to which the chansonniers are terrorised by the OAS.

What Father omitted to mention in his diaries is that whenever he came to Paris whilst I was a student there, he would take me to a night-club or to see a strip tease - always of the highest quality such as the Crazy Horse. He would explain that it was a form of art. Now that I looked like an adult I noted with amusement that if we met with people he knew, he would introduce me as a niece or a cousin! The diaries continue:

> After a stop in Brussels when I saw our Ambassador Roland Ouang and his wife and son, I left at three p.m. and arrived in New York at five p.m. local time. On the way we almost followed the sun and I was able to read without electric light during the whole trip.

261

My new job is interesting but has two drawbacks: I am always under pressure like the rest of my colleagues. Everyone has two or three jobs to finish at the same time so that we always finish at the last moment and the work is done badly. We are so accustomed to working to schedule that when there is no deadline the work is not done at all.

In the second place, being under de Seynes means I have to represent him at all the meetings he doesn't go to and act for him when he is away from Headquarters. Were I in his position, I would have taken on the whole responsibility for Technical Assistance but he is interested in it himself and deals with the government representatives. This diminishes my responsibility as Commissioner and frankly makes me feel rather useless.

The irony was that in de Seynes' absence I read the opening speech at the Social Commission, which presented the new idea that social and economic development ought to be linked. The Speech contained completely new ideas and I was congratulated on it, though in fact it had been drafted by Julia Henderson [Director of Social Welfare] without any contribution from me at all!

Fortunately, there were occasions when he was able to take more creative liberties with the material presented to him.

At the ECA in Addis Ababa, I made two speeches by cutting up and modifying the one which had been prepared for me in New York and I made another speech at the meeting of the Resident Representatives. In a fourth speech I said there was no better way for me to learn to keep my head above the water in my new functions, than to plunge headlong into the pool of knowledge, experience and frustration represented by them.

Whilst in Addis Ababa I went to visit Aklilon whom I had known since the Geneva days. He has become Prime Minister and told me that the Emperor would want to see me. I had an audience with Haile Selassie and he said that

China was the only country which did not recognise the conquest of Ethiopia by Italy.

Less arduous and more entertaining was a meeting with the owner of a Chinese restaurant who turned out to be a Chinese dentist without a diploma. He told me Ethiopians have good teeth because they do not eat sugar and only go to see him when they have broken their teeth in a fight with the long sticks they always hold in their hands.

In June 1962 he spent a few days in Oslo where he was reunited with his old boss, Trygve Lie, now President of the " agency" for international co-operation. Victor recalled:

Trygve was really touching. He had arranged for me to meet all the important people, including Lange, the Foreign Minister. He excused himself for not taking me to the theatre but invited Sonia Henie to a dinner instead, after which we visited her splendid house with its abstract paintings. She is quite stunning. So, incidentally, were the pictures.

The house was on the shores of a fjord and if there had been sun I could have gone fishing. Unfortunately the weather wasn't great but even without sun it was daylight at 10.45. Lie said he liked me because when he was Secretary General I did not always say yes and when he gave up the post I was kind to him and offered him hospitality every time he came to New York.

In August 1962 Victor took a decision that his biographers would later welcome:

As my handwriting is becoming more and more illegible, I aim to start typing on the Olivetti the Conference Department gave me on the eve of my presumed departure. This will hopefully prepare me for the day when I have no secretary, although I only type with my two index fingers.

The trip to Europe had gone well and Victor planned to follow it up the next year with a round of official visits to Latin America. However, the penny pinchers at the UN stepped in. Victor complained:

> I had arranged everything, including the necessary briefing and Arditti planned to join me in Buenos Aires. To my surprise, the Controller thinks we should economise on our travelling expenses as according to him there is not enough for the second semester of this year. De Seynes has been told by U Thant to travel only when it is absolutely necessary and has given up his trip to the Near East. I have the feeling Dharman and Kirkbride are responsible. Dharman does everything to save and is more difficult that the Controller himself. Once in the lift, Kirkbride criticised the numerous trips for Technical Assistance. They don't understand; it is not the necessity but the usefulness which counts. Nevertheless, my trip to Brazil, Argentina and Peru would not have been as useful as it would have been if these three countries were not in the midst of a political crisis. To be frank, I regret having missed a trip which would have been useful, in countries I do not know, and at a pleasant time of year.
>
> To compensate, I took two weeks leave to go to Stockholm by car via Germany and Denmark. Returning to New York I still took four days leave because at this time of year, we have neither conferences nor too much work and most of our colleagues are absent.

The Cuban Affair in November, which had brought the world to the very brink of nuclear war, had been a nerve racking time. Victor wrote:

> ... at least it proved to Russia and to the world that Kennedy, with the support of the American people, is ready to have a nuclear war when they feel their security is threatened. I knew that Khruschev would back down but in such a way that it looked to the Russian people as if he had saved the peace rather than almost provoking a war. Another two or three such incidents and the Swedes might well give him

the Nobel Prize! Those who will benefit from the affair are Kennedy, de Gaulle during the Referendum, U Thant for his role as Mediator and perhaps Khruschev. The world is also now agreed on the usefulness of the UN when neither of the two parties involved want war.

He made a similar observation a few years later, following the Six Day War between the Arabs and Israelis. Although the Assembly was unable to vote any of the resolutions to settle the situation, it was at least clear, on that occasion too, that neither the US nor Russia wanted war.

The conflict in Cyprus that year between Greeks and Turks confirmed Victor's judgement on the UN and its role in such circumstances:

First, we find out at the Security Council whether the disagreement allows for a peaceful solution. If not, then the UN resolution allows the countries involved to save face if they have to make concessions. This is what happened in the missile affair in Cuba and again in Cyprus.

Some of the more bizarre off-shoots of the negotiations were also recorded by Victor:

The sessions of the Security Council during the Arab-Israeli War were televised, often at night, with millions of viewers following them at home. Tabor, the President, who is Danish and very good looking, received hundreds of love letters and marriage proposals from American viewers. As he smoked a pipe, he also received pipes as gifts from men who watched television in Europe. Tabor was so popular as President of the Security Council that he was appointed Minister of Foreign Affairs in Denmark soon after the sessions.

Perhaps, at the time, the Cuban Affair had represented a crisis of such magnitude that the months and years that followed seemed to contain little of note. Alternatively, perhaps learning to type on the Olivetti proved more difficult than he had anticipated. Whatever the reasons, and although Father's notations in his diaries were always erratic and inconsistent, with gaps of several weeks or months, the most significant gap was between 1962 and 1966, when not a word was written. World-shattering events such as Kennedy's assassination went unrecorded, although other indications suggest that this period coincided with good health and a very full social life. He continued to play tennis at the UN, winning the Veterans' Cup year after year until he found no more competitors for the title! One year they just gave him the Cup without asking him to play. Thereafter he concentrated more on his golf.

It was not surprising, perhaps, that some of his colleagues, particularly those who felt he should give way to the next generation, were heard to remark that, "Victor Hoo is getting paid to have fun!" Indeed, his life at this time seemed to consist entirely of trips abroad, peppered by prepared speeches, dinners and parties with old friends everywhere in the world. During this period, perhaps with the instinct of someone who knows that time is running out, Victor tried to see those countries he had not visited before. There were not many but his fascination and curiosity were more those of a young man than one in his seventies.

At that time too, he started his involvement with Beatrice which was to last to the end of his life. This was the person who gave him unconditional love. She was neither pretty, nor young, nor intellectual. She was a wealthy American widow with an apartment on the East Side of Manhattan and a big country house in Westchester which she called Bumble Bee Farm. She loved Victor unselfishly and totally, and gave him all the comforts and reassurances that every man needs, while in return she asked for nothing. Her existence was well-known to all Victor's colleagues; he would often hold official parties at Bumble Bee Farm and occasionally she would travel as a private person on his official trips abroad. She was aware of his infidelities but never broached the subject.

During 1963 he visited the Far East, followed by a trip to Manila, where he met his old friend Liu Chieh, the Ambassador. Victor's youngest sister, Clementine, was married to a prominent business man in Manila and Victor often went to the countryside with them and their three children.

Before returning to New York that year, he came to visit me and my husband at our home in Suffolk where I was, as always, kept busy holding parties for him and his friends. The house had a swimming pool and Victor encouraged everyone to join him in the pool, splashing them if they didn't. The level of activity and enthusiasm seemed, if anything, to grow with age and he took a perverse delight in dragging my husband out of bed before dawn each morning to go duck shooting. It always took us several days to recover from his visits, me in particular, as I had to act as his secretary and travel agent as well as hostess.

In the summer of 1967 Victor went to Geneva via Stuttgart, where he bought a new car. As far as cars, as opposed to women, were concerned, he was a creature of habit and it was the usual light-coloured Mercedes, though Mother endlessly pleaded for a different colour so that neighbours would know he had a new car!

He drove to Geneva via a small village in Switzerland near the German border to visit Martha, our former Governess, and they spent a happy evening reminiscing over old times. She was overjoyed by his visit and still speaks about it as if God had condescended to call in on her.

––––––––––

Back in New York, Victor was invited along with other members of the Secretariat to a performance of the *Magic Flute* at the Met. He took with him Marcelle Courtney, who, as Marcelle Denisa, had once sung three roles in this opera. Victor recalled:

> She was delighted and very touched that I should have asked her, although my friends there said they had never seen me out with such an old woman. This is the price one pays for doing the gentlemanly thing.

It wasn't the only occasion on which Victor's gallantry had backfired on him. In New York he had an elderly friend, Margot Walbaum, whom he had saved from Hitler's gas chambers during the war. Margot was very grateful and Victor enjoyed the opportunity the association gave him of speaking German, a language he had no chance to practise within the UN. Unfortunately, Margot could also be very irritating. After being abandoned by her husband in favour of his young secretary, she increasingly became a millstone around Victor's neck. She had lost a comfortable income and relied on him to save her again. Victor obtained for her the job of Manageress of the UN gift shop, a very suitable position, given her knowledge of languages. Regrettably, she felt it was beneath her dignity and whenever she saw Victor in the Secretariat, would shout: "Hello, Viktor Dahling. Come and have a chat. When are you taking me out to dinner?"

267

Making the most of a situation that was mortifying and embarrassing, Victor took advantage of the opportunity to practise his curses in German under his breath.

In spite of the privileged social life that his work still offered him, by 1968 there were signs that Victor was beginning to feel marginalised. In January he noted:

> They only think of me when it is a question of inviting someone or giving a reception.

At this juncture in his life, when he perhaps had more time and opportunity than ever before to gather his impressions into a readable form, he confessed sadly that he was becoming increasingly unenthusiastic about writing anything:

> I rarely write letters. Since I've been at the UN I no longer have a chance to write memos because others do it better than I and my speeches are so technical that they need a specialist to gather the data and to draw conclusions. Reading Harold Nicholson's memoirs, edited by his son, moved me to note down some of my impressions but this did not last. I prefer reading to writing when I have the time. If I had only recorded my thoughts and impressions on the events of each day during my life, I would have the basis of my memoirs. However I am not vain enough to think these could be interesting or have any real historical worth.

This candid self-assessment did not make him any the less sensitive to the implied criticism of others, however.

> One evening Philippe de Seynes asked me to dinner and delicately implied that I wrote little and had few ideas. He referred to the coloured cards I've carried with me for the past fifteen years and asked what they were for. I said they were for noting down ideas. He laughed and said: 'They aren't ideas that you write down, Victor, but addresses.' I was actually very hurt.

Still, his travels compensated for the shortfall elsewhere in his life. In April 1968 he embarked on a world trip, embracing Los

Angeles, Honolulu, Western Samoa, Fiji, Ceylon, Jakarta, Bali and Java. There were, as always, the pleasures of social intercourse to distract him:

> Here at Suva at the Hotel Tradewind, they gave a cocktail party in my honour with the most exquisitely beautiful waitress, completely like a European except for the colour of her skin. I naturally engaged her in conversation and discovered that he father is Chinese and her mother from Gilbert Island. Generally, the girls from Fiji are big and muscular, smiling but very hairy on the face.

As part of his more official duties, Victor was due to attend three conferences in Canberra, Vienna and Geneva. Whilst he was away, he received news of Johnson's speech ending the bombing of North Vietnam and announcing his decision not to be a candidate for the presidency. Victor recorded:

> We will see what happens. I myself believe it is a political election ploy, the result of his recent conversation with Generals from Saigon. He wants a complete change in foreign, domestic and military policy. Just as long as he doesn't play the Communist game and isn't taken in by them! He was due to arrive in Honolulu this morning, where a big parade was scheduled, but yesterday morning Martin Luther King was assassinated in Memphis by a well-dressed white man and Johnson has to delay his departure. This assassination will undoubtedly provoke violent demonstrations by the blacks and reinforce black power.

Following his return to the US in August 1968, Victor spent some quiet weeks at the office. It was a peace shattered by the invasion of Czechoslovakia. He recorded:

> It is, of course, a catastrophe, but the marvellous thing is that it demonstrates the patriotism and discipline of the Czechs and shows that the Russians have not succeeded in forming a government with Guilsing. They have to keep the present government but have imposed very hard conditions on it that we don't yet know about. The Czech

269

government had advised their intellectuals to leave the country and already thousands are emigrating daily. There is a black joke going the rounds of the UN: 'How long will Russian troops stay in Czechoslovakia? As long as it takes them to find the person who invited them to come.' The invasion has shaken the world and will probably help Nixon to become the next President. At the moment the American people are unhappy both with Nixon and with Humphrey. They are a divided nation and the lack of unity has toppled many stronger empires.

The declining standards of electoral campaigns were becoming all too obvious. Victor noted:

I have been in the US for several Presidential elections but never before has the fight between the candidates been as bitter and unforecastable as now. At first Nixon had the advantage of a better organised campaign but he now seems to be losing ground. The candidates are prostituting themselves to the public, promising the earth to get more votes. If Nixon and Humphrey were to keep their promises, the US would be ruined. The fact that Humphrey and his advisors have said they'll replace American soldiers in Vietnam with the UN Army shows how little he knows about the UN, as if their Army was at his disposal!

In November Nixon was elected President of the US. Victor wrote:

What a relief for the anti-Red Asians. What stumped Humphrey was Johnson's cessation of the bombing of North Vietnam before South Vietnam had accepted his conditions. John Wood, a Canadian who has just left Vietnam, told me that Russia's occupation of Czechoslovakia had completely changed the situation in Vietnam. Before the occupation Saigon feared a bargaining between the US and Russia at its expense. Now this is no longer possible and morale there is better. They think that the war will lose its intensity, the Vietnamese being ready now to denounce the Vietcong. The problem at the end of the war will be to know what to do with all the Vietnamese soldiers who do not want to work. The UN vote on Vietnam will depend on what the Americans want. The present Prime Minister in Vietnam, Huang, is honest and his is the best government so far but he was not the US choice.

As 1968 drew to an end, Victor's preoccupation with the passing of time and the need to document his life became more pressing. He took comfort from a colleague's observation that Bunche looked older than him and might soon lose his sight as a result of haemorrhages behind his eyes but neither man could claim to have youth on his side any longer:

> Many people have encouraged me to write or dictate my memoirs, but recently Khoman and Chef Adabo have used additional arguments. Khoman says that my memoirs would be more interesting than other people's because of my character and personality. Adabo says that if my memoirs do not interest me personally they would still interest others. In Taiwan, memoirs are very fashionable. It would be easy to find someone to take note of what I tell him and make a book of it. On the other hand, at Columbia University in New York, there is a section which gathers the souvenirs of personalities on tape. Still, I would have to find time to do all that.

The year ended with an epidemic of Hong Kong flu throughout the US and for once, Victor felt privileged to be isolated, although the effect on his social diary was less welcome:

> I wanted to give a dinner for the Gosfliers and had sent out invitations a month in advance. Of twelve guests, five, including the Gosfliers were unable to come due to flu. I could have avoided this expense! One in five in New York is ill. The President of the Association started his speech saying, 'Escapees of flu.' I suppose I should count myself lucky to be one.

In 1969 there was a trip to Africa, where the food was not to his taste, and for the first time he suffered from the heat. His morale was not improved by the comment of a member of the British delegation he sat next to at a lunch in Addis Ababa:

I told him I had stopped smoking a year ago and he turned to his companion and said of me: 'Obviously smoking can't be that bad, if he is almost eighty and only stopped a year ago!'

By March he was in Taipei, where he felt more at home and where his friends were happy to boost his ego:

Everyone has been very kind to me. Yen Chia Kam told me my heart was still young, which is why I get along so well with the young.

With one eye now on retirement, however, he took the advice of another friend to heart:

Jimmy Wei said something very true: if you are looking for a hobby, it is best to choose one for which one needs no partner. This rules out bridge, chess, etc. since one is then dependent on others. Something like calligraphy or painting is better.

The Taiwanese say it's pleasant to live amongst the Chinese because they always help each other. If you ask your friend for money, he doesn't mind if you don't return it. You can always find another way of doing business. Habits are also changing here. They are starting to eat sandwiches at lunch because it is simpler than cooking.

Gerry Wen who is our specialist in community development said that the living standard of the villages here is now amongst the highest in the world. Many houses have televisions and all have a radio. Apparently India is the worst. Once Gerry was the guest of honour in an Indian village and they served him a dish with a dark crust that turned out to be flies!

Whilst I was in Taiwan, I visited the FAO Project to rear cattle on sloping land that cannot be cultivated. They have castrated bulls who still recognise cows on heat. A coloured band is put on the bull's snout so he leaves a spot on the cows he smells. They showed me the metal sheath they use for artificial insemination and an enormous rubber condom to gather the bull's sperm when he mounts an artificial cow. I feel sorry for the bulls being used like this. To prevent the horns from growing, they put a liquid on the place where the horns grow.

In April Victor had an interview with Chiang Kai Shek:

I told him I come here on leave every two years and that I wanted to quit but the Government and U Thant wanted me to stay. He thinks I should stay.

I advised him to increase our contribution to the UN as requested and explained why it would be desirable. Japan, for example, is paying $1 million, compared to our $127,000. He agreed to an increase and asked how much it should be. I did not dare to say what Hoffman suggested ($750,000) and said I would discuss it with the Minister responsible.

When he asked me about the American elections, I said it was lucky for us that Nixon was elected because with Humphrey or a Kennedy our situation at the UN would have been more precarious.

When I told him that I was looking for a place in Taipei to install my house, he smiled and told me he would give me a house if I came back. I hope he doesn't forget and is still alive! He is still the highest authority in Taiwan, as I discovered when I wanted to photograph two women in national costume who were sweeping the park. In order to impress them, my driver said I was the President's representative. I don't suppose he could very well say I was the President!

Victor returned to New York on 3rd June 1969. The trip had lasted three months and his verdict on it demonstrated that his former hunger for work was all but spent:

In retrospect, the best moments were those spent at the Sun Moon Lake in Taiwan and at Waikiki Beach in Honolulu.

A week later he was in Europe, and August was spent alone in a furnished studio in Geneva where he made his own breakfast and often lunch too, and was able to take the afternoon naps that had become a necessary part of every day. He was pleased to note that his monastic existence had at least reduced his waistline which had started to expand alarmingly in New York.

Returning via Baden and Kassel, he noted wryly that he had obviously aged since his last visit, since he elected to stay in his hotel rather than going to the movies as he always had before.

> On the other hand, in Fribourg, I started reading a copy of *Emanuelle* given to me by Rose Marie d'Escagne and was pleasantly surprised at the effect it had on me. Not that I was able to take advantage of it, being unfortunately alone!

In 1970 changes such as that in American policy towards Peking, which Victor foresaw as having far-reaching consequences, made him lament anew the fact that he had let his diaries lapse:

> I am becoming more and more idle, indifferent and possibly senile. I rarely keep a diary any more and yet so many important events are occurring. Nixon has now authorised a limited commercial exchange between the US and Peking and a limited purchase of Red Chinese goods by American tourists. In Vietnam American public opinion is forcing him to prepare the retreat of fighting American troops. These things will change the course of our history and possibly the world's and should be charted as they happen.

On a personal note, 1969/70 marked the beginning of Victor's insomnia.

> It started in Geneva during the Ecosoc, when I seemed to be waking up every night around two or three a.m. and was unable to go back to sleep. I cured myself with Doriden tablets and as soon as I left Geneva everything was normal. Then it started again towards the end of October and Doriden was not enough. I then started taking Valium and Lotusate until I had to stop for the operation on my hernias. After the operation I took honey and that was enough but last night I again slept badly.

Last December U Thant asked if I would accept the prolongation of my contract by another year. I said yes because since my meeting with Chiang Kai Shek in Taiwan I had decided that if he wants me to stay, then I must.

I felt bound to suggest to U Thant, however, that at my age I would be better resting. He says I must stay as long as he does and that if I can't do all the work, I should simply give more work to the others.

He reckons the Chinese Reds will enter the UN within the year. The change in American policy is starting to worry the Chinese press. Although the American-Peking meetings in Warsaw did not result in anything, the fact that they are taking place more frequently irritates the Nationalists. Recently there was a meeting of our Ambassadors in Taipei to discuss the consequences for us of the new situation in Indochina: the extension of the war to Laos, the expulsion of Sihanouk from Cambodia, hostilities between the Cambodians and the Vietcong and North Vietnamese, and the policy of appeasement by the Americans. Chiang Ching Kuo is coming to the US on 20th April to see Nixon and discuss the situation with him.

Three weeks later as Chiang Ching Kuo was entering a building in New York, a Taiwanese tried to assassinate him. Victor recorded:

His bodyguard deflected the shot by hitting the arm which held the gun. If the attempt had succeeded it would really have complicated the question of the succession to Chiang Kai Shek. I did not think the Taiwanese would go so far in their demonstration for independence.

There were other indications that year that the world was becoming an increasingly dangerous place for a diplomat. In April the German Ambassador to Guatemala, Count Karl von Spetie, was executed. Victor wrote, scandalised:

This has never happened before in diplomatic history, that a diplomat should be kidnapped and ransomed by

adversaries of the regime in order to obtain the release of
their comrades. What is the world coming to?

In May 1970, his wallet, two credit cards and memorandex agenda
were stolen from his hotel room during a stay in Italy.

They were on my dresser when I took a shower. Aside from
that time I had not left my room. This has never happened
to me before, though I suppose it could have been worse.
But why did they take my diary?

Victor might have interpreted this as proof that others found his
diaries more interesting than he did but he concluded that the
thief was simply in a hurry and had no time to look at what he was
taking.

The Biafran War in 1970 and the total defeat of the Biafrans
had been a source of great international concern for the
fate of the Ibos but by August the situation in other parts
of the world was improving:

Finally, things are going better. In the Middle East,
negotiations are starting between Israel and the United
Arabs. In Cambodia, American troops have been
withdrawn but the present government is still holding.
According to Georges-Picot, who came to see me in
Geneva and who thinks that Nixon's decision to penetrate
Cambodia was right, the Reds have been weakened and
will not be able to start an offensive against the
Vietnamese as they had intended. Thirdly, negotiations
between the Russians and Bonn for a non-aggression
treaty seem to have ended satisfactorily. Lastly, the
inflation of the dollar appears to have slowed down. All
things told, one can't complain.

At an exhibition in Geneva of documents relating to the peace
conferences at The Hague, Versailles and San Francisco, Victor had
been moved to see his father's signature in Chinese on a photograph
of the 1899 Hague Conference.
The incident brought home to him the sense of mortality that
had started to afflict his spirits, and consequently his health, over

the past two or three years. He was relieved to be told in Geneva that he was in better health as a result of not smoking any longer but in 1970 he had begun to experience waves of dizziness. He wrote:

There is a name for it but the good news is that it does not signify anything and isn't dangerous.

More of a disaster, potentially, was an accident that I had outside a pharmacy in Geneva where I went to buy some Formocarbine Naphtholée for Margie. I started to get out on the street side and a car coming from behind smashed into my door. If I had been coming out more quickly I would have been hit. Luckily the driver of the other car, which was also damaged, was very calm and polite and did not make trouble for me, unlike the Swiss Ambassador Humber in Geneva. On that occasion I had parked my car to go to a reception. He had just stopped his car in front of me when mine rolled forward and broke the glass of his rear light. He started to shout abuse at me but then calmed down when he discovered who I was. I gave him the 4.40 francs for repairs and he then gave me ten francs for the victims of the earthquake in Peru, thus suggesting that every cloud does indeed have a silver lining, though it's not the best way to collect for charity.

In August Victor spent a weekend with the Landeggers, old friends whose home he had often used, not only as an escape from his own but as an alibi when in fact he was spending time with Beatrice who lived near the Landeggers.

Karl Landegger's wife, Munling, was Chinese, the niece of Cardinal Yu Pin. Victor had been the matchmaker in this union and it had seemed a happy marriage but, that August, Karl had asked for a Mexican divorce. The terms were generous. What is not mentioned in the diaries is that Munling caught Karl in bed with the child's nanny and this propelled the already shaky marriage towards the rocks. Victor wrote:

Never before has a Chinese woman had such a profitable divorce. All expenses for their daughter will be counted separately, regardless of whether Lingling lives with her father or her mother. Karl told me that what he could not stand in Munling were her constant lies and pettiness. He leaves her 300 designer dresses and $100,000 in jewellery. What this will mean to me personally in terms of freedom of movement, I have yet to discover.

Other considerations arose in September which further restricted his liberty: He wrote despairingly:

I have again to be operated on, this time for haemorrhoids. I had a sudden haemorrhage which lasted about twenty minutes at Bumble Bee Farm around 9.30 a.m. On Dr Irwin's advice, they took me to the North Westchester Hospital where the surgeon advised an operation. I took an ambulance back to Yonkers which cost $77. Margie advised me to see Dr Quan and on the same day I went to New York in the evening, this time by taxi. He told me there is no trace of cancer and confirmed that it was the haemorrhoids which were bleeding. The worst part of it is that Margie was under the impression I was with the Landeggers at the time. To be discovered in the perpetuation of a lie is uncomfortable.

From 1971 Victor's preoccupation with his own problems was matched only by his increasing anxiety over the possibility of Red China's recognition. In November 1970 Canada recognised Red China and broke with the Nationalists. Italy followed, and Belgium and Austria announced they would do the same. Victor wrote:

It is what the Americans call 'jumping on the band wagon'. In these circumstances, next year or the one after, according to U Thant's prediction, the Reds will take our place in the UN. And what will become of us if we break with all those who recognise them?

In April 1971 he wrote:

I spoke to Chang Chun for an hour and a half. He is for the two Chinas at the UN because then the Reds would not come in. He agrees that we cannot retake the whole of China, but after Mao's death China will disintegrate among the military and perhaps we will be able to go to Canton or

278

Fukien even without American help. In Taiwan the independence movement is not widespread. The Army, with a large Taiwanese Party, had been indoctrinated in favour of the status quo because the majority profits from the present situation.

Our new Foreign Minister, Chow Shu Kai, agrees that we must not leave the UN because it would diminish our international status and give us more domestic problems.

Nixon is flagrantly flirting with our Reds. In the latest move he allowed an American Ping-Pong team to go to Red China accompanied by journalists. The American press is naturally giving this great publicity. Chou En Lai was very pleasant, unfortunately, and even added that he had never been to the US. Heaven forbid.

In July the world was shaken by Nixon's decision to go to Peking to see Chou En Lai. Victor wrote:

Of course, the Russians were furious. They are afraid of a Sino-American rapprochement but in the US the majority of people welcome this visit. I said from the beginning that Nixon wanted to be re-elected in 1972 and is resorting to any means to capture the imagination of the American voters. This is a severe blow to our representation at the UN. Our best friends are recognising the Chinese Reds who in turn demand that they break off relations with us. The *coup de grace* is the announcement of Kissinger's second visit to Peking to arrange the details of Nixon's agenda, just a few days before the vote. Khoman predicted privately to me on 26th September that we would lose the resolution by five votes.

It was exactly sixty years ago that the Republic of China was created. What an anniversary!

On 25th October Victor's worst fears were finally realised:

Peking was admitted to the UN and the Chinese Republic expelled.

After twenty-six years in the UN Victor was at last being asked to resign. The timing could not have been worse:

> Liu Chieh advised me to write a letter of resignation to U Thant but, apart from the shock of having to leave, this puts me in a domestic quandary. I am waiting for the new maid from Taiwan, whom Margie badly needs, to secure an American visa. U Thant has agreed, therefore, to try and get me special paid leave until the end of my contract.

> The Chinese Communist flag has already replaced ours. There was no ceremony because it is considered that there is no new country joining the UN. U Thant sent a cable to Peking asking if they wanted to be listed under China or The People's Republic. They said China. On 2nd November I called on Yang Hsi Kuen at the Chinese delegation. he was very frank and said that Taiwan would deteriorate economically. Peking can manufacture our products just as well as we do and cheaper. All is political in the world, even trade, and therefore economically we will suffer from our political isolation. The price of land in Taiwan has already dropped. He says that Argentina and Peru were bribed by Peking for their votes. Liu Chieh believes that the second Kissinger visit to Peking was timed deliberately by Chou En Lai.

Although not unexpected, the sudden fulfilment of Red China's manoeuvrings to gain entry to the UN had thrown the families of Nationalists abroad into confusion. Victor wrote:

> Yang advised me to stay abroad. He said his life was ruined: his wife had left him and his twenty-five-year old son, who is in the US, has no college education. He feels I should leave the UN in order not to have to consort with the Reds. I explained about the maid.

There were indications that, if it did choose to remain, the Chinese delegation would be helped to obtain permanent visas. Victor himself was approached with the offer of a teaching job at the University of Ohio, where U Thant had also been offered a research fellowship. Other offers came from publishers and PR Officers:

I had a drink at Terry Mayers'. She said I could write a very successful book and get an advance of $7-8,000 from the publishers who would also provide assistance with editing.

But, although welcome, the offers of help could not dispel the shadow that had fallen over life at the UN for the Chinese delegation.

Yesterday, at the Assembly, the Peking delegate, Chiao, and Malik, the Soviet delegate, shouted at each other over the disarmament conference proposed by the Soviets and rejected by Peking, the US and the UK. There has never been such an angry exchange of words at the UN before and even Bavardy invited them to temper their language, quoting an Arab proverb: 'the wind and the ocean had a quarrel but he who paid the price was the sailor in the boat.'

On 14th December, my last day of active service at the UN, I called on U Thant at six p.m. to thank him for all his kindness. He asked me several times whether he could do anything for me.

His final communication from U Thant, however, was depressingly remote:

On 12th February 1972, I received U Thant's letter thanking me for my services to the UN. It was drafted by the Personnel Office and though it praised me for services rendered, it was an official document without any warmth.

There is little to disguise the sadness and despair of the entries for 1972. The previous December Victor had discovered that the scar in his left lung had increased in size. Doctors were in favour of an operation, even if tests revealed that the scar was not malignant.

In February, coinciding with U Thant's final letter, he was told that he had cancer.

It was established by various tests. In the first, a bronchoscopy, breathing and pedalling tests showed that I have cancerous cells and that my breathing is not strong enough to risk an operation of the lung. Dr Alexander

281

prescribed Cytoxin tablets that he said are very potent. Following Dr Quan's advice, I went to see Dr Pool, a famous lung specialist. He advised other tests at the Memorial Hospital: brain, bone and liver scans, all of which were negative, as was a bone marrow test carried out later. This means that my cancer is localised in the left lung. Dr Pool prescribed two doses of cobalt a week. I was lucky that during that month I did not have flu.

After the radiation treatment Dr Pool said that the spot in the left lung had shrunk and what remains may be only a scar but one cannot be sure without a preventive operation, which is not worthwhile in my case. He said at the very beginning, when I went to see him, that my cancerous cells could be cured better by radiation and medicine than by surgery. Now he wants me to wait two weeks before starting medication.

Later in the month, Nixon left for his "China Trip". Although Americans were disappointed that there were no crowds to meet him at the airport or in the streets, Victor wrote:

America's new infatuation remained intact, nourished by an unexpected interview between Nixon and Mao and what was described as a 'cordial dinner with many toasts' given by Chou. All in all, the trip was a great propaganda success.

The joint communiqué that resulted stated categorically that Taiwan was part of China. Victor commented:

That certainly complicates the possibility of having two Chinas. Probably, without the paragraphs on Taiwan, Chou would not have agreed to any communiqué and this may explain the one hour delay in Nixon's take-off when he left Peking. Chou got what he probably considered most important and was greeted by a crowd of several thousands when he returned to Peking from Shanghai. It really is a triumph for him.

Those Americans who understand the Reds and the world situation and even many others, criticise the 'sell out of the Republic of China'. Our Ministry of Foreign Affairs issued a dignified statement, repeating the old claim that we will retake China. It was said in the press that this Peking meeting was as important for the world as Yalta. Yes, and in both cases, it sacrificed us, China.

Never have I seen a joint communiqué in which the strongest side - the US - makes concessions without gaining anything in return. What the American people like is the fact that twenty-two years of deadlock between the two is finally broken and they can talk - but at what price!

CHAPTER SIXTEEN

Postscript: Going Gently Into That Dark Night

Red China's Admission to the UN - The End of A Career - Disappointment

Victor's life had been full by any standards, the best years glittering with success and the material and spiritual rewards that were its natural accompaniment.

His last years, by contrast, were overshadowed by sadness, financial worries and disappointment at the fate of his country and its inability to rise from the ashes of defeat. Red China's admission to the UN in 1971 was the final blow, doubly painful because it meant the end of his career there.

This sword of Damocles had been ever present for the past two decades. Despite the Nationalist Government's official position as permanent member of the Security Council with veto power, the admission of new member states mostly of the Third World, now meant that the *de facto* position of Red China would inevitably become *de jure*.

On the 25th October 1971 Victor wrote:

> This was the blackest day of my career. Peking was admitted to the UN and the Chinese Republic expelled. Everybody agrees that it was American bungling that brought this about: Nixon's prospective trip to Peking, Kissinger's second trip just before the voting. American high-handed 'steam-rolling' attempts to obtain more votes, the adoption of the Albanian resolution - all add up as much to a defeat for America as for the Chinese Republic.
>
> In the past, defeats such as that of Shantung in the Versailles Treaty, the Mukden Incident and our retreat to Formosa,

still left us as the Republic of China. Now for the first time this is denied us. Of course we still have staunch friends and of course American public opinion and a great number of important Americans will support us but how long will the mutual defence treaty remain in force? The Reds will try to isolate us, ruin us economically and politically infiltrate us. Hopefully they will stop short of invading us.

Red China's admission represented a double blow for Victor, not simply because it demonstrated once and for all that Communism in China was not just a passing phase but because it signalled the end of his working life. All his efforts and struggles over so many years seemed to have come to nought and for once he allowed himself to give way to pessimism.

His last few days at the UN were made still more unpleasant by a contretemps with his old colleagues in the Chinese delegation. On 25th October, when the Peking delegates were admitted to the UN, the sitting Chinese delegation naturally walked out. Victor's contract, however, was due to run until 31st March 1972 and financial concerns impelled him to stay to the end. He felt, moreover, despite expressions of disapproval from Chinese colleagues, that a member of the Secretariat could behave as a neutral international civil servant as other Chinese members of the Secretariat did. When it was pointed out to him that he was the only political appointee, however, he had to agree to their reasoning. Nevertheless, a compromise was reached allowing him to stay until 31st December with paid leave for a further three months until the end of his contract. In spite of this minor victory, the episode further contributed to the bitterness of his departure.

Victor had always dreaded the prospect of retirement. His appetite for life remained undiminished well into his seventies. He had sufficient intellectual interests to keep him busy in retirement and there was always the prospect of writing his memoirs. His social life, however, was inextricably bound up with his work. He loved to travel and his work afforded him ample opportunity to do so. His status and position in society likewise depended on his official capacity.

The insecurity that he had expressed in letters to Augustin following their father's death, was never far from the surface. In old age he had the bitter certainty that, once he stepped down from the platform, the world would turn its back on him. The reassurance given by his family and friends could not dissuade him.

There were other more subtle and complex reasons for his reluctance to step down. His marriage to Margie had been a love match, filled with high expectations for the future. In many ways she might have been an ideal diplomat's wife. But the two were temperamentally and intellectually irreconcilable. Soon after the marriage, Margie had taken refuge from the demands of diplomatic life and her husband's neglect, in ill-heath. The sickroom became her kingdom.

In the mid-60s, when I had left home to study in Europe, and Peter was married with a family, my parents decided to adopt a little girl, Cindy, from Taiwan. She was very bright and deserving of a good education in return for providing company for Mother who spent her days in bed. By the time Father retired, Cindy was in high school and she proved to be a great solace to him, caring for him with genuine affection.

Shortly before his retirement, Victor confessed to his old friend Margot Walbaum, whom he had known since 1922 and whose life he had saved during the war:

> Looking back, for all my success, I failed on two counts - as a husband and as a father.

> 'No-one can be good at everything,' Margot replied generously.

In many ways, perhaps, it would have made very little difference if my parents had been happy in their marriage. Victor's zest for life, his constant need for change and activity, meant that domestically he could never have remained a "family man" in the conventional sense. He and Margie came to a mutually acceptable arrangement which gave him freedom and excused her from the official functions other diplomats' wives were expected to participate in. There were indeed occasions when Victor deliberately introduced his personal friends into his professional life whilst still maintaining an apparently stable home base.

The lung cancer suspected in December 1971 and confirmed in February of the following year was undoubtedly triggered by the events leading up to his retirement and the torment of deciding where to retire to. Although he would have preferred to stay in New York where most of his friends lived, Victor was not prepared to remain there in reduced financial circumstances. He had many rich friends and, if he could not keep up with them, he preferred to be out of it.

Left to himself, he would have accepted Chiang Kai Shek's invitation to return to Taiwan, where he could have lived like a king on his UN pension and where a high-ranking function would have given him not only status but the possibility of further serving his country. Although the prospect should have been attractive to Margie since she liked a hot climate and they would be able to afford several servants, the idea of a major move and the long journey presented enormous, insurmountable obstacles to her. By this time she had achieved a very agreeable lifestyle in New York. Her sister, her son and his family all lived nearby and she had a group of faithful friends within reach. Going to a new and strange environment, where she might have to adapt to conditions not to her liking and outside her control, was unacceptable to her.

Discussions at home from the late sixties onwards were heated, at times acrimonious, neither of them able to decide what to do for the best. Friends argued on both sides, making the situation even worse. If they did decide to stay in New York, which Margie wanted, it was essential to apply for residence before the loss of their diplomatic status.

On 7th November 1971 Victor had confided in his diaries:

> These are the unhappiest days in my life: worry about what will happen to Taiwan and my friends and relatives there and worry about whether I'll be able to live with Margie and Cindy in New York on my pension and small savings. It is worse than my unhappiness in Paris in 1918 over the loss of Shantung to Japan and in Chungking during the war. At that time we had a government, however weak and bad. Now, the very government to which I belonged all my life and even the existence of Taiwan as a separate entity from Red China is threatened. I have not yet reached the stage of being happy and proud of my country and my people with its Red government because it has not yet proven to have contributed anything towards the happiness and well-being of the Chinese nation.

The atmosphere at home underwent a change when Victor's illness was diagnosed as lung cancer. At first he was told that they would operate. Then the doctors decided against it, although his condition had not improved. We understood then that there was no hope of a cure. Within a few weeks there was a marked deterioration in his physical and mental state. He suffered several small strokes which at first were not very noticeable. His worries over his health were aggravated now by anxiety over hospital bills.

At this point my mother finally decided to go along with Father's idea of moving to Taiwan. Knowing the end was near, she made definite moves to sort out their belongings, put the house on the market, make travel arrangements, etc. Father had three brothers in Taipei all offering their assistance. Margie even came to believe that perhaps this was, after all, the best for both of them.

From April to June Victor was in and out of hospital. By this time he was starting to have difficulty breathing. Plans to return to Taiwan were stepped up. In hospital he had a constant stream of faithful friends and relatives visiting him during the day, and it was during one of these visits at Yonkers Hospital on June 9th that he died suddenly of a heart attack. It was swift and certainly a better way to die than by the slow process of cancer.

―――――――

The last time I saw my father was on 28th July 1971. It was his habit to visit me in England every summer, either on his way to the Economic & Social Council meeting in Geneva, or on his way back. Sometimes he stayed at our house in Suffolk for two or three days or I would meet him for a meal at Heathrow between flights.

In July 1971 he stayed with us for three days and we entertained some friends for a barbecue. He was still the life and soul of the party but I sensed that he had worries on his mind. He knew his term of office would probably not be renewed and his trips abroad would therefore cease.

As I drove him to Heathrow, he said several times: "I wonder when we will see each other again." I promised to visit New York the following year if he did not come here. As he passed through to the departure lounge, he turned to wave and there was a desperately sad expression on his face which has haunted me ever since.

I learned of his death through my brother Peter. Although not altogether a surprise, the shock was still great. My father had been many things to many people - an icon, a lover, a diplomat, a peace-maker, a bitter opponent of Communism and corruption and, finally, a human being as vulnerable to fortune as any other.

―――――――

The funeral took place at a fashionable church in New York's East Side, packed to overflowing. Many women sobbed openly. Colleagues and friends of my father, including his old mentor Dr Wellington Koo and U Thant, delivered moving tributes. Victor would have been gratified by the eulogies accorded him on his death

His wish had always been to be buried in China after the Communists had left. In accordance with this wish, his body was deposited at Ferncliff, outside New York, to await his return home. A slot very near to his, contained the remains of Judy Garland. He would have liked that. The casket is still there, joined in November 1997 by one containing my mother. These two, who were not ideally matched in life, would finally be united in death.

What Victor would have made of his own life, had he and not I been writing this postscript, can only be surmised. Like all human beings, he had weaknesses: he could be vain, self indulgent, licentious and worldly. Yet he was also noble in his aspirations, with a capacity for work and self-sacrifice for a just cause that left lesser men trailing behind him. His love of his country and his desire to serve it remained supreme. Had China been a greater country, his own contribution would have matched it.

Bibliography

Bartlett, Vernon, *Struggle for Africa*, New York, Frederick A Praeger, 1953

Bernadotte, Folke, *To Jerusalem*, London, Hodder & Stoughton, 1951

Bilby, Kenneth, *New Star in the Near East*, Garden City, New York, Doubleday, 1950

Boorman, Howard L & Howard, Richard C, eds, *Biographical Dictionary of Republican China*, New York, Columbia University Press, 1967

Byrnes, James F, *All in One Lifetime*, New York, Harper & Brothers, 1958

Ch'i, Hsi-Sheng, *Nationalist China at War, Military Defeats and Political Collapse, 1937-45*, The University of Michigan Press, 1982

Chiang, Kai Shek, *Soviet Russia in China: A Summing-Up at Seventy*, New York, Farrar, Straus & Cudahy, 1958

Chu, Hung Ti, *China and the League of Nations*, Illinois, 1937

Cornevin, Robert, *Des Origines à Nos Jours*, Paris, Académie des Sciences d'Outre-Mer, 1969

Cottrell, W F, *Better Born Lucky*, London, Regency Press Ltd, 1984

Crozier, Brian, *The Man Who Lost China*, Angus & Robertson, 1977

Crum, Bartley C, *Behind the Silken Curtain: A Personal Account of Anglo-American Diplomacy in Palestine and the Middle East*, New York, Simon & Schuster, 1947

Dell, Robert, *The Geneva Racket 1920-39*, London, Robert Hale Ltd, 1941

Eytan, Walter, *The First Ten Years: A Diplomatic History of Israel*, New York, Simon & Schuster, 1958

Fairbanks, John K, *The Great Chinese Revolution*, New York, Harper & Row, 1986

Gage, Berkeley, *It's Been a Marvellous Party!*, London, 1989

Granados-Garcia, Jorge, *The Birth of Israel*, New York, Alfred A Knopf, 1948

Gunther, John, *Inside Africa*, New York, Harper & Bros, 1955

Han, Woo-keun, *The History of Korea*, Seoul, The Eul-Yoo Publishing Co, 1970

Higgins, Trumbull, *Korea and The Fall of MacArthur*, New York, Oxford University Press, 1960

Hoare, James & Pares, Susan, *Korea, An Introduction*, London & New York, Kegan Paul International, 1988

Hoffman, Paul G, *World Without Want*, New York, Harper & Row, 1962

Horowitz, David, *State in the Making*, New York, Alfred A Knopf, 1953

Katz, Samuel, *Days of Fire: The Secret History of the Irgun Zvai Leumi and the Making of Israel*, New York, Doubleday, 1968

Koo, Wellington V K, *The Wellington Koo Memoirs*, New York, Columbia University, 1978

Lee, Chong-Sik, *The Politics of Korean Nationalism*, Berkeley, University of California Press, 1963

Lee, Ki-baik, *A New History of Korea*, Seoul, Ilchokak Publishers, 1984

Leighton Stuart, John, *The Forgotten Ambassador*, ed Kenneth W Rea & John C Brewer, Boulder, Colorado, Westview Press, 1981

Leighton Stuart, John, *Fifty Years in China, The Memoirs of John Leighton Stuart*, New York, Random House, 1957

Lie, Trygve, *In the Cause of Peace*, New York, The Macmillan Company, 1954

Macdonald, Donald Stone, *The Koreans, Contemporary Politics and Society*, Oxford, Westview Press, 1984

McKay, Vernon, *Africa in World Politics*, New York, Harper & Row, 1963

Mann, Peggy, *Ralph Bunche, UN Peacemaker*, New York, Coward, McCann & Geoghegan Inc, 1975

Miller, Richard I, *Dag Hammarskjold & Crisis Diplomacy*, New York, Oceana Publications, Inc, 1962

Oliver, Robert T, *Syngman Rhee, The Man Behind the Myth*, London, Robert Hall Ltd, 1955

Payne, Robert, *Chungking Diary*, London, William Heinemann Ltd, 1945

Pratt, Sir John T, *War and Politics in China*, London, Cape, 1943

Sih, Paul K T, *Nationalist China During the Sino-Japanese War, 1937-45*, New York, Exposition Press, 1977

Sze, Szeming, *Memories of An International Life*, IBSN, 1992

Tickner, Fred, *Technical Cooperation*, New York, Frederick A Praeger, 1965

Tong, Hollington K, *Chiang Kai Shek*, Taipei China Publishing Co, 1953

Townley, Ralph, *The United Nations, A View from Within*, New York, Charles Scribner's Sons, 1968

Tuchman, Barbara W, *Stilwell and the American Experience in China, 1911-45*, New York, Bantam Books, 1989

Tung, William L, *Revolutionary China, A Personal Account, 1926-1949*, New York, St Martin's Press, 1968

Tung, William L, *V K Wellington Koo and China's Wartime Diplomacy*, New York, St Martin's Press, 1977

U Thant, *Towards World Peace*, New York, Thomas Yoseloff, 1964

United Nations Year Books

Urquhart, Brian, *Ralph Bunche, An American Life*, New York, W W Norton, 1993

White, Theodore H, ed *The Stilwell Papers*, New York, Sloane, 1948

Wilson, Dick, *The Long March*, Revised ed 1977

Index